The Changing
World of Fashion

The Changing World of Fashion

1900 to the Present

Ernestine Carter

Introduction by Diana Vreeland

G. P. Putnam's Sons New York

First American Edition 1977
All rights reserved. No part of this publication
may be reproduced, stored in a retrieval system, or
transmitted in any form or by any means, electronic,
mechanical, photocopying, recording or otherwise,
without the prior permission of the Publisher.

Designed by Sandra Shafee for George Weidenfeld and Nicolson
11 St John's Hill, London sw11

Library of Congress Catalog Card Number: 77-309
isbn 0–399–11969–8
Printed in Great Britain by
Butler & Tanner Ltd, Frome and London

Contents

To Doris Langley Moore
*whose penetrating eye and mind have illuminated many
obscure corners of fashion, and to whose perseverance
and generosity Britain owes its unique Museum of
Costume at Bath*

Author's Note

*Actually I wanted to call this book 'One Bird's Eye View of Fashion (although I ceased being a bird in the strict
meaning of the word some years ago). We ran the title up on a flagpole but only the Editor of British
Vogue and I saluted. So. But in such a vast panorama one must select the peaks, and selection is a personal
matter. For example, I have not attempted to encompass the mechanics of dressmaking nor the techniques of
mass-production. I have left to the specialists the minutiae of fashion: the fans, the shawls, the gloves, the
handbags. . . . Most conspicuously, I have skirted round the enormous area of fabrics, for the progress from silk
worm to test tube, sheep's wool and cotton boll to laboratory with its triumphant consummation in the marriage
of natural fibres with man-made, the dramatic diminution in weight, the development of uncrushable materials;
the advances in printing, in weaves and in knitted structures, as well as the saga of the silks and satins of Lyons,
Zürich and Como, the laces of Calais, the cottons of the USA, not to mention the worsteds and tweeds of
France, Italy and England, seem to me to deserve a book to themselves. So, as Dormeuil, Bianchini, Staron,
Lesur, Ducharne, Rodier, Linton, Abraham, Agnona, Forster Willy, and designers like Brossin de Méré,
Sache and Mahlia may agree, this is in effect an opinionated book.*

Author's Acknowledgments

'I generally find that nothing that is asserted is ever true, especially if it is on the best authority.' This remark of Lord Melbourne's has been a great source of comfort to me as I found myself sucked into a whirlpool of contradictory statements while researching for this book. The deeper one dives, the wilder the eddies become: few dates agree, attributions seem dictated by partisanship, recollections vary. Among the most deceptive sources of information are the advertisements of the time (except as a study of advertising itself), for they merely represent what the advertiser wishes to sell. As, in general, advertisements deal with merchandise which is available, they are inevitably later than the date of the actual birth of a fashion, and, too, many promote fads or gimmicks – the lunatic fringe of fashion – irrelevant to what is really being worn. In the area of internationally marketed products, things are even worse: the launching of a new product can take place in London, Paris or New York at sometimes widely differing dates. What date do you choose? Although I dug until I thought I would reach China, I have had, in the end, to settle in some instances for what might be called 'consensus dates', i.e. dates on which three or more sources agree.

In my wish to avoid, if possible, further perpetuation of errors I have been a merciless gadfly, and I am deeply grateful to those who bore patiently with my persistence. I thank particularly Mr Seymour Leslie for sharing his prodigious memory; Mrs Doris Langley Moore, Miss Eleanor Lambert, Mr J.G.Links, Mr David Liney of Hudson's Bay Company & Annings, Mr D.Martin of Campkins Camera Centre Ltd for vetting the chapters dealing with their special fields of interest; Mr Geoffrey Squire for so handsomely sharing the fruits of his research; Mrs Anne Wall of the Buckingham Palace Press Office for the specifications set out for Presentation dresses; Miss Sue Baker and Mr P.McIntyre of the EMI Publishing Company and Mr George Smith of Chappell Piano Company Ltd for checking the words of old songs; Mr Barry Sandland of the Arthur Murray Dance Studios for the low down on hoe downs and other dances; Miss C.C.Singleton and Mr J.A.Smirfitt of the Hosiery and Allied Trades Research Association, Miss Beverley Alt of Pretty Polly and the Courtauld Public Relations Office for their guidance through the meshes of hosiery history; Mr Edward Rayne for special information on shoes; Miss Joan Chaumeton, Miss Ivy Sharp, editor of *Fur Review*, Mr Francis Weiss, Mr Leslie McMillan, M.Jean-Noël Ghigonis of Revillon and Mr Percy Savage for their generously shared knowledge of the fur trade; to Mr I.A.Clarke of Kodak, Mr Geoffrey Crawley of the *British Journal of Photography*, Mr Denis Knowles of Leitz, Mr Norman Parkinson and Mr Julian Allason and the press offices of Nikon, Olympus and Canon for their help in translating the arcane mysteries of the camera into laymanese; Miss Susan Shanks, Mr Fred Radford of the National Hairdressers' Federation, Mr Norman Bloomfield of the *Hairdressers' Journal*, Miss Dorothy De Roy of the *Retail Chemist*, Mr Patrick Maxey of *Soap, Perfumery, Cosmetics*,

Miss Iris Wade of Elizabeth Arden, Miss Linda Sampson of Revlon, Miss Deborah Bennett of Estée Lauder, Miss Jennie Dodds of Helena Rubinstein, Miss Elizabeth Motts and Mlle. M. Tessier of Roger et Gallet, and Miss Stephanie Thomas of Cologne Perfumery Ltd, for assistance in unravelling the various skeins of the beauty business; Miss Susan Farmer of De Beers and Miss Betty Britten of Cartier for light shed on jewellery; Mr David Burger-Wise, archivist of the Ford Motor Company for the technical details of old cars; to Tautz & Company for habits of riding; Miss Dorothy Rook, librarian of the Royal Society for the Preservation of Birds for the facts on the depredations of our feathered friends; Mr David Robinson, Miss Elizabeth Leese and the Library of the British Film Institute for checking out the dates of films and the names of their designers; Dr Robert Burchfield, editor of the *Oxford English Dictionary* for the provenance of 'winklepicker'; and finally Madame Propper de Callejon for the quotation by Jean Cocteau used in the Epilogue.

I would also like to thank Mrs Judy Bolland for transcribing my typescript into neat copy and Mrs Sue Simon for minding my ps and qs.

Introduction

by Diana Vreeland

Ernestine Carter, in her inimitable way, and in her clear and descriptive prose, has given us a concise resumé of fashion in the twentieth century up to 1977. Whether it is good or bad, neurotic or buoyant, fashion and ornamentation will be forever fascinating to both men and women, for fashion is a mirror of the times that reflects what is invented and worn. Ernestine Carter has not given us a description of bad fashion in good fashion times. Oh no, she has carefully selected, as the decades of our century go by, the best of the best (and the most typical) of the particular time she is describing.

All fashion is part of social history, and we know how fluctuating and mercurial social history is, hence the never ceasing changes of silhouette and appearance. For an illuminating description of the youthquake and change read her chapter on the turbulent years of the sixties, and as you perhaps can remember all this, you clearly realize that the appearance of the girls and boys was a violent, revolutionary gesture. They were lost in never ending threats of wars, in a miasma of drugs, against a background of violence in music, art, films, television and the theatre.

In the traditional area of Couture, Mrs Carter always knew where were the ripest plums, and her reports, although one may have been sitting directly across from her at the Collections she has carefully described in *The Sunday Times*, were always a delight and a surprise. Her clear point of view and trenchant prose, made them always refreshing to read and absorb.

This book is a small encyclopedia, livened by vignettes of periods past, and original theories on why certain silhouettes evolved, with analyses of American, English, Italian, French and Irish fashion scenes. Sometimes the designers create for the *haute couture*, sometimes for 'off-the-peg' or ready-to-wear, all of which are a reflection of the times. Mrs Carter's book is written by an expert. She is a greatly respected and influential force for the many people who eagerly seek her point of view and absorb her thorough experience on both sides of the Atlantic and everywhere that Ernestine Carter feels fashion is making its way.

It is a unique work and will be invaluable for many years to come for all those concerned with fashion – designers, students, social historians, as well as those who are fascinated by the never ending changes in this extraordinary century.

Beginnings

The twentieth century began in the reflected glow of the pyrotechnical burst of inventions that shed an incandescent light on the closing years of the Victorian Age. As Sir Edward Playfair wrote in *The Times Literary Supplement*, 'Progress in scientific discovery was explosive; it was more accessible then than now to the ordinary man; it excited emotion and aesthetic delight.'[1] We, who think of ourselves as children of an era of technological advancement, do not always realize how much this century owes the last. Of course not all the inventions had a direct influence on fashion. Some just gave it a glancing blow, but each of them, as they changed the shape and pace of our lives, changed the shape and pace of fashion.

Alexander Graham Bell and his telephone, Morse and his telegraph, Marconi and his wireless, speeded up communication and revved up the dialogue between the fashion capitals of the world. The photographic experiments of Fox Talbot and Daguerre pioneered the means to document the ephemeral moods of fashion (although it was Eastman's first roll film developed for the new Kodak camera that really fathered modern photography) while that Danish Pastor's device, the typewriter, helped to record them. (Pastor Hanson had his brainwave in 1870; eleven years later the first British typewriter was designed by Maskelyne the magician.) These were indirect influences, but Scottish

Kirkpatrick MacMillan's bicycle and the motor car, the child of many fathers, among them the French Lavassor and De Dion, and the Germans Daimler and Benz, demanded a fashion of their own. Thomas Alva Edison's electric light, his phonograph and motion pictures each made its differing impact on fashion (especially the latter), although more than probably this was the last thing that massive genius had in mind.

Of all the inventions of this incredibly productive period the sewing machine was the one that changed most drastically the whole history of clothing. In that first awkwardly designed contraption lay the seeds of mass production, of fashion for the many instead of fashion for the few. Like most major inventions it was the result of a series of ingenious minds, each of which added some essential component, and, like most major inventions, the eventual winner was the one who managed to make it a commercial success. The history of the sewing machine is as complicated as that of the motor car, its genesis a double-pointed needle patented in 1755. The first to invent a machine that worked was a French tailor, Barthélemy Thimmonier in 1830, but neither he nor, a few years later, Walter Hunt of New York, who contributed the essential element of the eye-pointed needle, reaped the rewards they deserved. Elias Howe of Massachusetts was more fortunate, although he too suffered the vicissitudes that seem to attend the birth of a new idea. Ignorant, as far as is known, of Hunt's curved eye-point needle and the under-thread shuttle, Howe incorporated both of these into the model which he patented in America in 1846. (Poor Hunt, when he eventually applied for a patent in 1853, found he had allowed too much time to elapse and the patent was refused on the grounds of abandonment.) Howe's early days were in the tradition of inventors. He took his model to London where the English rights to his patent were sold for £250 to a tailor who patented it under his own name. Howe was reduced to pawning his American patent rights and in 1849 returned home penniless where he found that others had caught on to the idea, and were manufacturing sewing machines. The most successful was Isaac Singer, who had patented his in 1851. Singer remained the Goliath in the field but Howe, although no David, managed to retrieve the patents he had pawned, and, with whose help or by what means history does not relate, was able to institute a series of law suits which were triumphantly successful. All, even the redoubtable Singer, were forced to pay him royalties estimated, at the expiry of his patent which had been extended to 1867, at around two million dollars. This is the happy end of Howe's story. Further improvements continued to be made based on Hunt's and Howe's principles and on Singer's developments, but the years 1846 and 1851 can be taken as the historic milestones on the path that changed an art into an industry.

1

The Lotus Years

As the Edwardian years recede ever farther into history they become bathed in an increasingly golden glow. The privileged few who typify these years – the noble and (ennobled) families who surrounded the King and who themselves lived like kings – enjoyed a world which no longer exists, a world in which there were no shadows, where it was always afternoon, a world of wealth and security which enabled its fortunate inhabitants to live with no thought of tomorrow.

The nostalgia for these sunlit days set in early and has lasted late. Rarely have so many books been written about so few years, for the reign of King Edward VII was brief, from 1901 until his death in 1910, yet so strong was his imprint that the years until the First World War are usually referred to as the Edwardian period. It was perhaps the abruptness with which the War snuffed out what Michael Holroyd called 'the last brilliant afterglow of Edwardian England'[1] and put a full stop

The door that this pretty lady is facing opens on the 1900s. Although she was photographed in 1893, she shape of her dress, with its high collar, small waist and jutting behind, her parasol and her large, plume-laden hat, will be just as fashionable in the early years of the new century as they were in the declining years of the old, for fashion does not change with the calendar.

*Sir Willie's luncheon party, photographed, in 1910, seems eminently
conventional in grouping and clothes, until you spy the gentleman in the last
row ; clearly a 'card' and note what he has on his head.*

to what James Laver more prosaically referred to as 'the last good time of the upper classes,[2] which
has produced such a prodigality of memoirs and continues to provide material for a continuing
stream of studies.

As the memoirists were aristocratic, the view is inevitably circumscribed, a limitation which has
affected most of the subsequent writers. It is not hard to see why these years are so tempting to write
about : such luxury and grandeur, and such capacity for their enjoyment; such consuming passions,
such delicious scandals, such royal liaisons (and such a capacity for *their* enjoyment), such glorious
freedom from the restraints of social conscience (of the beauties who revolved around the King, only
Daisy, Countess of Warwick, seems to have been aware of the distress the others ignored and actually
to have done something about it).

It was a time of excess. As Virginia Cowles wrote,

'Everything was larger than life-size. There was an avalanche of balls and dinners and country house
parties. More money was spent on clothes, more food was consumed, more infidelities were
committed, more birds were shot, more yachts were commissioned, more late hours were kept, than
ever before.'[3]

To keep up with this sumptuous programme, clothes were sumptuous too, and as every sub-
division of the day demanded its correct costume, wardrobes were vast. A country house visit could
only be accomplished with a retinue of maids and valets, and an array of trunks. Fashion, too, was

Mercia who so proudly signs her sketch of one of Messrs. Charles Lee & Son's 'Evening Gowns in Chiffon *and* Novel (sic) Guipure *and* Embroidery Chenille', *although she gives the impression that not only the whole intricately wrought confection but also the lady's anatomy has melted like a candle down to its widely spreading ruched base, she has actually only slightly exaggerated the grotesque distortion of the S-bend, and faithfully portrays the fashionable Alexandra dog-collar held rigid by painful diamond bars and the cottage loaf hair-do, new in 1904.*

necessarily aristocratic, limited to those who could afford not just the cost of such luxurious finery but the skilled ladies' maids to keep that finery in order (a survivor is reported by Geoffrey Squire to have said that it took her a whole day just to 'get up' the ruffles inside a court train) and to help the wearers in the complicated ritual of attiring themselves.

Vita Sackville-West, who in *The Edwardians* has left us the most romantic evocation of this period, describes this arduous process as the Duchess' daughter watches her mother prepare for the evening with the aid of her personal maid, Button :

'Button knelt before her, carefully drawing the silk stockings on to her feet and smoothing them nicely up the legs. Then her mother would rise, and standing in her chemise, would allow the maid to fit the long stays of pink coutil, heavily-boned, round her hips and slender figure, fastening the busk down the front, after many adjustments; then the suspenders would be clipped to the stockings;

then the lacing would follow, beginning with the waist and travelling gradually up and down, until the necessary proportions had been achieved. The silk laces and their tags would fly out, under the maid's deft fingers, with the flick of a skilled worker mending a net. Then the pads of pink satin would be brought, and fastened into place on the hips and under the arms, still further to accentuate the smallness of the waist. Then the drawers; and then the petticoat would be spread into a ring on the floor, and Lucy would step into it on her high-heeled shoes, allowing Button to draw it up and tie the tapes . . .'

The Duchess is now ready for her dress:

'Button, gathering up the lovely mass of taffeta and tulle, held the bodice open while the Duchess . . . dived gingerly into the billows of her dress. Viola watched enraptured the sudden gleam of her mother's white arms and shoulders. Button heaved a sigh of relief as she began doing up the innumerable hooks at the back.'

In the same book, Lady Roehampton instructs her maid to lay out various costumes 'with their adjuncts', that she might choose what she would wear that day.

'And so, eight or ten selections might be displayed on chairs ranged round the room, complete with shoes, stockings, hat, veil, boa and parasol . . . It often happened that after standing and turning before her cheval-glass, completely dressed, she would declare that she could not possibly go out looking like that, and would change again from head to foot, for she would rather keep a luncheon-party waiting for three-quarters of an hour than fall below the standard of her perfection. It was a worship, a rite, that she performed in the service of a double deity: her own beauty and the society she decorated.'

Only the later and legendary American, Rita de Acosta Lydig, outdid this fictional ladyship. Sir Cecil Beaton has described the wardrobe of this great beauty – the first woman to appear in public wearing a dress cut to the waist at the back – who, he says, 'independent of time . . . dressed in her own fashion' in clothes of fantastic luxury made for her by the Callot Sisters, whom she financed.

'Her wardrobe included black velvet dresses for day; low-cut, barebacked evening dresses; jackets and coats made of rich and rare materials and worn with velvet skirts by day or satin culottes for evening; nightdresses and underclothes trimmed with medallions incorporating classical figures in lace as delicate as the skeleton of an autumn leaf; black lace mantillas as light as gossamer; heavy lace tunics that appear like armour; blouses of embroidered batiste, needlework, or bobbin lace . . . cobweb thin stockings with rare lace insertions; rose-point petticoats, small sable hats, fezzes of unborn lamb . . .'[4]

Mrs Lydig's shoes, of which she possessed literally hundreds of pairs, were made for her by Yanturni, an East Indian who was Curator of the Cluny Museum, of antique velvets, brocades, or lace. They were kept in shape by shoe trees made of violin wood. Fiction pales before fact.

When fully attired to their satisfaction beauties like the Duchess and Lady Roehampton would

This watercolour sketch for a street dress by Lucile in 1904, to which are attached swatches of the fabrics to be used, came from her own sketchbook in the collection of Mrs Doris Langley Moore.

Right *The dazzling Mrs Rita de Acosta Lydig photographed by Baron de Meyer in the barebacked dress, well in advance of her day, that shook the occupants of the Diamond Horseshoe of the old Metropolitan Opera House.*

Opposite left *Miss Carroll McComas, the American actress, adopts in 1905 the typical photographic pose of the time, one arm artfully arranged to soften the protruding rear view. Miss McComas went on to become a star on Broadway, playing the lead, among other roles, in Zona Gale's Mrs Lulu Bett in 1920.*

be armoured from their high-boned collars to their toes. One can but wonder where the gargantuan meals were stowed and how the many seductions were achieved. Is it possible that the passions which consumed these frail creatures may have been in some way inflamed by the very constriction of their clothes, just as presumably the risk of being found out with its threat of social ostracism may have heightened their ardour?

Parisians were similarly iron-clad. Proust describes Odette de Crecy:

'... as for her figure, and she was admirably built, it was impossible to make out its continuity (on account of the fashion then prevailing, and in spite of her being one of the best-dressed women in Paris) for the corset, jutting forwards in an arch, as though over an imaginary stomach, and ending in a sharp point, beneath which bulged out the balloon of her double skirts, gave a woman, that year, the appearance of being composed of different sections badly fitted together; to such an extent did the frills, the flounces, the inner bodice follow in complete independence, controlled only by the fancy of their designer or the rigidity of their material, the line which led them to the knots of ribbon, falls of lace, fringes of vertically hanging jet, or carried them along the bust, but nowhere attached themselves to the living creature, who according as the architecture of their fripperies drew them towards or away from her own, found herself either strait-laced to suffocation or else completely buried.'[5]

Jean Cocteau concluded that to contemplate undressing a fashionable cocotte would be as complicated an undertaking as arranging to move house.

The one time of the day when these whaleboned palisades were breached was the tea hour, when it was permissible to wear tea-gowns; soft, seductive confections of satin, accordion pleated chiffon, or fine silk, first introduced in the Paris World's Fair of 1900 where they evoked a naughty thrill of excitement. Proust describes Odette wearing such a déshabillé, redolent of promised intimacy; 'of crêpe de Chine, white as the first snows of winter, or, it might be, in one of those long

Above *Queen Alexandra in her Coronation robes – a glittering icon festooned in jewels, preserving in 1902 the frizzy fringe and jewelled dog-collar she made popular as Princess of Wales in 1863.*

pleated garments of mousseline-de-soie, which seemed nothing more than a shower of white or rosy petals . . .'[6] In England, the tea-gown, although undoubtedly also worn for tête-à-tête assignations, was the accepted wear at grand house parties after the exertions of the afternoon, riding, driving, hunting or shooting, and before the final change for dinner. In France, according to Alison Settle,[7] the most beautiful were made by Madeleine Vionnet before she was the great couturière she was to become. In England the mistress of the tea-gown was Lucile, the leading English dressmaker, in private life Lady Duff Gordon and sister to Elinor Glyn, whose book, *The Visits of Elizabeth*, a delightful *faux-naif* account of Edwardian house parties seen through a young girl's eyes, is replete with references to these important garments.

Queen Victoria is said to have frowned on modishness which was felt to be a perogative for ladies of easy virtue. This disapproval must date from her mourning years, for in 1835 as a young

Overleaf left *Jacques Doucet has been dressmaker to Duse and Rejane at the end of the nineteenth century. By the twentieth he had become the doyen of the Couture, a dressmaker whose interest went beyond clothes to furniture and art, of both of which he made distinguished collections. The fanciful elaboration of this at-home dress of 1913 was painted by Robert Dammy for* La Gazette du Bon Ton.

Overleaf right *Paquin's version of Poiret's pagoda tunic shows the wit and chic which attracted the young fashionables – English as well as French – of the time. Drawn by Georges Barbier for* La Gazette du Bon Ton, *1914.*

AH! LE BEL OISEAU !

Robe d'intérieur de Doucet

Opposite *On Derby Day
parasols bloom with the
inscrutable frequency of
mushrooms, c.1907.*

*Hats of tea tray size were worn
by ladies lunching out, but the
taffeta coats, which Bradley offer
in this advertisement of 1910,
would not have found favour
with Mrs Eric Pritchard who in
1902 considered 'the daintiest and
most becoming of blouses'
appropriate for lunch in a 'well-
heated restaurant'.*

Princess she was 'in raptures over two boxes of dresses and hats sent her from Paris . . . "made by Mlle
Palmyre the 1st Marchande des Modes in Paris"', and as a young Queen, five years later, 'she flew
on to the ballroom floor like a tiny hummingbird in her blue satin gown from Paris . . .'[8]

With the Queen's death, and King Edward's long-delayed accession to the throne, the way was
open for ladies of fashion to dress in the *dernier cri* from Paris, and to deck themselves in silks and
satins and velvets, sparkling jewels, furs and feather boas, and with sleeves so exaggeratedly puffed,
their wearers had to go through doorways sideways. 'Not since the florid days of King George IV',
concludes Sir Osbert Sitwell 'had fashion been similarly triumphant.'[9] The result was an ostentatious
illustration of Veblen's canons of taste: conspicuous consumption, conspicuous leisure, conspicuous
waste.[10] Quentin Bell adds 'conspicuous outrage';[11] we might add 'conspicuous artifice'.

It is hard to think of a fashion in this century as remarkably distorted as that which prevailed at
the beginning. It was, of course, the dying echo of what had gone before, for fashion by and large
tends to evolve and it is only rarely that an event or a towering talent can stop it in its tracks and
make it change gait entirely. The events which changed the course of fashion in our time were the
Ballet Russe, and the talents were Paul Poiret, Chanel and Christian Dior.

But we are still in the 'Naughty Noughts', ruthlessly laced into a cinched-in waist, above it,
protruding in front in a low slung pouch, below it, bulging out behind. No wonder, when being
painted or photographed, the beauties of the day adopted a characteristic pose, their hands clasped
behind their backs, emphasizing their unbroken expanse of snowy bosom and minimizing their
steatopygous rear view. Even idealized fashion plates could not entirely prettify this curious
silhouette, and when by 1902 the cruel eye of the camera gained sway, a sense of discomfort was even
more painfully evident.

LE RENDEZ-VOUS DANS LE PARC

Grande Robe de soirée, de Worth

Only from the back could these hour-glass figures look romantic – and only Queen Alexandra somehow managed to give this rigid fashion the impress of her own delicate distinction. To some, like Jean Worth, she seemed over-dressed. As Sir Cecil Beaton observed, she would wear in the daytime 'clothes which most women would have worn at night, but the fact that she wore them during the day removed her from reality and only helped increase the aura of distance that one associates with the Court.'[12] Thus she fulfilled Joseph Chamberlain's dictum: 'Simplicity is all right in a republic but a sovereign must bring splendour.'[13] The last British queen to lead fashion, her innovations were widely copied: the dog collar, a choker necklace of many strands of precious stones, sometimes garnished with a tulle bow at the back, and less happily, a frizzy fringe which her imitators could, if they wished, buy ready-made and simply pin on. As Princess of Wales, Alexandra has also been credited with introducing the full-length coat, buttoned from collar to hem – 'the first', according to J. Anderson Black, 'really practical day coat suited to the English weather.'[14]

The prevailing hair-do, like everything else, was exaggerated, upswept to a forward jutting pompadour plumped out by 'teasing' or pads of combings or horsehair, vulgarly known as 'rats', amplified with 'switches' and ornamented with decorative combs. (This upswept style, appropriately called 'Edwardian', made a reappearance in 1937, to be followed during the Second World War by a version of the Alexandra fringe.)

Hats were large, heavy and plume-laden, skewered on by lethal but elaborately ornamented hat pins. For dining out at restaurants these hats were considered 'infinitely more becoming', according to Mrs Eric Pritchard, in 1902, 'than the best dressed *coiffure*'. Mrs Pritchard goes on to advise 'for the benefit of her country readers' that 'where the dinner costs *3s. 6d* to *5s.*, a pretty hat and light, becoming blouse should be worn. An elaborate demi-toilette or the decolleté frock of convention is more suitable when the dinner is priced at half a guinea and upwards.'[15]

One truly pretty accessory was the narrow stole or tippet with matching muff, usually in ermine or chinchilla, to which could be pinned a bunch of the newly popular Parma violets.

Just as ladies' maids seem to have existed in abundance, so did trained needlewomen. Between the two, lingerie in these years reached an apogee of exquisite workmanship, both beneath, in wonderfully wrought underwear, frilled, pin-tucked, embroidered, lace-trimmed and ribbon-laced, and on top, in whole dresses, coats and especially blouses. The hand-made blouse, at its highest expression in Paris, survived two wars and only recently expired.

England, that is fashionable England, now looked only to Paris for fashion, where across the Channel the French were revelling in the ostentation and extravagance of what James Pope-Hennessy called 'the delicious atmosphere of the second-rate'. Whereas in England the Court led fashion, in Paris, it was the courtesans – the *grandes cocottes* like Liane de Pougy, actresses like Sarah Bernhardt, music hall entertainers like Gaby Deslys and Polaire, opera singers like Lina Cavalieri – whose influence spanned the Channel.

The great names of dressmaking were Paquin, Doucet, Drecoll, Doeuillet, Chêruit, Maggy Rouff, the Callot Sisters (although in Proust's opinion they went in too freely for lace[16]), but, to the English and Americans, Worth led all the rest. The lustre of that name had not dimmed since the middle 1860s when Charles Frederick Worth became the first King of Couture. The English took a natural pride in his being English and the Americans were impressed by his regal clientele. Two other

Worth's romantic ball gown inspired the artist to give it a romantic title.
Drawn by Paul Meras for La Gazette du Bon Ton, *1912/13.*

Englishmen had also made their mark in Paris, both in tailored clothes; Charles Poynter (who worked under his firm's name of Redfern) who introduced the 'trotteur', a briskly tailored coat and skirt, and Charles Creed who made his name as a maker of riding habits. Premature Women's Libbers could take pride that of these leading lights of Couture – the Callot Sisters, Maggie Rouff, and Chêruit were women, as was Reboux, who became and remained until the twenties the commanding milliner, while both Madame Worth and Madame Paquin played important parts in their husbands' businesses.

Although English eyes were trained on Paris (and on Vienna as well for expert tailoring) at home, in another woman, Lucile, they possessed a remarkable dressmaker, a designer of truly ravishing, feminine clothes. She gave her confections names as romantic as the colours she preferred: 'Passion's Thrall' (purple and pink chiffon) was designed for Mrs Brown Potter, a reigning beauty and super-clothes horse of the time. 'Marvellously amorous colours', says Doris Langley Moore, through whose kindness I was able to study two of Lucile's sketch books complete with samples of fabrics, braids and laces. Another, 'Consolable Sorrow' (mauve chiffon over pale grey, with a deep-sleeved short coat in horizontally pleated black chiffon edged with silver lace) was also intended for Mrs Brown Potter. Both were topped with wide flat hats like outsize mortar boards dripping with lace veils.

As the century wore on, corsets remained unyielding, but although they retained their straight fronts, they grew longer below and briefer above, the space created filled in by the camisole. By 1908

'Five o'clock chez Paquin' painted in 1906 by H. Gerveux.

the high boned collars had given way to a wide low neckline, revealing alas, necks long neglected in the safety of concealment. This radical change is attributed to Vionnet then working at Doucet, although others give credit to Poiret's designs for *Le Minaret* in 1912. The waist had moved up by 1911 into what was thought to be an Empire line (pronounced, naturally, 'ompeer'). Hats grew even wider to make the figure seem more slender.

Freedom was in the air, for the great inventions in mobility of the previous century were beginning to come into common use. The motor car was to have the most immediate effect on fashion, creating a paraphernalia of its own, making the name of Burberry world famous. Proust, with his sensitive and concentrated eye was one of the first to perceive what a challenge the Métro and motor would be to the Couture. Another cross for the couturiers was the increasing appetite for active sport. Bicycling had already become a rage in the 1890s, giving birth to bloomers (named after Mrs Amelia Bloomer). Swimming was to replace the more sedate bathing. Bathing dresses were supplanted by the one-piece swim suit, introduced by Annette Kellerman in 1900. Tennis was ceasing to be pat-ball, although freedom of movement was still impeded by skirts long enough to

In 1908 both the rigid hour-glass corset and the high-boned collar had been banished. Décolletages appeared and waists were lifted 'à l'Empire', the longer line often broken by a tunic. The jewelled circlet spouting osprey feathers was the smartest hair ornament, pushing the conventional tiara into the shade. From The Queen, The Lady's Newspaper, *15 April 1911.*

Emancipation from corsets may have been a boon to the wearers, but, as seen at Longchamps, the sudden release from restraint produced a result that must have brought little joy to Poiret.

Opposite *Anna Pavlova,
supremely elegant from her
osprey trimmed picture hat to her
buckled slipper, was a postcard
beauty of 1914.*

*The rich Orientalism of Bakst
and Poiret was clearly the
inspiration for this photograph by
E. O. Hoppé in 1914 of Lady
Lavery draped in rich brocade,
lavishly fur trimmed,
accompanied by her exotically
caparisoned page.*

conceal flat tennis shoes which were considered unfeminine. Golf too was gaining popularity.

Activity was not confined to outdoors. Indoors the world was dancing, first to the lilting tunes of *The Merry Widow* and later to the throbbing rhythms of the tango. Both had their effect on fashion, as we shall see.

But the great revolution was hovering in the wings. The curtain was about to go up on the Ballet Russe, and, with a leap as breathtaking as Nijinsky's as the slave in *Scheherazade*, onto the stage of fashion there sprang a new designer, Paul Poiret. Poiret denied that he was inspired by the designs of Bakst and Benois, asserting that he had already wiped his palette clean of the delicate sweet-pea tints which Lucile's costumes for Lily Elsie, the beautiful star of *The Merry Widow*, had made fashionable, in favour of the bold, primary colours preferred by the Russians and the group of painters known as Les Fauves ('the wild beasts'). Still, without the overwhelming enthusiasm which the Ballet Russe aroused, it is doubtful if Poiret's designs would have found such immediate acceptance, or he himself such immediate fame. His theatrical innovations paved the way for glorious individualists like Lady Ottoline Morrell, whose predilection for the dramatic was ridiculed by her disloyal literary protegés. D.H.Lawrence describes her:

'A strange figure . . . wearing a large, old cloak of greenish cloth, on which was a raised pattern of dull gold. The high collar, and the inside of the cloak, was lined with dark fur. Beneath she had a dress of fine lavender-coloured cloth trimmed with fur, and her hat was close-fitting, made of fur and of the full, green and gold figured stuff.'[17]

Although to Lawrence she may have looked eccentric, it seems clear that Lady Ottoline, one of the first Society hostesses to welcome the Ballet Russe when it came to England in 1911, was aware of Poiret.

Poiret may not have invented the brassière nor have been the first to abolish corsets, but, by

In 1909 the Ballet Russe took Paris by storm. The costumes by Benois and Bakst, especially the latter's for Scheherazade, first performed in Paris in 1910, took Paul Poiret by storm too. The turbans with their extravagant plumes, the harem pantaloons encouraged his natural inclination toward Oriental extravagance. To these he added the short hooped 'lampshade' or 'pagoda' tunic for a costume for Madame Poiret to wear at his 1002nd Night party in 1911. According to Poiret's biographer, Palmer White, Madame Poiret was placed in a gold cage from which, when the guests had assembled, Poiret as Sultan released her. Georges Lepape commemorated the costume with this gouache of Madame Poiret escaping from her prison which he presented to her as a souvenir of the occasion.

The incredible Poiret himself, drawn by Georges Lepape for the cover of the Poiret Album.

'Bakst-in-the-home' was less happy than Bakst in Bon Ton as this so-called 'smoking suit' of 1922 shows.

Poiret's hobble skirt had been abandoned by 1915 and full rib-seamed-skirts ballooned like half-unfurled umbrellas, a resemblance emphasized by the real umbrellas. Left to right: tailored suits by Paquin, Lanvin, Doeuillet; coat by Paquin. Drawn by Valentine Gross for La Gazette du Bon Ton, *entitled 'Il Pleut Encore'.*

breaking the carapace in which women had for so long been imprisoned he created the contemporary woman. With their Protean capacity for changing shape, women fell with ease and delight into his soft, slender dresses dropping from gently moulded bosoms above high waists. The mature, voluptuous beauty vanished. Poiret set women on the quest they still pursue, like Ponce de Leon, for the Fountain of Youth. Artificial constriction was banished, to return only twice in the years that followed: in the early twenties with the brutally flattened bosom and hips, and in 1947 with the *guepière* (a tiny wasp-waisted corset) which Christian Dior introduced as the basis for his 'New Look'.

So these somewhat absurd years passed in a strange confusion as the twentieth century freed itself from the shackles of the past and attempted to assimilate the technological present with such arch and ineffectual devices as concealing electric lights in Chinese lanterns and telephones under the skirts of elaborately dressed dolls, escaping from conventional clothes into Poiret's fantasies, sublimely unaware that it was moving toward catastrophe, secure still in an optimism which the First World War was to relegate once and for all to the mothballs of history.

2

When Paris Ruled

From the crinolined heydays of Charles Frederick Worth, Paris ruled fashion. What Paris decreed was the last word on what was worn, what was to be worn. In the Chambre Syndicale de la Couture Parisienne the top designers had a powerful association, part trade union, part public relations, part training school. Under Gaston Worth, son of Charles Frederick, the Chambre had from 1885 represented the French Couture; from 1911 it represented the Paris Couture only. In 1936 it reorganized itself again into a tightly knit protective professional group. The change in 1911 enabled it to survive the First World War, that of 1936 to survive the German Occupation of the Second World War.

It is to the Chambre that we owe the definition of Haute Couture. It is not just simply supplying rich women with expensive apparel; it is, according to the Chambre, 'not only the art of sewing but the art of inventing, assembling, creating everything that goes to clothe a woman.' That might seem

Christian Dior's New Look, with which he opened his own House in 1947, restored Paris as a centre of fashion after its isolation under the Occupation. As Balenciaga found inspiration from the flamenco dancers and the bullfighters of his native Spain, Dior found his in the peasant dress of his native Normandy. His tragically early death in 1957 robbed fashion of one of its greatest – and happiest – talents.

Far left *The Ranee of Pudukota snapped at Aix-les-Bains in 1923 wearing a dress by Jeanne Lanvin and a hat by Reboux.*

Left *The Ranee of Pudukota in a coat by Patou from his winter collection 1926/7.*

Below left *Balmain has always understood the art of piquant contrast: here he belts the softness of chiffon in wide gilt leather, bares one shoulder, floats a panel from the other. Jean Shrimpton photographed at Versailles in 1962.*

Right *Jules François Crahay has been one of the most inventive designers of the Paris Couture. At Nina Ricci he startled with the lowest plunge necks in 1959, pioneered gipsy dresses in 1960, the first maxi coat in 1963. In 1964 he moved to Lanvin, succeeding Antonio del Castillo. For Lanvin in 1970 he designed this double evening cape in black taffeta, its fullness spreading from cartridge tucks.*

enough, but as in all art, there is something else – the artist's handwriting. Proust, with his almost obsessive interest in clothes, attempted to define this something else through Albertine in *Within a Budding Grove*. Asked if there is a difference between a dress by Callot and one from a shop, she replies, 'Why, an enormous difference . . . Only, alas! what you get for three hundred francs from an ordinary shop will cost two thousand there. But there can be no comparison; they look the same only to people who know nothing at all about it.' Twenty-five years later Nancy Mitford undertook to explain the same thing. In *Love in a Cold Climate* Fanny's profligate mother gives her a little scarlet jacket by Schiaparelli, which the worldly Cedric Hampton identifies at once. 'Cedric, how can you tell?' 'My dear, one can always tell. Things have a signature, if you use your eyes!' Cedric also makes a shrewd guess at the cost. Fanny is appalled: 'Twenty-five pounds for this? . . . Simply silly. Why I could have made it myself.' 'But could you? And if you had would I have come into the room and said "Schiaparelli"?' 'There's only a yard of stuff in it, worth a pound if that.' . . . 'And how many yards of canvas in Fragonard? . . . Art is more than yards . . .'

This explains Haute Couture, but why Paris? Couture exists in other countries which have designers with equally identifiable signatures. The answer lies in an observation attributed to Quentin Bell that 'if Paris did not exist, it would have been necessary to invent it.' Paris has always been uniquely a centre for the arts, and its intellectual and social climate provides the right temperature in which fashion can flourish. Paris is the focus for a proliferation of exquisite crafts which the existence of the Couture attracts. The Italian designer, Simonetta, when she made her ill-fated sortie from Rome to Paris, was overwhelmed. 'In Italy', she said, 'if you want a button or a bow, you have to design it, work out how it is to be made, oversee the production. In Paris, every day someone comes to you with trays and trays of fabulous buttons, belts, buckles, bows, with ideas for handbags, feathers, embroideries, new and fantastic fabrics.' A delicate part of the art of the Couture is the selection from amongst this embarrassment of riches.

The workrooms of the pre-First World War days could – and did – produce miracles of delicate needlework – tuckings, insertions, ruffles, ribbon bows, faggotting, satin bindings . . . Labour was not only skilled but cheap, and plentiful enough to supply the minor as well as the major Houses (to Proust the major Houses were Callot, Doucet, Chéruit, Paquin – 'the others are all horrible'[1]) and even the little woman round the corner. The standard of workmanship persists, but the supply has dwindled and the cost has soared.

In the fabulous hothouse of Paris, new blooms flower, hardy perennials fade away, leaving behind the fragrance of their memory in bottles still bearing their names. Not all the talents are French. Native blood is enriched by foreign injections: Balenciaga was Spanish, Jean Dessès was Greek, Yves Saint Laurent is Algerian; Schiaparelli was Italian; Redfern, Creed and Molyneux were English, Mainbocher American. Some Houses like Lanvin, Patou, Dior and Nina Ricci whose founders have died continue to function with new designers. Lanvin has sheltered the Spanish Antonio del Castillo, then Jules François Crahay. Crahay had been at Nina Ricci where Gérard Pipart now reigns. Patou has had a succession of designers of whom the most distinguished have been Marc Bohan (now at Dior) and Michel Goma. At Dior, Yves Saint Laurent succeeded the great Christian and Marc Bohan succeeded Saint Laurent. Pierre Balmain and England's John Cavanagh started with Molyneux. Balmain went on to Lelong where the young Christian Dior was also working. What gave Paris its dominant position was not merely this mobile agglomeration of talent, but the powerful personalities who changed the language of dress – the movers and shakers as well as the serene sculptors and architects of clothes.

Although crêpe was Vionnet's favourite medium for her bias cut, she could bring it off in lawn as well, here used for a skirt of tiered petals on a lilac dress, 1920. Presented to the Victoria and Albert Museum in 1971 by Sybil, Marchioness of Cholmondeley, for whom it was made.

One of the first movers and shakers was Poiret. It has become conventional to point to him as the pivot on which fashion in this century changed direction. He certainly claimed to be, but there is the strange fact of the simultaneity of ideas. Just as when two scientists in different countries unbeknownst to each other find that they have each been working toward the same solution of the same problem, so in different fashion capitals an urge to liberate the body from the rigid confines of corsets was asserting itself. In both London and Paris the tea-gown was a harbinger of freedom. There was also a third capital – Vienna. 'The hang of a Viennese skirt'[2] was appreciated in Edwardian England. Amongst the best known Viennese Couture Houses was that run by the three Flüge sisters, one of whom was a friend of the artist Gustav Klimt. As Geoffrey Squire of the Victoria and Albert Museum has pointed out, as early as 1902, Klimt was designing for her soft, flowing, uncorsetted dresses. In Paris, Vionnet as well as Poiret had staked her claim to being the first to abolish the corset. But all this is academic. Credit does not necessarily go to the originator but to the person who brings the innovation to the world's attention, and there is no doubt that it was Poiret who publicized, popularized and epitomized this dramatic change. His passion for the exotic, the dramatic, and sometimes the absurd – the hobble skirt, the minaret tunic, the pantaloons, the rich embroideries and richer brocades, the glitter of tinsel and metallic threads, the exaggerated tassels, the voluptuous fur trimming, the little aigretted turbans – combined to overshadow the adorable simplicity of his dresses and tunics falling softly from their high waists. Inspired or not by Bakst and Les Fauves, Poiret changed the palette of fashion from pallid muted shades to violent primary colours. While Poiret reigned, he reigned supreme, but tastes change. He died in 1944 having lived to witness his own eclipse.

Left *The Chanel suit, worn by Chanel in 1929.*

Above *The Chanel suit in 1958: braid-trimmed in British Linton tweed it became a classic and by 1962 was copied throughout the Western world.*

As Poiret changed the shape of women, Chanel changed the shape of fashion. Although she had started her career as a milliner before the War, it was in 1919 that, as she said, she 'woke up famous'. Her gift was to understand the potential that lay in the poor little dress, the success of the minimum after the excess of the maximum. She was herself the essence of the post-First World War mood – independent, arrogant, a flouter of convention. What she liked to wear herself immediately became fashion. She took cardigans, it is said from the English cricket field, and put them over easy skirts, flared or sunray pleated, with pockets at just the right place for their wearers to achieve her own round-shouldered, hip-forward stance. She took from sailors their pants and sweaters – their berets too – and made them the rage. She took jersey, till then a 'poor' fabric and kasha, a specially woven wool, and made them into short straight dresses. She loved the contrast between her favourite Linton tweeds and the fine silks she used for blouses and matching linings. She trimmed her casual suits with marvellous braids, fine gilt chains and glittering buttons. And on everything she hung her imitation jewellery, just as she wore the real ones herself. She put feet into the sling-back Chanel shoe, beige with a black patent toe, made beige a colour, sun tan a vogue, *Chanel No 5* one of the most famous scents in the world. She closed her doors in 1939, reopened them in 1954 to a noisy lack of acclaim, but by 1962 her quilted tweeds with their quilted silk linings were being copied everywhere. She died in 1971 at eighty-eight having twice in her long career put women into a uniform of her own devising.

As Chanel was right for the early twenties, Schiaparelli was right for the thirties. Caught between a Depression and the approaching shadows of war, life had become brittle. The word was 'amusing', and Schiaparelli amused, and made amusement pay. Nowadays some of the fun seems to have evaporated: the hat like a stuffed shoe, or trimmed with a cutlet, the glove with fingernails, and similar surrealist fancies invented for her by Cocteau and Dali. Her other contributions are more impressive. She brought to Paris her Italian sense of colour: pillar-box red, scarlet, violet and royal purple and above all her 'shocking' pink. There was no flattery in her clothes, more of a masculine chic with their shoulders widened like the Guards' greatcoats whose actual cloth she used, their width often extended even farther with glycerined coq feathers, her severe dinner suits brightened with gold embroidery. She gave a new life to fastenings with inventive buttons (some designed for her by Jean Schlumberger), and was one of the first to use zippers and man-made fibres. She retired in 1954, the year of Chanel's return, and died in 1973 at the age of eighty-three.

It cannot escape notice that most of the talents concerned with fashion are remarkably long-lived, but one of the greatest, and certainly the happiest, was to die far too soon. He was Christian Dior whose untimely death in 1957 brought to an abrupt end a dazzling career.

All of these designers have had one thing in common – each expressed the mood of his or her time. As Chanel responded to the heedless, perverse post-First War world, Christian Dior

Typical of Schiaparelli's visual japes is this trompe l'œil *butterfly bow on one of the hand-knitted sweaters with which she made her name in 1928. It was given to the Victoria and Albert Museum by Madame Schiaparelli in 1971.*

Opposite Elsa Schiaparelli photographed by Sir Cecil Beaton, her hair feather cut to match her feather cloak, c. 1930.

Left *The Christian Dior strapless evening dress at its apogee in 1951, worn by Maxime Birley, then the Marquise de la Falaise.*

Opposite *By 1951, four years after Christian Dior had launched his New Look, all the couturiers in both Paris and London had adopted his cinch-waisted, full-skirted silhouette, as had Jacques Fath in this saddle-coloured taffeta late-day dress, worn with a scoop-brimmed hat of black velvet.*

interpreted the yearning for a return to femininity that followed the Second World War. After the *garçonnerie* of Chanel, the *belle laiderie* of Schiaparelli, and the years of wartime restriction and uniforms, women were ready to fall back into an ultra-feminine echo of happier days, back to tiny waists cinched by *guepières*, back to longer skirts, their fullness made fuller by petticoats and linings, back to shaped bosoms and padded hips. A New Look dress with its boned and stiffened lining could almost stand alone but on top everything was soft – collars lay easily open, shoulders sloped, skirts swayed. It may have been retrograde, but it was ravishingly becoming. Talleyrand said that nobody could appreciate the *douceur de la vie* who had not lived before 1789; it could be said that nobody could appreciate the *douceur de la mode* who had not lived through the New Look. It burst upon the world in 1947 and its influence survived until Balenciaga's chemise of 1956 killed it, a year before Dior's own death.

Balenciaga, dignified, as reclusive as Garbo, never a shaker although definitely a mover, moved so slowly that sometimes he seemed to stand still. When he opened in Paris in 1937 Carmel Snow of *Harper's Bazaar* was the first to understand, appreciate and support this proud Spaniard, the first to foresee that he would one day become a major force. Although after the War Balenciaga was showing rib-hugging jackets with puff-shouldered sleeves over full skirts, he began in 1952 to release the body, first by loosening the backs, only gently shaping the fronts of his jackets and tunic dresses, progressing step by step and stitch by stitch to a minimally shaped chemise in 1957. In the hands of Balenciaga's disciple, Hubert de Givenchy, this chemise was exaggerated into a kite shape, wide at the top, tapering to the hem. Promptly christened the 'sack', widely and not too carefully copied, it caused shouts of male wrath in America, evoked acid comments from *The Economist* in England and disappeared, but the chemise in varying forms is with us still. Balenciaga retired in 1968, died in 1972. Although at the time of his retirement he had said that the world in which couture could flourish was finished, Givenchy continues against the odds to uphold the Balenciaga tradition.

Overleaf left *Jeanne Lanvin's interpretation of the aberrant hemlines of the twenties, 1924/25.*

Overleaf right *A rare sketch by Jean Patou himself of the low-waisted long skirted twenties, its tube-like simplicity softened by a transparent overdress of lace, 1923.*

"UNE MINUTE ET JE SUIS PRÊTE..."

From his arrival in Paris in 1937 from Spain when Carmel Snow of Harper's Bazaar was the first to recognize the strength of his talent until his death in 1972, Cristobal Balenciaga was in the eyes of his devoted clients, as well as in the opinion of fashion experts, a major force in fashion. As Diana Vreeland wrote in her foreword to the Exhibition, 'The World of Balenciaga', held at the Metropolitan Museum of Art in New York in 1973, 'He was the master tailor, the master dressmaker.' Balenciaga loved the drama of the lifted skirt that swoops down to a train at the back – made poetry out of what in 1927 was quite simply ugly. In 1957 he caught these full skirts high with narrow sashes and ruffle-edged the hems as shown here: by 1958 the line flowed from narrow shoulders into a peacock tail.

Pierre Cardin has been a shaker ever since he opened his House on the Faubourg St Honoré in 1953. Unlike the others, he responds less to mood than to modern techniques and technology. He has explored every permutation of drapery, exploited the total capacity of the sewing machine: cartridge tucks, smocking, scallops; in addition he has run a dazzling gamut of pleats. A preoccupation with bias cut resulted in spiral dresses of dizzying virtuosity. Frail, pale, intense, Cardin seems intent on his own inner compulsion – remote from the Balenciaga influence. From the moment the Russians shot Gagarin into space in 1961, Cardin too was in orbit. By 1964 his collections were directed toward the moon, anticipating the Astronauts' actual moonstrike by five years, with space helmets, leather stocking boots, dresses that were just lightly swinging tabards over knitted catsuits. Always given to exaggeration, his collars have been the widest, largest, tallest, his skirts slit the highest, his cut-outs the most. And by 1970 when he acquired the Théâtre des Ambassadeurs, which he rechristened L'Espace Cardin, his collections have been the longest. (Of one a journalist exclaimed 'I loved the first three hundred'.) He was the first couturier to start designing for men, in 1958, and now designs everything from radios, cars, jewellery to LPs. Ever unexpected, it was he who in 1965 executed the deliciously pretty Edwardian costumes designed by Ghilaine Uhry for Brigitte Bardot in *Viva Maria* – copies of whose high-necked, long-sleeved, lace-trimmed blouses swept through the English and American boutiques.

Opposed to these explosive forces are the great classicists: Vionnet and Grès. Madeleine Vionnet, who died in 1975 at the age of ninety-eight, had her own concept of couture: 'to dress a body . . . not to construct a dress'. She chose clinging fabrics: crêpe de Chine (which had previously only been used for linings), soft velvets, sleek satins, which, to achieve her end of moulding the shape, she cut on the cross. This revolutionary bias cut was one of the great inventions in dressmaking in our time, a technical triumph. Pure in principle, it was eminently sexy in execution. Molyneux used it to create the famous satin dress in which Gertrude Lawrence made her entrance in *Private Lives*; Adrian used it to make Jean Harlow into a pre-Marilyn Monroe sex symbol. The cut kept Vionnet's name alive long after her retirement in 1939, and will keep it bright as long as clothes are sewn and not extruded from a tube.

Madame Grès began her career in 1934, when she was known as Alix. Although as Mainbocher once said of himself, Madame Grès sniffs the breeze, her vision is so concentrated on the range of stuffs which she is pre-eminent at handling – the jerseys, both silk and fine wool, chiffon and paper taffetas – that her clothes are always unmistakably hers. Her bravura performances are in silk jersey which she folds and drapes into dresses of classic, sometimes breathtaking, beauty. These evening dresses are as near as fashion comes to the sculptured drapery of the 'Winged Victory'.

The Paris Press loves its legends. One was that Chanel always tore apart every suit the night before her opening show. Another is that Madame Grès is never ready. As her audiences, punctual to a dot, wait with varying degrees of patience, dresses can be seen being carried down the hall from the workrooms to the models' *cabine*, like corpses hidden in their white shrouds, as supposedly

Overleaf left *For the spring and summer of 1964 Yves Saint Laurent used the beguiling freshness of Provençale cottons for skirts deeply quilted at the hem, and matching head kerchiefs.*

Overleaf right *Gérard Pipart for Nina Ricci has created a Franglais combination, as the caption for this photograph from his 1977 collection clearly shows: 'un blazer de shantung façonné sur sweater de jersey de soie noir . . .' This 'style Anglais' could never happen in England.*

Right *Pierre Cardin, ever exaggerating, in 1971 scallops the longest revers as well as the hem of a black coat over a knee-length white shift dress.*

Opposite *In 1964 Courrèges stopped the show in Paris. As the fashion editor of* Figaro *said, 'He has outdated all the others'; what he had done was lift skirts to four inches above the knee, and started the climb toward the mini. By 1968 he had reduced the skirt to minimal proportions worn over a knitted catsuit.*

Madame Grès finishes putting in the last pin, re-adjusting the last fold. Perhaps both legends are true; there is no gainsaying the long waits.

It is true that Yves Saint Laurent's opening on his own in 1962 had the fashion world on tiptoes with anticipation, but the fact is that the strongest handwriting of the sixties belonged not to Yves but to André Courrèges, the pelota player from the Basses-Pyrénées. Courrèges had worked with Balenciaga for eleven years before he opened his small, narrow, clinically white salon in 1961 and incidentally started a new pattern of couture presentation by showing his collections to music throbbing sombrely in the background. (The music was not to remain either sombre or in the background and he was soon to move into larger premises but white has always been his signature.) Not unnaturally his first collections were echoes of the Master, but by Courrèges' next season he had found his own formula: short skirts (the shortest in Paris), clear Le Corbusier colours – pink, white, ice blue – neat, cap-sleeved shift dresses flaring from narrow tops diagrammed with welted seams, clean-cut coats with little half-belts – all worn with white calf-high boots or snub-toed Mary Janes. These and his tunic-topped trousers, seamed fore and aft, became the new uniform. With his four-inches-above-the-knee skirts of 1964 Courrèges anticipated the mini, and he was the first to put women into pants. His disciplined, hard-edge outlines filled a desire for order in a disordered world, but the mood changed. The midi, a feel for softness, a distaste for synthetics – the nylon and the vinyl which had begun to displace his worsteds and gabardines – combined against him. And he lost his lead.

It is ironic that Emmanuel Ungaro who had worked alongside Courrèges at Balenciaga, left in 1964 after six years to join Courrèges briefly, leaving him in 1965 and opening on his own in 1966, should have survived the changing mood more successfully than his friend and patron. Born in

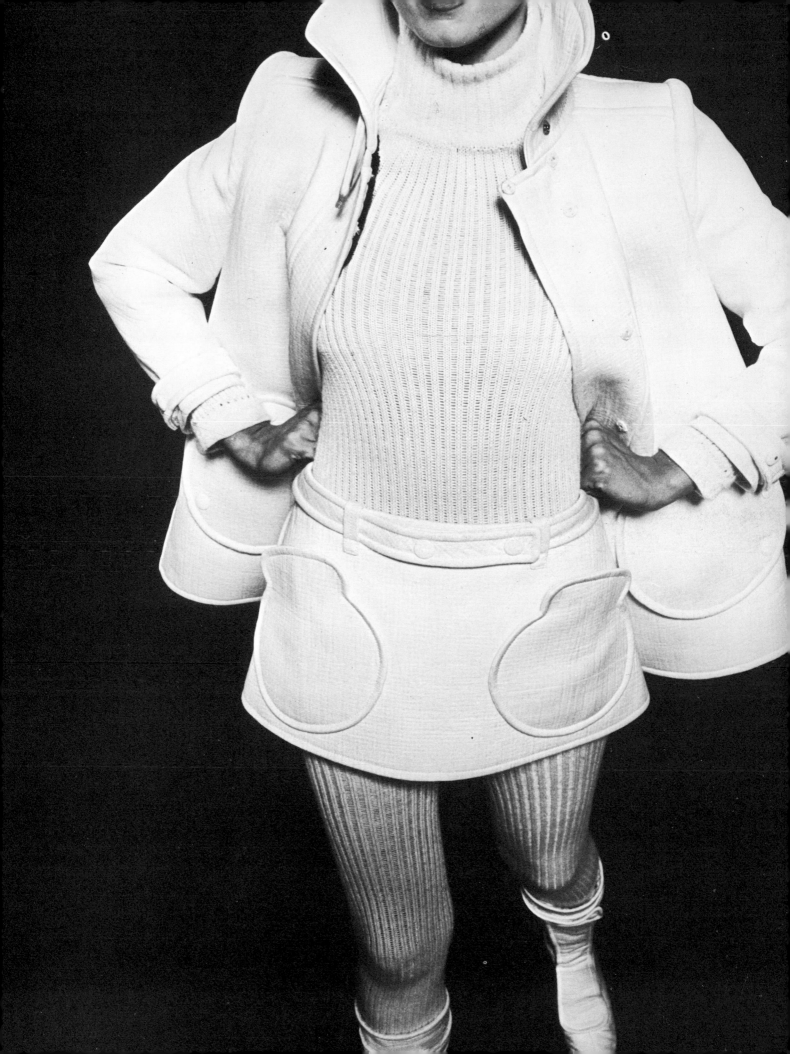

Provençe of Italian parents, Ungaro has the Italian feel for fabrics, and his close collaboration with fabric designer Sonja Knapp has resulted in a marvellous marriage of patterns, colours and textures which his combination of accurate cut and unorthodox ideas exploits to the full.

In retrospect, the first sign that the Couture was losing its commanding position was Saint Laurent's Beat Collection for Dior in 1960. It was not the collection itself, which was only important to the House of Dior and to the young Saint Laurent whose whole career it changed. What was important was that the collection showed that the powerful voice in fashion was not going to be that of the traditional clientele of the Couture – rich and middle-aged – but of the young; that instant fashion for an impatient public was going to replace painstaking perfection.

Gone forever were the halcyon days in the twenties described by Edith Wharton[3] when rich Americans were happy to cut short their holidays at the smart European resorts to swelter in Paris in July for what she called 'the most momentous period of the year: the height of the "dressmakers" season.' Now they jet in and jet out, and as Marc Bohan said, 'they all want their dresses yesterday'. Gone too are the days Nancy Mitford described in *The Blessing* when Grace, the English heroine, finds herself '. . . busy, an unaccustomed busyness, since it was all concerned with clothes . . . more and more dresses for more and more occasions: big occasions . . . little occasions, the voyage.' When Grace suggested that she might travel in her morning suit, the *vendeuse* replied sternly, 'It is always better to travel with brown accessories.' Poor *vendeuse*; soon travel accessories were to consist of an airline travel bag and clients like Grace to become as scarce as hen's teeth. The last of a dying race may be Mrs Paul Mellon who, according to a recent report in *W*, wears Givenchy exclusively, and entirely. She has her own atelier in the Maison Givenchy in Paris and it is said that he creates everything from her lingerie to her little tennis hats'.

What did happen? The Paris Couture had picked itself up after the trauma of Occupation. Led by the loyal stalwarts, American *Harper's Bazaar* Carmel Snow and American *Vogue*'s Bettina Ballard, the Press of the world regathered, most of them smelling deliciously of Rochas' latest scent, *Femme*. With the dazzling success of Dior, the buyers once more zero-ed in. It didn't really matter that air travel had widened the fashion horizon. Ireland had its charm but only Sybil Connolly's gossamer fine, pleated linens were worth the detour. Spain had Pertegaz and periodically produces a Berhanyer or a Mitzou but was never real competition. Italy came closest to being a worry.

Rome is as exciting a city as Paris, in some ways more so, with the glitter of its *Alta Moda*, all Marcheses, Duchesas, Contessas, Principessas, and their marvellously spoiling ways. In fashion it offers a splendour of colour, imaginative and luxurious fabrics, workrooms that produce seams of marquetry perfection, a sense of fantasy and drama, and a changing cast of talent. The aristocratic Simonetta, born Duchesa Colonna di Cesaro, and married to couturier Fabiani known for his expert tailoring, was the reigning queen from just after the War until she attempted to storm Paris, as did Roberto Capucci. Princess Galitzine made her name with her palazzo pyjamas. Mila Schön from Milan counterpointed bead embroidery of great elaboration with tailoring of exquisite simplicity. As interest began to sag, Valentino, who had made his debut in 1959, really hit the Big Time in 1968. Still, the most enduring Italian talent belongs to that reincarnation of Renaissance man, the Marchese Emilio Pucci. Literally snapped into fashion by photographer Toni Frissell on the ski slopes, Pucci combines a shrewd business brain with designing strength, but his forte is so specialized that Paris can afford not to be jealous. His headquarters are in the Palazzo Pucci on the Via dei Pucci in Florence where the showings at the Pitti Palace organized by Giovanni Batista Giorgini did at

Below *Ungaro's forte has been the handling of combinations of virtuoso printed fabrics, first by Nattier, then by Sonja Knapp. Here in his 1976/77 collection he marries a tunic in red challis printed in tiny green and yellow flowers to a divided skirt made of two scarves, largely checked and bordered in roses to make a very personal bow to the omni-present Russian mood.*

Left *Valentino after five years at Jean Dessès and two at Guy Laroche showed his first collection in Rome in 1959. By 1967 he had won a Nieman-Marcus Award; in 1968 he was in the midi and boots mood. Later that year he launched his gilt Vs as buttons, as trim on shoes and boots, embroidered on his stockings.*

Right *Givenchy has the supreme knack of presenting the startling in a guise acceptable to the conventionality of the very rich. Here he veils hot pants with a dress in Abraham's transparent navy organza scattered with field flowers, covers that in a matching double cape, ties the neck in a matching scarf, adds matching wedge-heeled shoes.*

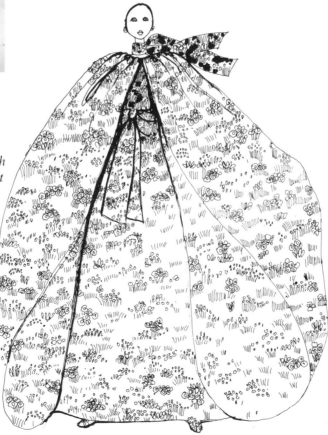

Above *P might stand for Permanent as well as Pucci, for this indefatigable Marchese has stayed at top level since he was first snapped by photographer Toni Frissell on the ski slopes after the Second World War. Printed silks are his signature, and the skill with which he translates exotic inspiration like this Javanese trousered skirt of 1964 into sophisticated resort wear makes this an area in which he excels.*

Left *After Christian Dior's death, his mantle fell upon the slender shoulders of the young Yves Saint Laurent. In 1958 Saint Laurent launched the trapeze; in 1959 he restored the hobble skirt, lifted to shackle the knees instead of the ankles, and added the dog collar beloved by the Edwardians.*

Opposite *Marc Bohan at Christian Dior takes a typically French delight in interpreting a popular fashion in couture terms and couture fabrics. In his 1976/77 collection he tops a long, wickedly slit black jersey dress with a khaki anorak – but makes the anorak of silk taffeta.*

one time nearly rival Paris in attracting attendance. The Italian temperament and the rivalry, bred in the blood between Rome and Paris, finished that off as far as the *Alta Moda* was concerned. The Pitti showings have been sustained by the rising success of the ready-to-wear, despite the competition of Milan where Missoni, Basile, Armani and Albini are increasingly flourishing names.

By the mid-sixties the ultimate authority of the Paris Couture was beginning to be eroded by the escalating workroom costs, the impatience of a jet-paced world, the declining demand for quality, the appetite for novelty and the heavy accent on youth. It was not as if the Couture had not realized that they must expand their market. The great Houses had long since begun to produce ready-to-wear collections as well as couture, Lucien Lelong was the first in the twenties, to nose their way into every possible aspect of fashion – men's clothes, children's clothes, lingerie, stockings, scent, nail varnishes, bibelots, household furnishings, shoes, stockings, tights . . . By the seventies the ready-to-wear after many bosh shots had found its feet, or rather its designers – Emmanuelle Khanh (by then a veteran), Karl Lagerfeld for Chloé, Jacqueline Jacobson for Dorothée Bis, Sonia Rykiel, Corine Bricaire, Jean Charles de Castelbajac for Amaraggi, the remarkably inventive Kenzo Takada of Jap, and above all, Yves Saint Laurent. And it is increasingly the ready-to-wear showings that are attracting the buyers.

The success of Yves Saint Laurent makes a nonsense of theories. Unlike Chanel, Dior, Mary Quant, his is a name that does not come trippingly to every tongue. Unlike them, he was not an instant success. He was not, to begin with, the right person in the right place at the right time. He was in fact the wrong person at the wrong place at the wrong time. The House of Dior was too massive, too grand, and, with too much at stake; too inflexible to respond to the violent changes which Yves rang. After his first success with his Trapeze line, he dropped his hemline to mid-calf (ten years too

soon) and a year later hobbled them above the knee (five years too soon). The first produced roars of rage; the second screams of outrage. The next year, 1960, Yves' antennae were quivering toward the Left Bank where the young French were giving their imitation of the Chelsea Beats. That collection was the end of Dior for Saint Laurent.

His departure from the Avenue Montaigne gave feud-loving Paris a field day: real Montague and Capulet stuff, the embers briskly fanned by *Women's Wear Daily*, rather hard on Marc Bohan who was chosen to take Saint Laurent's place. By 1962 when Saint Laurent was ready to open on his own in the pretty little house on the Avenue Spontini in Neuilly as far away from couture-land as possible, he was followed by defectors from Dior – a top *vendeuse* and a favoured model – but the most valuable recruit to his forces was Pierre Bergé. Bergé had been known as the entrepreneur whose clever promotion had propelled the artist Bernard Buffet into artistic and financial success. He was to do even better for Yves.

In his autumn/winter collection of 1976 Yves Saint Laurent paid tribute to Catherine the Great and the 'rich peasants' of ancient Russia; in his spring/summer collection of 1977, he seemed at last to have left the steppes, and turned for warmer weather to a warmer climate with a mixed salad of Carmen flounces, can-can corselets and velvet ribbon ties at the neck. It is hard to keep up with this changeable talent, but there is no doubt that he has started something big with those corselets.

That Saint Laurent has talent is incontrovertible. He has made lasting contributions to the vocabulary of fashion, the pinafore dress for day and evening, the heavy knit poloneck, the Trapeze (which, incidentally, revolutionized maternity clothes), the egg-cosy knitted cap. He has produced some delectable ideas – like the crisp organdie collars and ties that highlighted his collections of 1963 and 1964, his porters' smocks, his pea jackets, his 'smokings', his fur coats, their horizontal skins alternating with strips of suede or ciré. On the other hand his course has been erratic, veering from Robin Hood to the defiant clothes of the Occupation, from Chanel to the Hollywood forties, from see-through shirts and dresses to little Lord Fauntleroy velvet knickerbocker suits, from tarts' clothes to demure so-called Proust dresses, from Mondrian to chongsams. He reached for headlines with brides, the traditional finale to French Couture collections, in untraditional bikinis, pants suits, or got up like a bouquet in a cornucopia of white organdie, the bare legs the stalks. Even his most fervent admirers were confused.

He has found his *métier* in the ready-to-wear which suits his volatile talent. He opened his first Rive Gauche shop in 1966; by 1971 there were thirty-nine throughout the world. By 1976 YSL boutiques numbered one hundred and eleven. He has spread his designing skill to cover fifty-eight products (roughly par for the course today), rakes in from America alone some fifty million dollars from his men's clothes, and lives in a palace in Marrakesh. Although his fortune is made in ready-to-wear, he has not deserted Couture, and attendance at his collection is a must, although after the initial swooning enthusiasm, there have been second thoughts. Saint Laurent has always cast around for inspiration. He was early on the ethnic kick with Russia and never seems able to tear himself away from the steppes for long.

In his Couture winter collection of 1976, Saint Laurent was once more back in Russia, but this time with Catherine the Great. There were the ever-present babushkas and boots below mid-calf and ankle-length skirts, but the peasant look he has loved for so long was interpreted in sumptuous fabrics and exaggerated splendour as befits an empress. By contrast his spring/summer collection three months later, with short (just-below or well-above-the-knee) full, flounced and ruffled skirts, laced black velvet corselets and shawls seems to have taken a southerly direction toward the flamenco dancers of Spain, compliments of 'Carmen', while black velvet ribbon neckbands made a bow to Toulouse-Lautrec.

YSL has a great sense of drama, a fantastic talent for accessorizing, but is what he is doing fashion, theatre or folklore? Some critics have been ecstatic, some caustic. Either way he makes headlines, for his is the most charismatic personality since Dior. As for his short skirts, his fellows (Cardin, Ungaro, Kenzo, Lagerfeld *et al.*) hiked theirs up even shorter.

Paris may no longer rule but it survives as a centre – that it is now a centre for prototypes, for the ready-to-wear and for the promotion of lucrative licences does not matter. You could say that it is the same only different. To succeed there is still the ultimate accolade as Valentino's decision in 1974 to quit Milan and show his ready-to-wear only in Paris testifies.

3
Where America Leads

Periodically the United States of America changes the image of its national bird from a nobly brooding eagle to a lustily crowing cock, whose message is that America leads the world in fashion. Actually this ought to be true when you consider the sheer size of the country, the degree of overall affluence, and the astronomical number of human bodies to be clothed. In 1965 it was estimated that twenty-five billion dollars were spent on all clothing – men's, women's and children's; in 1975 women's fashion alone accounted for twelve billion. Thus the American ready-to-wear industry is the largest, the most competitive, the most highly geared, the most innovative in marketing methods. In this capacity it is the envy and model for every country with a developed or developing need for mass-produced clothing. But although the wholesalers are masters at producing instant fashion at all price levels, although the industry now possesses an ever increasing cadre of highly

*Bonnie Cashin's favourite fabrics are skins – leather and suede – and wool
jersey: used separately or together. Here in 1967 she combined an orange suede
smock coat to a hooded jersey dress, striped in green and yellow, belted in green
leather, for a characteristic timeless Cashin look.*

professional and talented designers, the actual influence of their output on international high fashion has been minimal. The impact of America has rested on its popular or folk fashion, Cape Cod fishermen's oilskin slickers and sou'wester hats, cowboy gear from boots to stetsons, T-shirts, denim, and above all jeans.

Hearts have been bruised and pockets lightened by the attempts of successful American manufacturers to sell their wares abroad, whether directly to stores or through manufacturing under licence. Nor have they been more successful on the continent. Their proponents blame this on high import tariffs, but the fact remains that *Time* magazine, one of the most enthusiastic flag-wavers, could in 1976 point only to Japan, with a potential market even more teeming than that of the United States, as the country where the 'New York Look' has made its mark.

One of the reasons is obvious: there is no universal life-style, it varies inevitably from country to country. The success of American manufacturers and that of their designers depends on their being attuned to the changing life-styles of their own country.

Another is that although American designers and manufacturers excel in sleek packaging and brilliant promotion, they are more dependent than they care to admit on Europe for the ideas which it is their special talent to absorb, streamline and project.

Paris had been the cynosure of fashion eyes ever since Americans discovered Worth at the beginning of the Third Republic – alas after the Commune had swept away his most glamorous client, the Empress Eugènie. Fashion then was strictly limited by income and social position. New York was the capital of capitals, the social and fashion centre of the country, an irresistible magnet which drew the ambitious in every field from the furthest reaches of the hinterlands. Boston was the most aristocratic and insular; Chicago the brashest. But all three capitals took their fashion cues from Paris. The grandest ladies crossed the ocean slowly and elegantly by ship to obtain their wardrobes at the source, although Boston matrons were said to put away their new Paris gowns for two years to mature, for there it was considered vulgar to be in the forefront of fashion. Others purchased imported models from expensive shops. The less affluent studied fashion magazines and pattern books with their seamstresses in the hope of duplicating the glamour they craved.

Import snobbery was as strong then as now, and the ladies with their eyes beamed on Europe seem not to have realized that one of the most powerful influences on the fashions they were expensively acquiring from abroad was their own Charles Dana Gibson, who through his illustrations not only established an ideal of beauty, but encouraged, if not invented, the S-bend stance, as a ditty by Leslie Styles sung by Camille Clifford, England's Gibson Girl, corroborates:

> Why do they call me a Gibson Girl,
> A Gibson Girl, A Gibson Girl
> What is the matter with Mr Ibsen
> Why Dana Gibson, Why Dana Gibson?
> If you want to lead the fashion
> In an independent whirl
> Walk with a bend in your back
> And they'll call you a Gibson Girl.

The democratization of fashion in America as in England began with the sewing machine. The power of the needle trade began with the formation of the International Ladies Garment Workers' Union in 1900. New York, the centre of the garment industry, was first made aware of the

An early fashion parade 'glorifying the modes in an Egyptian Hall . . .' at Wanamaker's in Philadelphia. From The Illustrated London News, *10 December 1910.*

hideous conditions under which exploited labour had to work when the union called its first strike in 1909 – a strike which, perhaps because the strikers, mostly shirtwaist workers, were mainly women and young women at that, attracted the support of the suffragettes, social workers and the Church. The nation was also made aware two years later when a fire swept the building in which five hundred employees of the Triangle Shirtwaist Company were trapped, taking a toll of one hundred and forty-six lives. Out of the ashes of the Triangle fire the ILGWU emerged a giant. That same year, 1911, there arrived in New York from Russian-Poland an immigrant named David Dubinsky who was to become president of the ILGWU twenty-one years later. This was a fortunate bit of timing for the election of Franklin Delano Roosevelt as President of the United States six months afterwards inaugurated a new climate in labour relations – a climate in which Dubinsky flourished.[1] The subsequent history of the ILGWU as it widened its horizons to include a notable degree of social responsibility, and that of Mr Dubinsky who became a national figure is fascinating but not relevant here, except to note the shaming fact that 'sweat shops' which the ILGWU was founded to abolish were both in name and actuality of British origin.

Still, whether interpreted by machine or by hand, by union or independent labour, the ideas stemmed from Paris. In 1914, as the War separated America from the fount of inspiration, Mrs Edna Woolman Chase, editor of *Vogue*, made a gallant attempt to carry water on both shoulders. She decided to put on a fashion show with living models, an idea which she thought her own, happily unaware that Jay's, a London store, had preceded her as had Wanamaker's in Philadelphia, as well as designers Poiret and Lucile. The aim of her show was to boost home-grown 'original designs', and at the same time to be in her words 'a reaffirmation of America's belief in and dependence on Paris'.[2] Mrs Chase deserves credit for a nice *Vogue* promotion, but her definition of 'original designs' apparently did not include the original designers, for none were mentioned, only the names of the luxury speciality shops participating.

It was not until twenty-seven years later that Dorothy Shaver of Lord & Taylor, the first woman store president, featured four American designers (all women as it happened) in an advertisement. Only one is known outside her native shores – Elizabeth Hawes – mainly because she wrote in 1938 a debunking book called *Fashion is Spinach*. (The title was derived from a cartoon by Carl Rose in *The New Yorker* showing a child facing with distaste a plate of broccoli, then a novelty. The caption read, 'I say it's spinach and I say the hell with it.')

Miss Shaver, a pioneer in everything, who was to be the first store president to present a British week in 1958, also gave house-room to the late Claire McCardell, like Bonnie Cashin, an intrinsically American designer. Miss McCardell who died at the untimely age of fifty-three in 1958 has become a legendary figure.

In between there was a long struggle for recognition, for it was the fate of designers for the ready-to-wear to work anonymously, and even if they had their own firms, stores more often than not removed designers' names and substituted their own to prevent rival buyers from discovering their sources.

Geoffrey Beene is another exponent of pared-down simplicity. In 1976 he included this dress in his first European showing – a chemise in white and navy striped wool, scarfed in navy and white.

Adolfo, like Halston, is a milliner turned dress designer. Born Adolfo Sardina, he is known by his first name as Halston is by his last. From fantasy, he has made in 1976/77 a volte-face, a return to Chanel, even putting his model in Chanel shoes against a Chanel Coromandel screen.

Halston in less than ten years has become America's Number One boy.
His specific ability is the juxtaposition of luxury with devastating simplicity, like
this silk jersey halter-necked jumpsuit worn with a tailored coat of ultrasuede, 1972.

Opposite *Ralph Lauren's recipe for play clothes 1977 goes 'take one blue singlet, combine with white lumber jacket, add short shorts belted in navy'.*

Left *Calvin Klein, in his early thirties, is another dazzling success. He understands the chic of negligence, well illustrated here from his 1976 collection: a scoop-necked cotton knit blouse, the neck worn open and the short sleeves rolled up, belted in plaited twine, over a full grey poplin skirt.*

That the names of American designers are known abroad at all as well as throughout the United States is due in large part to Eleanor Lambert. Miss Lambert, among other major services to fashion, is the inventor of the Fashion Critics Awards, known familiarly as the Coty Awards, which are to the fashion industry what Oscars are to films. Tireless in her promotion of native talent (well, if not exactly native, talent working in America), her most ambitious European venture was to organize a fashion show by American ready-to-wear designers in the Palace of Versailles, as near as never mind to the heartland of fashion.

But American designers really do not need European *réclame*, for the financial rewards in their own bailiwick are astronomical. For example, Halston, a young Middle Westerner who, starting as a designer of hats became the reigning hat maker in New York, only a few years after deciding that he preferred making clothes to hats, found his label worth twelve million dollars to Norton Simon Inc., one of America's largest conglomerates. That was in 1973. Two years later *Time* reported that Halston Enterprises, including boutiques, scent and franchises (that is manufacturers making Halston designs under licence) did ninety million dollars worth of retail trade – a slightly misleading figure taking in as it does varying store mark-ups, but still not a sum to be sneezed at.

Halston may be top of the class of 1976 but Oscar de la Renta is stepping on his heels and there are others, too, that are no slouches: designing giants like James Galanos, Bonnie Cashin, Pauline Trigére, Bill Blass, Gus Tassell, Geoffrey Beene, Jacques Tiffeau, Adolfo, Calvin Klein; commercial giants like Anne Klein (whose firm runs up a total of one hundred and fifty million dollars, retail again, and who sold half her business to Japan for twelve million dollars), Mollie Parnis, Albert Nipon, Adele Simpson, Jerry Silverman, Jack Lazar of Kimberley Knits. And new names like Carol Horn, Cathy Hardwick, Mary McFadden, Britta of Cinnamonwear, appear and are hailed every year. In this particular way, American fashion differs from American politics. Russell Baker, writing in *The New York Times* in May 1976, said 'newness is a powerful selling point among Americans but its defect is that it wears off very quickly ... We live in the land of total and instant consumption, and its proto-typical figure is the instant has-been.' The proto-typical new designer is the latest Coty Award winner, but a remarkable lot of these bright stars stay in orbit.

Still despite the efforts of dedicated protagonists, despite this wealth of talent, despite the gloss which seems to come with the rent of premises in 550 and 530 Seventh Avenue, the two buildings which house the cream of America's ready-to-wear, stores continued to sell line-for-line copies of couture models, first from France and then fromthe top names in Italy as well. As the ready-to-wear in these countries began to come of age, the buyers, always in search of novelty began to push, and manufacturers to copy, this merchandise. By the mid-sixties the most successful of the new breed of European ready-to-wear designers like Yves Saint Laurent got the message and began setting up boutiques in America (and other countries) to sell their own copies of their own clothes. This, however, does not seem to hinder the bi-annual pilgrimage of American buyers and manufacturers to Paris, Italy (with several centres) and London, but where they used to come only for the couture they now mainly concentrate on the ready-to-wear.

Besides inspiration (which is only reluctantly admitted) there are other reasons for this bi-annual hegira. To go to the European collections is a status symbol for buyers and manufacturers, and, once there, they are given VIP treatment: wined, dined and catered to. 'After all', said M. Gorin when he was President of the Chambre Syndicale de la Haute Couture Parisienne, rubbing his thumb and middle finger together in a typically French gesture, 'it's the figures that count.' Americans were the biggest spenders; the French now bow lower to the Germans and Japanese. Paris is the constant lodestone, Italy next potent as an attraction with all those principessas and contessas. In the mid-sixties swinging London was a draw and in 1976 it became a draw again – alas, in some measure due to the shrinking pound.

These powerful spenders with the prestige of their great stores behind them inevitably have an influence on fashion, for no designer can afford to ignore the market they command, to resist the temptation to please so much money. Even the aloof Balenciaga in the early fifties adjusted the first examples of what became his famous 'Loose Look' to suit the buyers.

In the van of this army of dollars come the American journalists whose reports can influence even these mighty spenders. This was most dramatically demonstrated in 1957, when, after less than enthusiastic notices which caused some buyers to skip their expensive attendance, Balenciaga and Givenchy, followed in 1964 by Yves St Laurent, barred the Press from their Collections until the 'livraison', a month after the buyers' shows. The 'livraison' is the date the clothes bought are delivered, and by then, buyers' money was safely in the designer's till. Balenciaga and Givenchy had always shown after all their colleagues anyway but never as long after as this, a delay which necessitated return trips, not so bad for those on this side of the Atlantic, but expensive and time-wasting for the Americans. After havering from a month to three weeks to eighteen days, the three mavericks finally slunk back into the corral.

Anyone who further doubts the American journalists' importance has only to see where they are

*Pierre Cardin in 1977 follows the leader back to the strapless tops of the late
forties, here flatteringly allied to a high Empire waist.*

643 x-42
MGM

*Opposite By the thirties 'It'
had been superseded by sex
appeal and Jean Harlow was its
chief exponent. The Blonde
Bombshell's bleached platinum
hair must have sold enough
peroxide to float the QE II. For
her, Adrian designed the slinky
bias-cut satin dresses which,
along with her hair, became her
signature.*

*By the fifties nascent Women's
Lib had changed sex appeal into
'sex symbol' and, from her
appearance in John Huston's
Asphalt Jungle, Marilyn
Monroe was established, until
her tragic death in 1962, as the
sex symbol without equal. Her
provocatively wriggling walk
changed the rear view on
pavements and in offices round
the world.*

seated in the luxurious salons, to note the care laid on for them, the flowers that pour in to their rooms at the best hotels. But these chroniclers of fashion deserve a chapter to themselves – and we have given them one.

These are the indirect influences. More direct ones are due to the technological advances that have given this century not only the means of instant recall but made it the most fully documented in history. The invention of the camera, motion pictures and television has made the recent past immediately available. And it is these three media of record and dissemination which are responsible for the vast influence of America on popular fashion.

Hollywood was the first and most powerful disseminator. The early days of flickers exerted little if any influence – neither Mary Pickford's sausage curls nor Lillian Gish's wistfulness had any real impact on fashion. That was left to Theda Bara. The first movie 'vamp', a sobriquet coined for her to boost her first film *A Fool There Was*, made in 1915 and based on Kipling's poem, 'The Vampire', she was born Theodosia Goodman. An energetic publicity office not only dreamed up her pseudonym which they insisted was an anagram of 'Arab Death' but invented for her an aura of sinister wickedness. This reputation made her the idol of the tango addicts who copied her powdered pallor, kohl-rimmed, heavily mascara'd eyes and dark red lips. The vogue for vamps, however, was brief and by 1918 the reign of Theda Bara, her predecessors and followers, was over. They were supplanted in the twenties by the *femmes fatales*, Pola Negri, Gloria Swanson, and Garbo. The bandeaux and tight-fitting cloche hats covering the forehead and descending to the eyebrows with which Pola Negri and Gloria Swanson accentuated the sexy looks they flashed from their heavily

*Overleaf left In 1977 Oscar de la Renta also
discovered the charms of cotton and matching
headscarves, and to underline their femininity, he
added a lace-edged petticoat.*

*Overleaf right Mary McFadden is the new
Golden Girl. Well-connected, she has a well-
connected clientele. Her finely pleated, butterfly-
wing printed tunic of 1976 opens at the back over
Chinese pants, a style which she also favours for
herself.*

Clara Bow had the luck to be around when Elinor Glyn descended upon Hollywood in the middle twenties. For Miss Bow, Madame Glyn invented 'It' and nominated her the 'It' girl. That sobriquet and Miss Bow's cupid's bow pout gained her more than 20,000 fan letters a week.

Although The Outlaw *which featured Jane Russell (for which Howard Hughes had designed the uplift bra) was made in 1943, it was not released until 1946; in the meantime publicity stills like this one had made her the Forces' pin-up girl and world famous before she even appeared on the screen.*

made-up eyes were copied by those who fancied themselves to be hot stuff. By 1929 Garbo's shoulder-length hair and slouch hats were part of every teenager's equipment,[3] but Garbo's magic remained inimitable. After Jean Harlow, the greatest sex symbol that Hollywood gave to the world was Marilyn Monroe who shot to fame in 1953, and with her tightly-covered wriggling walk changed the rear view on many pavements.

In the early impoverished days of movies, actors and actresses often wore their own clothes, and as David Robinson wrote in *The Times*, '. . . a smart coat or silk dress was more likely to land a job than acting skills . . . Indeed you could often earn more for your hat than your talent.' When the industry moved from barns and empty plots to Hollywood in the early twenties and the golden age of movie-making really began, there flowered in the lush climate of apparently unlimited wealth a group of remarkable designers: Howard Greer, Adrian, Travis Banton, Walter Plunket and Orry-Kelly, all of whom were commemorated in Diana Vreeland's exhibition of 'Romantic and Glamorous Hollywood Design' at the Metropolitan Museum in 1974. Of a vintage lot, Adrian was the most talented and the one who exercised a positive influence on fashion. His dress for Joan Crawford in *Letty Lynton*, a film made in 1932, of white organdie with wide ruffled sleeves to add breadth to her shoulders and diminish her waist, was copied all over America; R.H. Macy & Co. in New York alone sold half a million copies. This sleeve turned up in the collections of Madame Grès and Balmain thirty-one years later. His padded 'coat hanger' shoulders for Joan Crawford and his bias-cut dresses for Jean Harlow made their indelible mark too. His slouch hat for Garbo in *A Woman of Affairs*, 1929, and his small ostrich-trimmed over-one-eye hat for her in *Romance*, 1930, changed the millinery picture.

But by and large the chief influence of Hollywood was on make-up and hair styles and bras. Just as women had copied the vamp look, they were later, wherever motion pictures were shown, to copy the arched eyebrows and cupid's bow pout of Clara Bow, the 'It' girl, Joan Crawford's wide rectangular mouth, Jean Harlow's pencilled eyebrows and platinum blonde hair, Rita Hayworth's tawny mane, Marilyn Monroe's wide-eyed, open mouthed stare. The cantilevered uplift bra is credited to Howard Hughes who is supposed to have used his aero-dynamics know-how for the greater glory of Jane Russell in *The Outlaw* made in 1943 (but not released until 1946). Padded or wired, the bra made Miss Russell into a No. 1 pin-up and created the sweater girl.

As Hollywood declined and the star of television rose, the revival of old films, particularly Westerns, was a powerful combined influence on fashion everywhere. In England Mary Quant was one of the first to fall in love with the cowboy's buckled hipster belts, tight-fitting blue jeans and high-heeled boots in 1960. By the mid sixties jeans were the uniform for both sexes; by the mid seventies jeans boutiques proliferated, and from jeans sprang the vogue for denim – in overalls, in skirts, in work jackets. This great non-fashion is America's most powerful influence abroad.

Another folk fashion started spontaneously in the mid fifties when American teenagers took to wearing their brothers' or fathers' shirts outside their jeans. By 1957 this uniform of the young had become so universal that James Thurber, whose mind's eye missed nothing, wove a story of its inception. The whole thing started, according to Mr Thurber, when a young father tried to insert his small daughter into her one-piece sleeping garment. Defeated by its unfamiliar mode of entry, he eventually put her to bed in one of his own shirts.

'It had also a disturbing after-effect, [wrote Mr Thurber] for when the little girl got into her teens, she was more interested in wearing her father's shirts than in any garments of her own ... Why they insist on wearing them *outside* their blue jeans, nobody seems to know, but the fashion has the nation in its grip, and nothing can be done about it now.'

Actually, although it is too late to enlighten Mr Thurber, they wore them that way because they were too large to stuff inside. Soon, however, manufacturers were making shirts meant to be worn outside, and twenty years later a teenagers' whim has become established as a universal fashion – and not just for teenagers.

In Paris Marc Bohan for Dior had got the message in 1961 with a dress he called 'Blue Jeans' which he translated into couture language by outlining the saddle-stitching with brilliants, just as later, when he showed the cowboy back-to-front kerchief, it was in one of Brossin de Méré's most delicate flowered organzas. But it was American films that put French youth into jeans. They became the signature of the demonstrators, their wearers seeing themselves as John Wayne, Paul Newman, or either of the Easy Riders.

Old American films, too, are responsible for the wave of nostalgia for the thirties which began in England in the sixties, hit Paris and glanced off Italy. Ginger Rogers ostrich feathers, floppy fabrics, droopy dresses, mid-calf hemlines, Adrian's wide shoulders and slinky Jean Harlow satins – these were what took hold of young imaginations, forced the fad for second-hand clothes, generally stultified fashion.

But no Hollywood film has equalled the effect on fashion of *Dr Zhivago* in 1966 – to the delighted amazement of the young English designer, Phyllis Dalton.

Another, stranger, influence was that of the Hippies. All the way from the Haight-Ashbury slums of San Francisco, the Hippies' trailing agglomerations of body coverings swept the streets of Europe. Their most positive and lasting effect has been in England where what could be called a commercialized home industry to reproduce their tatty, long skirted garments sprang into being and

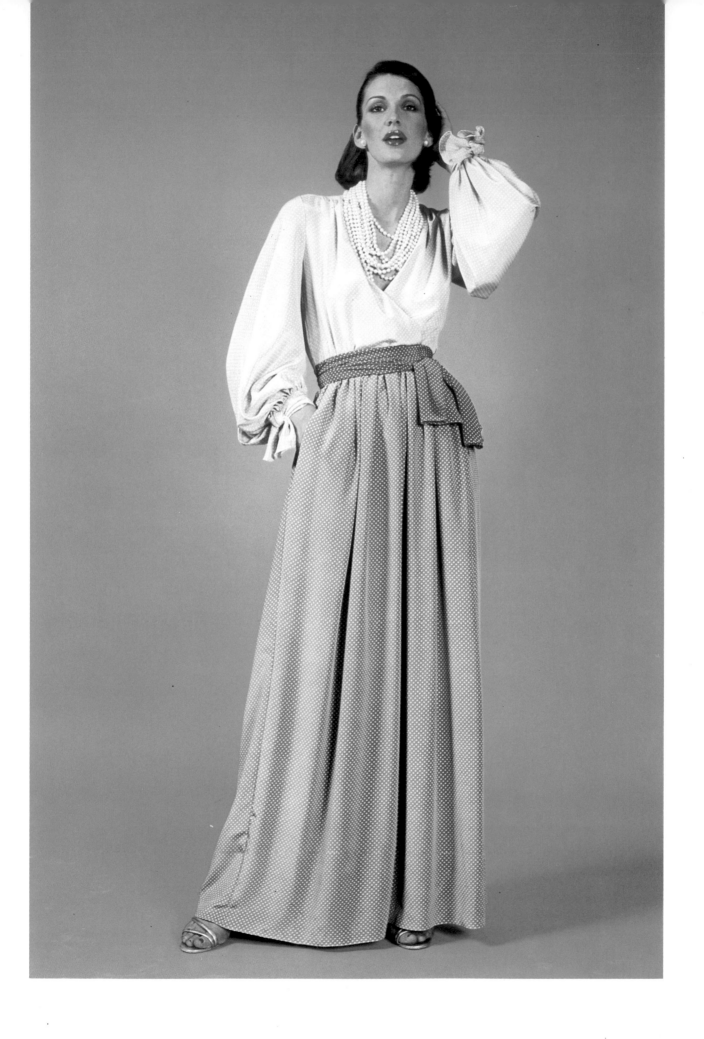

still flourishes, now more tidily and most successfully in the Laura Ashley boutiques.

Even more strangely, the Hippie translation of mix-and-match into mess-and-muddle made another positive contribution to British fashion. Here their magpie assemblages of clothing defying orthodox canons of taste, the happy anarchy of their accidental combinations of patterns, textures and colours were distilled by the imaginative talents of Bill Gibb and Zandra Rhodes into a new dimension of poetic fantasy.

One of the most impressive characteristics of American fashion is the constantly renewed reservoir of talent from which every year new names emerge. Of this vast army, from the perspective of distance, a select few stand out as unique in their different fields: Hattie Carnegie, Mainbocher, Valentina, Charles James, Claire McCardell, Bonnie Cashin, Sylvia Pedlar and Helen Lee.

Hattie Carnegie, from her first fashion collection in 1918 became an institution. Even in 1928 when she added her own ready-to-wear to her made-to-order models, thus following Lelong in setting a pattern which was later to become widespread, her shop remained a synonym for elegance. Her hey-days were the twenties and thirties when the neat, shaped, instantly recognizable Carnegie suit in grey worsted with its straight skirt, tidy little collar and jewelled buttons became a status symbol. All her clothes had an identifiable stamp – akin to England's Eva Lutyens – although she employed various designers. Like Elizabeth Arden, she was an astute picker of talent, and many of those she chose found fame in their own right – Claire McCardell, Norman Norell, Gus Tassell, and in a different milieu, the late Pauline Potter who became Baroness Philippe de Rothschild and the pet of the Paris Couture. Miss Carnegie died in 1956, having carved a special niche in American fashion history, although her influence rested on her side of the ocean.

As Miss Carnegie had a special clientele for whom her clothes were a uniform, so did Mainbocher. Any other resemblance is purely coincidental. Chicago-born Main Rousseau Bocher is the only American ever to have established a successful Couture House in Paris which he opened in 1930 and closed in 1939 when the War forced him to return to his native shore. As Mr Bocher was editor of French *Vogue* when he decided to design clothes, he must also be the first journalist who turned from reporting fashion to creating it. His Paris House flourished in the Molyneux days, and his clothes had the same well-bred, whispered, elegance. Molyneux designed the wedding dress for Princess Marina when she became the Duchess of Kent; Mainbocher designed the wedding dress for a more controversial bride: Mrs Simpson when she became the Duchess of Windsor. In New York he rapidly acquired a glossy clientele. Modest, soft-spoken, white-haired, Mainbocher maintained a gentle supremacy until his retirement in 1970. He died in Munich in 1976 at the age of eighty-five.

Valentina arrived in New York from Russia, married to George Schlee, a fellow Russian. These are the only uncontroversial facts about this extraordinary woman who likes to wrap herself in layers of mystery. It is said that she came in 1922 with the Revue Russe,[4] that the year was 1923 and the entertainment the Chauve Souris,[5] that both she and her husband George Schlee were White Russian refugees.[6] In any case, in 1928 backed by friends, she started a new career as a dressmaker. From that time until she closed her doors (the same doors behind which Elizabeth Hawes had decided 'fashion

Bill Blass is a master of seemingly negligent but adroitly calculated simplicity.
In a poll taken by W in November 1976, two Bill Blass outfits came first and
third out of forty-seven fashions by thirty-five top American designers shown in
the paper. His is a thoroughly American look – in 1977 too.

Left *Mainbocher with a
Mainbocher, drawn by Eric in
1934 for French* Vogue, *of which
American-born Mainbocher had
been fashion editor then editor
from 1922 until 1929, when he
opened his own House in Paris.
He closed in 1939 on the outbreak
of War and opened in New York
in 1941.*

Opposite *Mrs Charles James
photographed in her husband's
Salon wearing one of James'
typical grand dresses for evening.
A dress like this was heavily
reinforced beneath to create a
shape to his liking, not
necessarily that of the client: as
one of them said, 'it existed on its
own'.*

was spinach') in 1960, she reigned as America's sole true couturière, owing nothing to Paris, impervious to fashionable artistic influences, creating clothes of baffling and dramatic simplicity. Among her clients were Garbo and Lynn Fontanne, and of course the cream of Society, but no one wore Valentina clothes as well as Valentina herself. Although inimitable, like Mainbocher she set a standard which filtered down to the mass market. Beautiful and imperious, she became a legend in her lifetime.

Another original is Charles James – half-American, half-British, a Harrovian whose father had been to Eton, an aesthete in a family whose sons traditionally went either into the Army or Navy, and as such disowned by his father, a Colonel, who became an instructor at the Royal Military Academy. James made his start as a designer of hats in Chicago where he had been exiled at the age of eighteen. He moved to New York and there, with the aid of Sir Cecil Beaton, a school friend, quickly made his name with the chief roarers of the Roaring Twenties. Paris was his next objective which he reached via London where he penetrated the Bloomsbury enclave, acquiring as a client among others, Lady Ottoline Morrell. In Paris he found patrons in Poiret and the fabric manufacturer Colcombet. Another client was producer Charles Cochrane who commissioned James to design the clothes for Clare Luce in 'Follow the Sun'. At the dress rehearsal, according to artist Adrian Daintrey, a contemporary, Miss Luce complained that one of her costumes was

too tight to dance in. 'That's funny,' piped up James from the stalls, '*I danced in it all last night*'.

Both his couture and attempts at ready-to-wear were equally disastrous financially, although his patrons included women of supreme elegance who were prepared to wait as long as two years for his elaborately structured creations, and his clothes are enshrined at the Smithsonian Institution, the Brooklyn Museum, the Costume Institute of the Metropolitan Musem of Art in America, and at the Victoria and Albert Museum in London. His is a talent as unique and personal, and as out of the mainstream, as Gaudi's buildings are to the architecture of his time. The trick is where to put this gifted and eccentric man – London, Paris or New York. I've plumped for the latter where he still lives.

Claire McCardell is a purely American phenomenon. Born in Maryland, a graduate of the

Clair McCardell in the mid-forties, when other designers were frozen into an exaggerated version of Schiaparelli's nipped-in waist and stiffened shoulder pre-war silhouette, went her own soft and infinitely feminine way. Typical of her immediate pre- and post-war designs is this easy, high-sashed, button-through dress in red calico, its loose matching coat thoughtfully lined in wool c.1949/50.

Parson's School of Design in New York, with a successful career in the sportswear firm of Townley, plus a spell at Hattie Carnegie's sandwiched in, she was ripe to become the creator of the American Look when the Second World War threw America back on its own fashion resources. Early in 1940 she had been one of the first of the few to oppose the Schiaparelli legacy of padded shoulders, by then exaggerated both out and up, which so disfigured most of the wartime clothes. She was ready for wartime restrictions: Sally Kirkland in her spirited summing-up of Miss McCardell's life and achievements[7] quotes Norman Norell, the doyen, until his death in 1972, of America's ready-to-wear, saying '. . . Claire could take five dollars worth of common cotton calico and turn out a dress a smart woman could wear anywhere.' Her taste was for humble fabrics. As Vionnet had brought crêpe out of its shadow as a lining fabric, and as Chanel had made a lady of cotton jersey, Miss McCardell used then neglected materials like mattress ticking, cotton voile, seersucker, dotted Swiss, cotton georgette . . . She admitted to having been influenced when she was young by Vionnet (and who wasn't) and later by Grès, but, with her, inspiration never resulted in imitation. Rather it was like the grain of sand which an oyster turns into a pearl, and in her hands Vionnet's bias cut and Grès' draped jerseys came out as pure McCardell.

It is invidious, as well as nearly impossible, to say who was first at a fashion innovation, but Miss McCardell was undeniably early in her use of jeans stitching and her affection for denim. She pioneered the wearing of flat shoes, persuading Capezio, specialists in ballet shoes since 1887, to make for her in 1944. She was certainly first with her 'diaper' or baby's nappy draped bathing suit of 1942 to which one of Halston's which made the cover of *Time* in 1976 bears a startling resemblance. Because of the simple directness of her ideas, the softness of her construction (in a period of padded everything), the elegance of her proportions, her clothes look as fresh today as they did when the far-sighted Marjorie Griswold and Dorothy Shaver of Lord & Taylor first spotted her talent in 1940. Her death in 1958 deprived America of one of its rare indigenous designers.

Bonnie Cashin is of the same ilk as Claire McCardell; that is, she is completely American in her inspiration and invention. Born near San Francisco in California, after a brief stint in ready-to-wear designing in New York, she returned to the coast, this time to Hollywood where for six years she designed a number of films including the now classic *Laura* made in 1944. Despising 'a safe berth' as she called it, she returned to New York in 1949 and opened her own studio as an independent designer. On the West Coast she had absorbed the Chinese influence that used to be predominant in San Francisco and the easy casual style of ranch and rodeo life. The former inspired her layered look of which she was a pioneer, the latter her ponchos and fringed suedes. In 1950 the Brooklyn Museum began to collect her clothes and in 1962 gave her a retrospective exhibition. Four years later *Time–Life* gave her another in London. Of her the Brooklyn Museum wrote: 'There are very few in the markets of fashion who can afford to disregard their commercial milieu. Bonnie Cashin is unique in that she cannot afford to recognize it.' Despite this detachment, in each field of fashion she has tackled, including clothing, knitwear, gloves and leather articles, she has achieved commercial success as well as artistic acclaim. One of the first to be aware of the effect on fashion of exurbanite living, which her suedes and leathers, her leather-bound jerseys and tweeds exactly suit, she is one of the few to find a market, though a restricted one, beyond her native shores; she has had her own department at Liberty's in London since 1960. She is also one of the very few to influence international fashion. Her layered look has become a cliché of the seventies. Perhaps it is only coincidence that her ponchos would turn up across the ocean as part of Hippie gear, while her fringed suedes would be echoed in the American Indian protest uniform which, via Twiggy and the King's Road, would find their way into Saint Laurent's collection of 1968.

Sylvia Pedlar who died in 1972 was also unique. Her special field was lingerie and within these self-proscribed limits she attained the design status of a couturière. Although her collections were mass-produced under the name of Iris, she gave them a custom-made look with her delicate batistes, fine lace insertions, spaghetti thin rouleaux and satin ribbons. Nightwear had always been an American speciality and in the thirties Nancy Melcher, plus a brilliant advertising campaign had made the underwear firm of Vanity Fair famous with her permanently pleated nylon nightdresses. Miss Melcher was the first underwear designer to receive a Coty Award in 1950, Mrs Pedlar the second in 1951.

Mrs Pedlar brought a sophisticated and witty eye to the design of underwear, constantly devising changes in shape rather than simply in trimming. Amongst her innovations was the 'shortie' nightdress, toreador pyjamas, brief slips and half-petticoats in flowered nylon tricot (which she designed), the high-waisted nightdress, the long full nightdress dropping from a rectangular lace neck and the toga – which she called a 'bedside nightdress'. She was widely copied the world over, but what gave her particular pleasure was the annual visit of Hubert de Givenchy who always bought out her collection to take back to Paris as gifts.

Helen Lee is a pioneer in children's clothing. Overseas her direct influence is minimal. In 1962, under the aegis of Eleanor Lambert, Miss Lee put on a children's fashion show in London for charity, all the small models being strictly upper echelon children. After years of seeing little girls looking like bon-bons in smock-topped dresses and fondant colours, to see them in dark green or red or even black, in simple unfussy shapes, in dark or bright coloured tights instead of little white socks, in corduroy or velvet instead of silk or lawn was a revelation. London stores were reluctant to take up

Miss Lee's ideas, a reluctance they might well regret for Miss Lee now controls the designing of one hundred million dollars worth of children's clothes retailed through the giant mail order chain of Sears Roebuck.

It took the boutiques, whose owners had probably never heard of Miss Lee, to follow her lead. Tights were the turning point, pinafores the inspiration: jeans, polo-necked sweaters, dungarees and duffle coats rapidly diminished in size. Little English boys, once uniformed in grey flannel shorts and blazers (in school or out), or in dress tartans and buckled shoes for parties shared in the boom. Children's clothes became practical as well as fun.

Paris, too, woke up to a new deal for small fry. A boutique on the Left Bank, Le Petit Faune, was the pioneer. Inspired by clothes worn by working-class children, they made tiny black dresses, then swept on into other dark colours. Led by Madame Pompidou and reigning film stars like Catherine Deneuve, the mothers of the smallest smart set file through the door whose handle is a large safety pin.

In this special area, America was the instigator, England extended the repertory of ideas, and France added the wit. While giving the United States due credit, it is best to forget the interim period when little American boys were seen looking like sad little midgets, in miniature versions of their fathers' Brooks Brothers suits, a fad fortunately not taken up in other countries.

Perhaps the most beneficent and widespread influence has been in what is still technically called 'sportswear'. Casual clothes would be a better phrase. In the mid-fifties there began in American an exodus from the large cities to the suburbs – an exodus that gave birth to a new concept of sportswear.

The simplicity, the ease, the independence of this way of dressing has now come of age and dominates American design. Abroad it is expressed in the 'do-your-own-thing' mood, with its concomitant fashion creed of 'putting together', a latter day version of 'mix-and-match', which gave new life to separates. This has produced an amusing anomaly, for the most popular ingredients to 'put together' in England come from Paris, while in Paris such marriages are called *'le style Anglais'*.

Deserving far more than a postscript is a tribute to the great American retailers. From the giant mail order houses like Sears Roebuck to the luxury of I. Magnin with its Lalique counters and honey-coloured travertine floors, they have no equal. The tragedy is that the aptitude for clever buying and the inspired salesmanship of these imaginative retailers – the late Grover Magnin and Hector Escabosa of Magnin's, Stanley Marcus of Nieman-Marcus and Geraldine Stutz Gibbs of Henri Bendel – have had so little impact across the ocean.

Sylvia Pedlar, in her Iris lingerie, was the first to take a lighthearted view of nightwear – in 1964 printing the practicality of nylon tricot with a scattering of bright pink and green flowers.

4

When London Swung

London, despite strenuous and continuing efforts has never managed to achieve the fashion status that makes Paris an irresistible magnet, Rome so alluring, New York so exciting, yet there were areas in which London shone and periods when London led.

England possesses in the Monarchy and the Court a unique advantage, although Queen Alexandra was the only queen in this century who actually led fashion. Queen Mary evolved for herself a style of fashion for day, but her high-tee'd toques, pale-coloured coats and low-heeled criss-cross ankle-strapped shoes made her a figure to be admired rather than emulated. Norman Hartnell's clothes for the Queen Mother when she was Queen set a style for wives of functionaries – provincial mayoresses, aldermen's wives and the like – and her favourite flowery hats were still nodding on the heads of the kind of ladies who attend public luncheons until well after bouffant hair styles finally vanquished headcoverings.

It was the sight of Chelsea Birds like this one in 1964 striding along the King's Road in their leather boots that inspired American journalist John Crosby to invent the phrase 'Swinging London'.

Presentation at the Court of King Edward VII in 1905 demanded elaborate dresses like these worn by two American heiresses, Mrs Arthur Lee and her sister, Miss Faith Moore. Mrs Lee subsequently became Viscountess Lee of Fareham, and gave many of her clothes to Mrs Doris Langley Moore for her Museum of Costume.

Above *Cloche hats and low waists were new in 1926, but the sun on Regatta Day at Henley brought out old Japanese parasols and a sunshade.*

Left *Lucile, still going strong after the War, included this evening dress in her fashion show at the Hyde Park Hotel in 1920, its tango skirt veiled in filmy Oriental drapery.*

Occasionally a Royal figure can trigger off a mass fashion. Recent Royalties have also been unwitting grist for the copying mills. The Queen's wedding dress was reported by *The New York Times* to have been copied 'stitch-for-stitch' by American manufacturers (no mean feat when one considers Hartnell's fabulous embroideries) and swept up the aisles to many an American altar. When a sketch of Princess Margaret's wedding dress was published by the American trade paper, *Women's Wear Daily*, a week before her wedding, it was not only a journalistic scoop but a service to manufacturers ready and eager to reproduce it.

Queen Elizabeth II dresses in the manner of a modern queen. As far as is known, she is not particularly interested in setting fashion, and may have been surprised to find that her habit of tying a silk square over her head at horsey occasions would send the sales of silk head squares soaring and even inspire Pierre Balmain in one collection similarly to swathe his mannequins' heads – with a bow to Her Majesty.

The existence of a Court and its attendant ceremonials, and the magic aura that surrounds even the least ostentatious of monarchs provides a fertile, if specialized, field in which fashion can flourish. Until the Second World War a London Season demanded a lot of clothes. The Edwardian addiction to house parties was increased by the advent of the motor car which meant more clothes. Even today Royal Ascot spells for many at least four elaborate outfits, plus an alternative for rain and/or cold.

In the early years of the century, as we have seen, fashion meant Paris, and Paris meant Worth, although by 1910 Paquin had become a favourite label for young fashionables. But in Lucile England had a couturière whose fame like that of her sister, Elinor Glyn, soon sped across the Channel and the Atlantic as far as Hollywood. One of her assistants was the young South African, Edward Molyneux, who left in 1914 to join up. Although Lucile continued to produce collections well after the War (she died in 1935), by then she was not above appropriating sketches submitted by aspiring designers.

Norman Hartnell recalls that she carelessly left his name on one of several of his which she published as her own, for which oversight Mr Hartnell collected fifty pounds in damages and costs.[1] Less widely known Houses were those of Dove and Ospovat, the former echoing the Oriental flavour of Poiret and the Ballet Russe, the latter dressing the beautiful Lady Diana Manners. And of course there were Reville and Handley Seymour whose most impressive client was Queen Mary.

Captain Molyneux (he bore his rank and the scars of battle, which cost him the sight of one eye, for the rest of his distinguished career) and a few years later, Norman Hartnell, were swallows that did make a summer, the first of a group of extremely personable young men who chose to make their careers in fashion. Molyneux followed the signpost which Worth had pointed to Paris, and in 1919 after the end of hostilities, at the age of twenty-six he opened his first Salon on the rue Royale. In 1932 he opened a London House, but Paris remained his base until he escaped to England in 1940.

The between-war years were Molyneux's high period. Elegance, not then the discredited word it became forty years on, was his hallmark – the elegance of sophisticated simplicity and a feminine paraphrase of Sir Max Beerbohm's summing up of Beau Brummell's principles, 'certain congruities of dark cloth ... and the rigid perfection of linen', in neat navy or grey flannel with white. Royal clients (he made Princess Marina's wedding dress) gave him *réclame*; peripatetic actresses like Gertrude Lawrence and Lynn Fontanne spread his fame across the ocean. The debonair Captain, painter, collector (he made and sold for millions two collections of paintings), and, after his retirement in 1950 due to failing sight, successful grower of carnations for the scent makers, was one of the first English dressmakers to achieve social success.

His return to fashion in 1965, although he could not recapture the success of his pre-war days, he handled with customary gallantry, presiding over and encouraging younger talents. His death in 1974 was the close of a glamorous chapter in British fashion.

Norman Hartnell was infected with the designing urge in 1921 when he was at Cambridge, where he gravitated first to the Marlowe Dramatic Society and then to the Footlights Dramatic Club. Two years later, with a daring equal to Molyneux's, he opened his own Salon on Bruton Street. In this halcyon period of drawing-room comedies when the stage was peopled with well-dressed actresses he, like Molyneux, designed for the shining stars of the theatre, Lily Elsie, Evelyn Laye, Bebe Daniels, Binnie Hale, and shared Gertrude Lawrence with Molyneux.

The late twenties were the years of The Bright Young People and the endless parties memorialized by Evelyn Waugh:

'... Masked parties, Savage parties, Victorian parties, Greek parties, Wild West parties, Russian parties, Circus parties, parties where one had to dress as somebody else, almost naked parties in St John's Wood, parties in flats and studios and houses and ships and hotels and night clubs, in windmills and swimming baths ... dull dances in London and comic dances in Scotland and disgusting dances in Paris ...'[2]

Mr Hartnells' contribution to this list was the Circus party which he gave in 1928.

The London Season centred round the Court, culminating for a debutante in her Presentation at Court. Two of the loveliest debutantes of the thirties were Margaret Whigham and Lady Bridget

Molyneux's second most glamorous client (Princess Marina was the first) was Gertrude Lawrence, who in 1932 wears with her customary aplomb this dress and jacket in a dazzling arrangement of stripes, which against the spotted background provide a foretaste of Op Art.

Poulett, both of whom Hartnell dressed, as did South African, Victor Stiebel, also a graduate of Cambridge and the Footlights, who in 1932 had opened his Salon on the same street.

Presentation dresses for a debutante had to be designed within the rules laid down by the Lord Chamberlain's Office: low evening dress with a court train suspended from the shoulders, the train not to exceed two yards in length and not to extend more than eighteen inches from the heel of the wearer when standing. On her head it was stipulated that the debutante wore a white veil topped with three small white ostrich feathers, the centre one a little higher than the others, mounted 'as a Prince of Wales' plumes', the whole worn slightly to the left side of the head. Coloured feathers were inadmissible except in cases of deep mourning when black feathers were permitted. There were no restrictions on the colour of the dresses, nor of the gloves which were compulsory. Bouquets and fans were optional. The designer's scope might have been somewhat restricted, but at least the wearer knew that if all the rules were followed, she would look no odder than the rest.

From dressing debs for Presentations Hartnell was to move even closer to the Court. In 1935 he made the wedding and bridesmaids' dresses for Lady Alice Montagu-Douglas-Scott's marriage to the Duke of Gloucester. Two of the four small bridesmaids were the Royal Princesses. This was his first step into an area unique to England in which he shone uniquely. He was soon making dresses for the whole Royal Family, including Queen Mary, thus starting a career as a double Royal Warrant holder – Dressmaker by Appointment to two Queens of England – Queen Elizabeth (now the Queen Mother) and Queen Elizabeth II.

These startling evening pyjamas of chiffon, cuffed and banded in fur, overskirted in satin were an eye-catcher in Norman Hartnell's Collection of 1924.

A cartoon of Norman Hartnell in a dress he designed for the Cambridge University Footlights Revue of 1921 by C. Hildyard. As caption there is an early Clerihew which reads:

> *Mr Hartnell as Gwen*
> *Looks quite pretty now and then.*
> *You will agree that his dresses are divine,*
> *Made from his own design.*

It was dressing Queen Elizabeth that propelled him into world fame. The Abdication of King Edward VIII had left the Monarchy shaken – and shaky. The new Queen had led a quiet life as Duchess of York, in contrast to the junketings of the second Prince of Wales' set, and was little known to the public. It was one of Hartnell's triumphs that he invented a way for her to look, although he says that it was actually King George VI who guided him to Winterhalter and the idea of re-creating the crinoline.[3]

He met the challenge of great State occasions – Royal weddings, Coronations, State Visits – with an imaginative invention based solidly on a sturdy sense of the practical. Typical of the latter were the robes of viscountesses and baronesses which he was asked to redesign for the Coronation of Queen Elizabeth II, the cost of which he reduced from five hundred to thirty pounds, and Princess Margaret's wedding dress in 1960. It was one of the wonders of the time how that dress made of three hundred yards of fragile white organza had survived uncrushed the drive from the Palace to the Abbey in the tiny glass coach ('about as big', so Princess Margaret said, 'as the average Austin 10', one of the miniest of mini cars). Mr Hartnell had solved the problem by splitting the full skirt at the back over a flat panel so that it could be pulled apart when seated like a man's tail coat, and then fall back together, the fullness hiding the division.

Equally inspired was his solution to the problem presented by the death of Queen Elizabeth's mother, the Countess of Strathmore, three weeks before the Royal Visit to France in the summer of 1938. The designs had been accepted and the clothes were ready for fittings. Black or the purple usual for royal mourning would have cast a pall of gloom over the occasion and also have been unsuitable for July. Mr Hartnell came up with the happy suggestion of white for which there were precedents as a royal prerogative for mourning. He had, as he wrote, 'to pass, as it were, a magic wand over the whole collection and transform all the dresses into white'[4] in a fortnight. This all-white wardrobe for the Queen not only gained him the acclaim of Paris but the Palms of an Officer of the Academie awarded to him by the French Government.

His services to royalty were also recognized by the award of the Member of the [Royal] Victorian Order (MVO) in 1953, and his position as 'a world influence on fashion' by the Nieman-Marcus Award in 1947, the first English designer to be so honoured, and the only one until Mary Quant was given the same honour in 1973. In the New Year's Honours of 1977, Hartnell was made a Knight Commander of the [Royal] Victorian Order (KCVO) and became the first dress designer to be knighted. These accolades commemorate the two periods in this century in which English fashion achieved international recognition.

At seventy-six Sir Norman is a trifle more Hanoverian in outline, but his pixie wit is unimpaired and he looks with philosophical detachment on a changed world in which, even if his clients wanted them, it would be impossible to produce the magnificent embroideries for which he was renowned.

Although it was a slow process one of the aftermaths of the War was the changed face of the Monarchy and therefore of the Court. Formality and grandeur were gradually dissipated. In 1958 Presentations at Court were replaced by Garden Parties. Court dress for men (except for Garter Knights) simply vanished into the blackout, and in 1964 decorations were permitted to be worn with black tie. There was the occasional gala at the Royal Opera House like the one for the President of France and Madame Auriol in 1950 when the occupants of the royal box dressed by Hartnell eclipsed even the smartest of the *corps diplomatique*. State visits continue but the diminuendo of regal glamour has been steady – so steady that during the three-day visit of another French President, M. Giscard D'Estaing and his wife, in 1976, beginning with the traditional State dinner at Buckingham Palace

88

There is no doubt who is Sir Norman Hartnell's most glamorous client – Her Majesty Queen Elizabeth II, for whom he designed this elaborately embroidered ballgown for the State Visit to France in April 1957. Sketch by Norman Hartnell. A detail of the embroidery – Napoleonic bees, golden fleurs de Lys and field flowers, diamond chanticleer plumes, on cream satin – is shown opposite.

and ending with the equally traditional but outstandingly beautiful return of hospitality at the French Embassy, many felt as they gazed round on the flood-lit garden and lily-lined marquee that it might be the last time that so many dazzling tiaras and glittering decorations would be seen in such splendour and profusion.

As informality became the keynote of the Court, it seeped down to the people, and the descent like that descent to Avernus was swift. Suddenly white tie was no longer seen at Covent Garden opening nights, and soon even black tie disappeared except at benefit performances graced by royalty. Theatre audiences are a shambles. As debutantes could no longer be presented at Court, the Queen Charlotte's Ball, an annual charity event in aid of the hospital of that name, became a mild substitute. The debs making their first bows to society are required to wear white, but without the panoply of the Palace even the most doting mothers are rarely induced to have dresses made by the expensive couturières for their ewe lambs. Instead they mostly patronize the big stores who look forward to the occasion with mixed feelings, for, as the head of one of these stores said ruefully, 'The mums come in with their daughters and choose a white dress. The day after the ball, the dresses come back with the excuse that the deb's father didn't like it – usually with lipstick and champagne stains as well.' Until recently stores still thought it worth while to turn a blind eye to such ignominious tactics.

The change in the image of royalty is typified in fashion by the dressmaker who shares the honour of dressing the Queen. Hardy Amies, who received his Royal Warrant in 1955, has been dressing the Queen since 1951 when she was still Princess Elizabeth. With Sir Norman he provided the wardrobe for the Commonwealth visit that ended so tragically with the King's death. Mr Amies is in tune with the informality that permits television cameras to wander about the Royal residences, travel on the Royal train and on the Royal yacht photographing the Queen and her family as they did for the programme shown in 1969 – a humanizing counterpoint to the hieratic ceremonial of the Prince of Wales' investiture at Caernarvon that year. Mr Amies dresses the Queen in what the late Bettina Ballard described as 'current daytime smartness',[5] but he is quite up to his share of State occasions too which he handles in a contemporary style.

Mr Amies came into the Royal Enclosure of designers by a different route than Hartnell, perhaps a more natural one, for his mother had been a Court dressmaker. Besides the advantage of a Court, England also had a well-deserved reputation for tweeds and tailoring. In the pre-war thirties Americans made a beeline to London for tweed suits. The name at the time was Lachasse and the young designer who made it was Irishman Digby Morton. Mr Amies, who took Digby Morton's place when the latter left in 1933 to open his own House, generously credits him with revolutionizing the so-called classic tweed suit from its hairy, Harris tweed rigidity, 'into an intricately cut and carefully designed garment';[6] one fashionable enough to be as much at home at the smartest restaurant as on the moors. The peak year for Lachasse and Mr Amies was 1937 when the Coronation of King George VI attracted to London not only droves of American sightseers, but American store buyers as well. Alas, too soon afterwards, the Second World War transformed slim, elegant Mr Amies into slim, dashing Lieutenant-Colonel Amies of the Intelligence Corps. The early days of that war are best described in Evelyn Waugh's *Put Out More Flags* – a sort of in-and-out war for those who joined up bursting with enthusiasm and then, deflated, found themselves sent home to await another call-up for training. During one of these in-between intervals Mr Amies and Lachasse parted company, and Mr Amies was given, through his ineffable *vendeuse* Miss Campbell, a corner at Worth in Grosvenor Street in which to show models designed during his off-duty days until he was sent overseas. On the first of January 1946 he opened on his own in the beautiful house in Savile Row, built by Lord Burlington in 1835 in which Richard Brinsley Sheridan had lived and died. From that day Mr Amies has never looked back. In 1950 he was the first London couturier to open a boutique. His greatest success, however, has been with his clothes for men which he started with Hepworth's – a large ready-to-wear men's firm – in 1961.

In case it seems invidious to have selected these two designers from those who formed the Incorporated Society of London Fashion Designers, a group formally founded in 1942 in an effort to further exports, it is because these two talents reached beyond the British Isles: Sir Norman as a royal dressmaker, Mr Amies with his ever-growing licensing empire, totalling in 1976, one hundred and

Opposite The other Royal dressmaker, Hardy Amies, designed this neat suit in Cumberland tweed softly checked in peach and grey-brown for his ready-to-wear in 1962. It was, of course, the Queen who brought silk head-squares into fashion.

Overleaf left Zandra Rhodes designs her fabrics as well as her dresses – both as fragile as dragonfly wings. Her handwriting it so individual that the change from season to season is so subtle as to be difficult to date, but this dress is from her 1976 collection.

Overleaf right Bill Gibb marked 1976 with a swirl of tiered white embroidered net and organza.

Teddy Tinling and tennis have been synonymous for the nearly forty years he has been designing clothes for the courts. Ever since he designed the dress Suzanne Lenglen wore when she came out of retirement in 1938, he has been an innovator. In 1968 he launched his first tennis dresses in colour, not alas for Wimbledon. This one, scalloped at yoke and hem, is in pale lemon cotton.

sixty million dollars, and encompassing besides the United Kingdom, Canada, the United States, Japan, New Zealand, Australia, South Africa and the EEC countries.

A different kind of court dressmaker is another Englishman. Teddy Tinling, designer of tennis wear, has also been – and still is – on the world map. *Time* magazine in 1976 saluted him as being 'present at the creation', which presumably referred to his having designed the tennis dress Suzanne Lenglen wore when she came out of retirement in 1938. Mr Tinling had met Mlle Lenglen at Nice when he, a little over thirteen, was, he says, pressed into service to umpire a match in which she was playing. (Ball-boy somehow seems more probable, but as Mr Tinling is six foot seven, he was probably even then tall for his age.) During his nearly forty years of coping with tennis clothes of ever-decreasing dimensions, he has dressed nearly every female tennis champion from most countries that can produce a contender. He made world headlines in 1949 with the frilly lace panties he gave Gussy Moran to wear under her brief skirt. These caused a sensation at the time, but time has shown, and *Time* agrees, that this bold gesture in the face of the stolid conventionality of Wimbledon, 'liberated' women's tennis clothes. Now at sixty-seven, Mr Tinling has left England to work in America where he is revered as a practicing oracle of what to wear to play a game in a country which boasts 150,000 tennis courts on which over eight and a half million females are busy playing.

Other British designers, members of the ISLFD, the Incorporated Society of London Fashion Designers, whose numbers rose and fell like the *Financial Times* Shares Index, are delightful, intelligent and cultivated, and some like Digby Morton, Michael, John Cavanagh and the late Victor

Stiebel especially talented. Bettina Ballard, then fashion editor of American *Vogue*, found them in 1960 'charming, unegoistic men who seemed to brush their own talents off as if they were specks on their coats . . .' This diffidence may have been charming; to Mrs Ballard they lacked 'the hard realistic attitude of the French'.[7] Although she didn't realize it at the time, the mainstream of fashion was changing direction, and not even the dedicated chairman of the ISLFD, Edward Rayne, also holder of a Royal Warrant as shoemaker to the Queen, could play Canute.

The first faint rumble of the approaching Revolution that was to shake the foundations of fashion was the opening in 1955 of a small shop on the King's Road. The shop was called Bazaar and it marked Mary Quant's first step onto the fashion scene and the beginning of the transformation of the King's Road into the official playground of the Beat Generation in their uniform of brief, too tight skirts, long flying hair and black or white stockings. It was at the Royal Court which stands at the top of the King's Road that John Osborne's *Look Back in Anger* opened in 1956 and focussed overseas eyes on the British theatre and its 'angry young men'. That year Janey Ironside took over from Madge Garland as head of the Fashion School of the Royal College of Art. In 1958 Jocelyn Stevens bought the near-centenarian *Queen* magazine (founded in 1861) and set about transforming it into a saucy youngster. The Revolution had begun.

Mary Quant photographed in 1969 in the mini which she made famous – and vice versa.

Left *The mini on the King's Road in 1967 when the British Government approved the lowering of the age of majority from twenty-one to eighteen. The bill was passed in 1970. Some were shocked that such swinging youngsters would soon be able to marry without the consent of their parents – and even to vote.*

In 1960 the twenty-four-year-old Yves Saint Laurent presented in the sacred precincts of the late Christian Dior a collection which showed him in total tune with the cool, gone beats of Chelsea, and sounded the first knell of the dominance of the French Couture. The Revolution was under way and as the sixties raced on the tempo increased. Everything was on the boil. The theatre guyed the establishment in *Beyond the Fringe* in 1961. The Beatles changed the sound of music. In 1962 television discovered satire in *That Was the Week That Was* (incidentally also discovering Millicent Martin, David Frost and Bernard Levin), and *Private Eye* began its impudent career. By 1963 Carnaby Street had become a tourist attraction, its only rival, the King's Road. That year Pop Art was canonized when the Tate Gallery purchased Roy Lichtenstein's 'Wham'.

By 1964 Mods and Rockers were fighting it out on the beaches – the Mods in sharp Carnaby Street gear, brimless hats and Cuban heels, the Rockers in the boots and leather jackets which had inspired Saint Laurent. Ton-up boys were wreaking mobile havoc on their motor bicycles. Youth – angry, violent, iconoclastic – was in the driver's seat. The permissive society was born. That year an American journalist, John Crosby, writing from London, overcome by the King's Road and the leather-coated, leather-booted Chelsea birds who patrolled it, coined the phrase 'Swinging London'.

That year youth hit Paris. *Yé Yé* (the French version of the Beatles' Yeah, Yeah, Yeah' refrain) hit Paris, with designers like Réal, Ted Lapidus and Louis Féraud becoming the leaders of the *yé yé* set, while stores like the Galeries Lafayette and Au Printemps and boutiques like Dorothée Bis were packed with clothes by Mary Quant, Jane and Jane (Jean Muir), Gerald McCann, Tuffin and Foale, Caroline Charles and Roger Nelson. In 1965 New York got the message and American *Harper's Bazaar* devoted a whole issue to young London, with photographer Richard Avedon as guest editor, including a glossary of 'inmost lingo'.

These were the years when London swung and the world swung with it. It is hard to say just which finger triggered off the youth explosion. The times were right and the talents were right for the times. And Mary Quant was one of the rightest. Mary was more than just the fashion symbol of the sixties. Her unique position in fashion history, as the introduction to her retrospective exhibition at the London Museum in 1975 put it, is

'. . . that she was the first to understand and create a look for a new generation, that she jolted this country and a sizeable part of the world out of its conventional ideas about clothes, that she blasted an opening in the wall of tradition through which other young talents have poured, that in every area of fashion she opened windows which had been sealed tight far too long.'

The sixties were for her a decade of expansion: 1961, first fur collection, first wholesale company; 1962, first collection for the American market; 1963, inauguration of the Ginger Group; 1964, designs for Butterick patterns; 1965, rainwear, tights (and all hosiery), underwear and swimwear; 1966, cosmetics, boots and shoes. In the seventies she added household furnishing, towels and sheets, knitwear, men's ties, stationery, spectacle frames, the Mary Quant doll, hats . . . Mary's stated aim was a world market – this she has achieved with her cosmetics. (For 'Mary', please read 'with her

Laura Ashley is an English, or rather Welsh, phenomenon. Riding the wave of reaction against the tawdry sexiness of the thirties revival, the Laura Ashley shops feature a milkmaid innocence. This and the charm of their sprigged cottons are the bases of their success – and to be absolutely fair, the milkmaid look of pinafores and smocks was pioneered by Gina Fratini, and sprigged lawn has long been a staple of the Liberty fabric range, but the combination has hit the jackpot for the Ashleys. The formula varies little: this one is vintage 1975/6.

husband, Alexander Plunket-Greene and her manager, Archie McNair' throughout). Mary and the mini – 'the gym slip of the permissive society' – are indissolubly linked, yet the mini's life was shorter than that of denim and jeans which surfaced in 1963. The span (literally and figuratively) of her hot pants of 1970 was even briefer. What survives is her talent for tackling each problem in design as if it had never existed before, and her irreverence – like Dorothy Parker, inseparable her nose and thumb.

At the Royal College of Art a bumper crop of students pushed their way through the door Mary Quant had opened – and Janey Ironside had the wit to give them their heads – even if sometimes it seemed as if they were not screwed too securely on their shoulders. None of them has yet made it on the Quant scale, but Ossie Clark, Bill Gibb, and Zandra Rhodes and Gina Fratini are names known outside Britain (Marion Foale and Sally Tuffin, too, before they closed up shop), while Janice Wainwright, David Sassoon, Roger Nelson, Hylan Booker and Christopher McDonnell do all right at home. It should be noted that not all the successes were Professor Ironside's exclusive chickens – some had begun their training under Mrs Garland, some were to continue it under Mrs Brogden who succeeded Mrs Ironside in 1968. And although the RCA was identified with Swinging London, many of the strongest front-runners, including Mary Quant herself, Yuki, Jean Muir, John Bates, although they profited by the climate Mary and the RCA had created, came into fashion by separate and different routes: Jean as a sketcher for Liberty, John as a dogsbody in a ready-to-wear firm, Yuki via the London College of Fashion.

In the wake of this wave of talent came a burgeoning of boutiques. These were not the luxurious, scented off-shoots of the French Couture. Small, dark and loud with canned music, they could be told apart only by their self-consciously mad names: I Was Lord Kitchener's Valet (dedicated to the rage for old uniforms), I Spy, Hung on You, Count Down, Bus Stop, Take One, Eggs, Carrots . . . They spawned up and down the King's Road, from which Mary Quant had wisely withdrawn, making it into one long cheap bazaar, spread on to the Fulham Road, then north to Kensington. Like tumbleweed, they were there one day and blown away the next. Some, however, took root. And many have provided outlets for budding talents.

The swinging boutique of the sixties was Biba's, started by fashion artist Barbara Hulanicki and her husband, Stephen Fitz-Simon, as a small mail order operation in 1964. One of the darkest boutiques in Kensington, dimly lit by lamps in Tiffany-type shades, dripping ostrich feathers and beads, it sold off-beat clothes at down-beat prices. Queues formed outside their door like those at cinema theatres; Biba became a tourist attraction, and a magnet for shop-lifters of all nationalities.

Although the merchandise was new, the shop exuded the atmosphere of the second-hand, an appetite for which the young had acquired. Biba's final move across the street to what had been the premises of a department store unfortunately coincided with a dramatic change of mood. The Laura Ashley shops challenged the sexy Biba thirties image with their version of the granny look in pinafores and fresh, sprigged cottons. 'Où est Biba?', the standard tourist query, gave way to 'Où est Laura Ashley?'. Biba disappeared.

By 1966 before this milestone, the phenomenon of swinging London had attracted more journalistic attention. Anthony Lewis in *The New York Times* found England 'relentlessly frivolous' and noted that 'the talent that once went into government now goes more and more into clothes

Shirt of organdie, lipstick printed, the fabric designed and printed by Zandra Rhodes, for her first retail effort, The Fulham Road Clothes Shop opened in 1968.

design . . .' *Esquire* pronounced that 'London's persistence in coping with the uncopable has caused it to become the home of the modern idiom, the only truly modern city . . .' Bernard Leason, London bureau chief of America's *Woman's Wear Daily*, took a more jaundiced view: 'England is not really slipping into an historical era of debauchery and general moral decay . . . It only looks that way.' In 1968 Jean Muir returning from a triumphant trip to New York said: '. . . this Swinging London bit . . . it's so dead . . . The spark is gone.'

The sixties had been a decade of confusion, a confusion that extended even to a confusion of male and female, with unisex clothes, trousers and long hair for Him and Her. It had been a decade of anarchy and rebellion, and escape – escape into fancy dress, second-hand clothes, Hippie gear, nostalgia and drugs. Bill Gibb and Zandra Rhodes, emerging in 1968 like brilliant butterflies from their chrysalises, pointed the way to a new escape route: escape into fantasy – a bourne it seems, from which few travellers return.

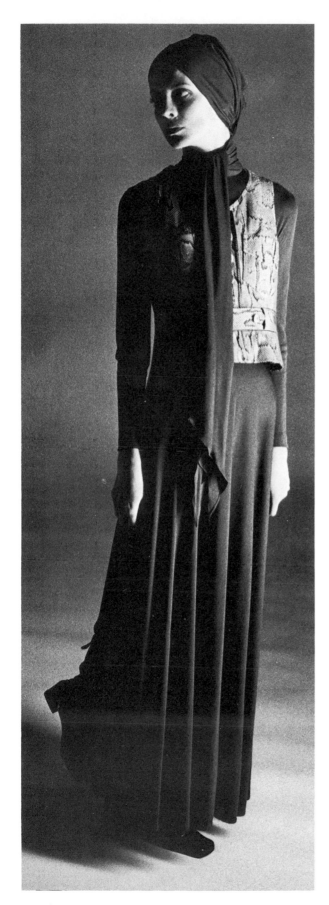

Above *Gina Fratini could be called the pioneer of the
pinafore, here in snuff brown velvet over a dress in white silk
organza, lace trimmed and ruffle-necked, 1972.*

Left *Jean Muir is Great Britain's greatest classicist, her
name is as well known in New York and Paris as in London.
This long, clinging rayon jersey dress, shown here in brown,
with matching scarfed turban and snakeskin gilet of 1969, is
typical of her disciplined restraint.*

Opposite *John Bates' handwriting is bold and definite.
Unusually tall and slender himself, he thinks in terms of tall
elegant women, the kind who can wear this coat and
capeline patterned in bold zigzags, from his 1975 collection.*

The swinging stopped. By 1971, with the success of Yves Saint Laurent's Rive Gauche shops, the lead returned to Paris.

The strong talents survive: Mary Quant, Jean Muir, John Bates, Bill Gibb, Gina Fratini, Zandra Rhodes, Ossie Clark and Yuki. Mary Quant's position is now more firmly based on her ancillary operations than on fashion. Jean Muir's qualities of fierce integrity, discipline and purity of style have made her name not only in England, but in America where she has been established at Henri Bendel since 1966 and where since 1975 she manufactures under the name Jean Muir America, and in France also where, after two successful years under the Mendès banner, she now exports directly. She is the leading contemporary classicist.

John Bates, after establishing a successful middle-market firm under the name Jean Varon, in 1974 started under his own name a top price line as well. His style is personal, more eclectic and more daring than Jean Muir's, but recognizably his. He is a designer of positive statement.

Bill Gibb and Zandra Rhodes deal in the poetry of fashion, are alike only in the originality of their thinking and their virtuoso handling of unexpected combinations of textures, colours and patterns. They are the proponents of fantasy. Zandra, too, has made her mark in New York. Gina Fratini (despite her name which was her husband's) is a purely English designer, happiest in the area she has made her own – that of deliciously pretty clothes, so simple that they have a fantastic age range from seventeen to seventy. Ossie Clark is an up-and-downer – but when up capable of producing, particularly when he is working with fabrics designed by Celia Birtwell, dresses of gossamer beauty. Japanese-born Yuki, who studied in England and trained under Pierre Cardin, is a master craftsman in that most demanding of fabrics, silk jersey which with seeming simplicity he moulds into fluid folds that move with the wearer. He has translated into the ready-to-wear the high tradition of Haute Couture but is happiest in the made-to-order world.

Under these great oaks, little acorns grow – some not so little. There are the Pallants, a husband and wife team operating under the name of Cucumber, Jane Cattlin, Pauline Wynne-Jones and many more . . . All are younger than their American opposite numbers and none of them have behind them the kind of money which in America insures top-flight production and projection. But their very innocence and lack of this gloss of professionalism gives their work a special freshness.

Other survivors are those edifices of British fashion erected in the latter half of the last century. The Victorians built well, as the endurance of these centenarians (give or take a decade or two) testify: Aquascutum (1851), Burberry (1856), Liberty (1875) and the comparatively youthful Jaeger (1884) – all alive and exporting. A fifth, unlike the others does not manufacture, but stands as a monument to retailing. Its name a by-word throughout the world – Harrods, founded in 1849.

Yuki, Japanese born, Cardin-trained, has become in a few years one of Great Britain's most distinguished designers. His forte is his virtuoso handling of silk jersey, and, as here, from his 1977 collection, of silk chiffon.

5

The Arts and Fashion

A lot of highfalutin nonsense has recently been talked about the relation between Fashion and Art. This emphasis on 'cross-fertilization' between the two is perhaps due, in part anyway, to a desire to upgrade the status of fashion as it makes its belated way into British museums. (American museums recognized its importance long ago: the Costume Institute of the Metropolitan Museum of Art in New York was founded in 1937.) The truth is that it is virtually impossible for even those most anxious to be convinced to find that fashion ever exerted any influence on the art of this century. Rather fashion has reflected the transitory phases of twentieth-century art as each has swum into fashionable ken. What cross-fertilization there has been has been mostly one-way.

Fashion has in fact battened on art, especially in France where artists have always taken a genial interest in clothes – it is said that Renoir, for example, helped his friends in that trade to choose the colours of their fabrics. And at a further remove fashion has simply adapted itself to the influence of art on interior decoration.

Boldini's ravishing portrait of Consuelo, Duchess of Marlborough, painted in 1906, typically exaggerated her long neck and graceful arm into a composition of attenuated elegance.

Charles Dana Gibson's pompadoured Gibson girl and centre-parted Gibson man inspired a repeat performance by Camille Clifford, known as England's Gibson Girl, partnered by Leslie Styles who composed the song that made her famous. Both the original drawing and the subsequent photograph of 1908 were made into postcards for which at that time there was an insatiable public.

The high period of portrait painting in the early years of the century, however, presents a teasing question: which came first, the chicken or the egg – the painter or the painted? It seems clear that until Charles Dana Gibson idealized his beautiful wife, Gibson Girls did not exist. His brush called into being a world of women, women of all classes from Duchesses and Dollar Princesses to shop girls, all of whom suddenly acquired handspan waists and upswept pompadours broken flirtatiously by a carefully stray curl. Was this also true of John Singer Sargent? Can one believe that all the ladies whose portraits he painted possessed those acres of unbroken marble bosom, those arms of extraordinary (and sometimes varying) length. Or did they develop them in delighted response to their canvas selves? Was his uncompromising portrait of Isabella Stewart Gardner the result of an unaccustomed fidelity to his subject, or her refusal to conform to his ideal? And were the ladies (sometimes the same ones) who sat to Boldini all swan-necked and of such exquisitely attenuated elegance as Sargent's were arrogantly opulent? In short, did these artists influence or were they influenced?

Boldini was the more faithful recorder of fashion, for he enjoyed the clothes of the time and astute students can identify the designers of the dresses his sitters were painted in. Helleu, too, delighted in the modishness of his sitters. Sargent, on the other hand, found contemporary fashion lacking in pictorial quality, and either had his sitters wear specially designed dresses or glozed over too identifiable detail. Although this vagueness may be a bore for those looking to him for source material, Sargent's talent, as *The Times* wrote in 1956, was to 'recreate an utterly vanished society, so near to us in time and yet so distantly removed from us in spirit, and to understand moreover what this society conceived itself to be.'

Contemporary taste tends to relegate Boldini and Helleu to the later company of van Dongen and Doumerge. The former may have over-flattered their subjects, may have over-commercialized their art, but they never descended to the slap-dash vulgarity of the latter in their mutual aim of capturing and preserving the appearance of their times.

Just as the Pre-Raphaelites put their models into mediaeval dress because the style of the time offended their romantic aesthetic, the fashionable portrait artists of a later day preferred to paint their sitters wearing evening dress and some, like Phillip de Laszlo, invented costumes for their sitters, draping them in lengths of brocade, velvet or chiffon, rather in the way window dressers achieve an effect of clothes by clever arrangements of uncut yardage. Augustus John, on the other hand, created real clothes for his wives and models (to use a euphemism) not only to be painted in but to wear, and in so doing produced the first Chelsea Look. In their full, gathered skirts below fitted corselets or buttoned bodices, their wide-sleeved smock tops and floppy brimmed black felt hats, to Iris Tree, John's women were 'angels dressed as peasants'.[1] But this far-sighted inspiration, although, immortalized in his paintings, had only a limited influence at the time.

Two early instances where fashion acted as an echo of art were at the beginning of the century. One was Art Nouveau, the other, the art of the Orient. Both had their roots in the previous century and the main effects of both were decorative.

Admiral Perry's trade treaty with Japan 1854, and the 'open door' policy (1902 for Britain and 1903 for the United States) with China had made the West aware of these distant countries. Japanese woodcuts as early as 1856 were influencing Impressionist painters and the followers of Art Nouveau, but the popular impact, expressed mainly in interior decoration, came via Liberty's in London, who by 1890 were having a success with their Eastern silks and Chinese porcelains, and through Samuel Bing's shop for Oriental art in Paris which he had opened in 1875 after a trip to the Far East.

Everything Oriental became the rage in Paris – Dumas even put a recipe for a Japanese salad into a play. The result of this unqualified enthusiasm often resulted in a strange mixture of East and West, a hodge-podge of the old and new if one is to believe the description of Odette's drawing-room as observed by Marcel Proust in *Swann's Way:* Oriental draperies, a Japanese lantern concealing a gas jet, enormous palms in Chinese porcelain pots, screens on which were fixed photographs, fans and ribbon bows, floor cushions of Japanese silk, a plush-covered easel holding a portrait of the hostess, and the inevitable Japanese chrysanthemums. Responding to backgrounds such as these, ladies discarded their tea-gowns for silken kimonos delicately embroidered with the exotic flora of Japan – sprays of wistaria, peonies, branches of flowering cherry. Echoed in fashion there was the same muddle, for the kimono sleeve with its deep armholes was awkward in coats and unhappy married to Western collars and cuffs, unhappier still topped by vast, heavily-trimmed hats.

The under-wrought, and to today's eyes, over-tasteful, simplicity of Whistler's Japanese-inspired interiors – plain curtains falling straight to the Japanese matting on the floor, plain walls painted in white and yellow, a few pictures or etchings simply framed, a few pieces of Chinese porcelain – seems to have been ignored, in Paris anyway.

Mr Bing appears again as the *deus ex machina* of Art Nouveau. Twenty years after opening his Oriental shop, Bing opened a shop for modern art which he called L'Art Nouveau. Originally from Hamburg, he with the German art critic, Julius Meier-Graeffe, had discovered van de Velde, who was to become a key figure in Art Nouveau, and commissioned him to design four rooms

*H. Thiriet uses the mannerisms of Art Nouveau to give style to an
advertisement for a White Sale in Paris, 1900.*

for his gallery. It became the talk of Paris, arousing enthusiasm and rage in equal parts.

Although Bing gave the movement the name by which it is known, its seeds had been planted in the Arts and Crafts Movement in England, and, like the discovery of Japanese and Chinese art, dated from the previous century. Professor Sir Nikolaus Pevsner characterizes it as 'a style which links the nineteenth with the twentieth century' and in his opinion *qua* design it was 'played out by 1905'.[2] If its influence on fashion was limited, for it was itself primarily a fashion of decoration, it defined the boundaries within which art was to influence fashion – that is mainly as surface ornament.

Accommodating themselves to their backgrounds, Art Nouveau ladies chose dress fabrics patterned in the sinuous curves of the stems and foliage of the water lily and the lotus, loosened their hair, became languid and self-consciously picturesque – what was later termed 'arty-tarty'.

Sir Osbert Lancaster writing in 1939, took Art Nouveau with less seriousness than does Sir Nikolaus, in fact with active distaste. And indeed as the inventions of the late Victorian years came into common use, a distressing miscegenation took place vividly described by Sir Osbert: 'From the heart of a tinted glass flower at the end of a terrifying sinuous brass stalk there now peeped the electric bulb, while in the fireplace a strange collection of stalactites embossed with a design of waterlilies, glowed with gas-produced heat'.[3]

As Sir Nikolaus said, and this truly horrifying caricature proves, as design the movement was

In this drawing of a cape by Madeleine Vionnet in 1922 for La Gazette du Bon Ton *the artist has borrowed a trick or two from Futurism.*

played out. In fashion it has survived in jewellery and ornaments, most fancifully – and remarkably – in those devised by René Lalique, who, like Louis Comfort Tiffany, was, in addition, a virtuoso performer in glass.

A sort of appendix to Art Nouveau was a group which called themselves 'the Souls' – a mutual admiration society composed of aristocratic beauties and their admirers, mostly statesmen. For their houses they liked Morris fabrics and pale colours, filled their vases with leaves rather than blooms (an economical taste perpetuated into the forties by Lady Colefax). They wore, like their Art Nouveau sisters, trailing draperies, and showed their admiration for the Greek ideal by an addiction to the laurel, a leaf of which, fastened by a brooch, was a sort of club sign. Some wore their hair *à la Grecque* in a chignon. Still, these Souls were a clique and their affectations were not contagious.

The most revolutionary influence on fashion came out of Russia in 1909 with the arrival in Paris (and two years later in London) of the Ballet Russe. The designs of Benois and Bakst with their barbaric vitality, bold primary colours and Oriental sensuality took hold of the imagination of both dress designers and their customers. Of the Paris couturiers, Poiret was the first to translate this exoticism into fashion. His success was instantaneous. Scheherazade moved into the Salons not only of dress designers but of the ladies themselves on both sides of the Channel.

The violent colours of the Ballet Russe and of the group of painters – Matisse, Vlaminck, Derain, known as Les Fauves (the wild beasts) annihilated the dainty pastel colours beloved by the Edwardians, and not only in clothes, but in décor as well.

The backgrounds against which the ladies wore their Poiret or Poiret-inspired dresses and turbans were, quite simply, ghastly. Paintings came down and walls were draped in brightly coloured fabric or painted midnight blue, black or garish shades of red, purple or orange. Armchairs made way for divans heaped with cushions. Carpets were banished and leopard skins or Oriental rugs were scattered on painted floors. In keeping with the theatrical origin of the inspiration, daylight was filtered out by tinsel and gauze curtains, their swags and festoons caught by huge tassels.

Sonia Delaunay translated her absorption in abstract art, which she shared with her husband, artist Robert Delaunay, into the fabrics commissioned from her by Bianchini Ferier in 1925. She is pictured here on the sands with Madame Taueber Arp (wife of Dadaist, Jean Arp) each wearing Delaunay creations. Nancy Cunard, right, one of her many famous clients, was photographed in 1930, the year Madame Delaunay returned to painting, in a Delaunay coat.

Sonia Keppel describes the transformation wrought by her sister Violet (later Trefusis), under the influence of what she dubbed 'Bakst-in-the-home':

'With her own skilful hands, over the fireplace she painted the head of a sphinx . . . Heavy gold lamé curtains shut out the daylight, and the electric light bulbs were dimmed to obscurity behind opaque shades. The room glowed redly, as though it were smoulderingly on fire. Persian missals [sic] gleamed on the walls, and an ikon faced the sphinx opposite the fireplace. Gorgeous Persian jackets lay about on divans ready for Violet's guests to put on when they entered. On top of the cushions lay casually a huge feathered turban . . . incense hung heavy in the air . . .'[4]

Wow! No wonder Violet kept the door shut.

Inevitably there came a reaction both in art and fashion. In their Cubist paintings of 1909, 1911 and 1912 Picasso, Braque and Juan Gris used only subdued colours – white, grey and browns, both dark and light. The lighter shade became translated into fashion as beige, but this may have been a coincidence and it is doubtful if otherwise Cubism exerted any real influence except, rather unfortunately on jewellery, replacing graceful curves with squares and triangles. Indeed beige became a fashionable colour through its use by Chanel who in 1919 had opened her shop on the rue Cambon. Two years before she had met the extraordinary Misia Sert. With her third husband, the

Spanish painter, José Maria Sert, Misia who had been painted by Renoir, Bonnard, Vuilliard, Vallotton, and was a friend of Toulouse-Lautrec and Mallarmé, gave Chanel what the latter called 'her Sorbonne years'. It was through the Serts that she met the poet Reverdy and through Reverdy that she met Picasso. He fascinated her, as he did everybody, but there is no evidence that his paintings influenced her even in her choice of colours. Beige in her hands became as personal a signature as decorator Syrie Maugham's famous off-white. Chanel's most active connection with the arts was in 1914 when she designed the costumes – contemporary beach wear – for Diaghilev's production *Le Train Bleu* for which Cocteau provided the libretto, Poulenc the music and Picasso the curtain.

Colour was to come back into fashion with the Exposition des Arts Decoratifs in Paris in 1925 which produced a startling new talent: the designer Sonia Delaunay, Russian wife of Robert Delaunay. Delaunay was an unorthodox Cubist who, revolting against what Alfred H. Barr Jr has called 'cubist scholasticism',[5] painted brilliantly coloured abstract compositions of discs. His wife, in tune with the new awareness of the aesthetic of the machine, applied his theories to fabrics instead of canvas, giving a new status to textiles and a new impetus to textile manufacturers.

Another exponent of colour was Elsa Schiaparelli whose shocking pink became as famous as Chanel's beige. Schiaparelli turned up in Paris from Italy just about the time of the Arts Decoratifs exhibition as a designer of hand-made knitwear into which she incorporated the abstract patterns

The dramatically strapless dress of Madame Gautreau in this study by John Singer Sargent in 1905 is amusingly echoed in Sir Osbert Lancaster's cartoon of fifty years later.

"I dare say Gina Lollobrigida *did* wear one just like it but Gina Lollobrigida wasn't going to a quiet little dinner-dance at the Fetlock-Smythes!"

The two great Surrealist exhibitions in 1936 at the Museum of Modern Art in New York and at the New Burlington Galleries in London exerted a powerful influence on photographers. That same year Salvador Dali held an exhibition at the Reid & Lefèvre Gallery in London when Sir Cecil Beaton gathered up him and his wife Gala for this Surrealist composition.

which the exhibition had brought into vogue. One of the first to use *trompe l'oeil* in fashion, her avant garde designs made her an immediate success. Witty though those *trompe l'oeil* collars and bows were then, they were to become a cliché with the development of the intarsia knitting machine, invented in 1923, which can reproduce mechanically such hand-wrought tricks.

By 1927 Schiaparelli had moved into more ambitious sportswear and out of her hotel bedroom into a top floor on the rue de la Paix. By 1934, when she established her House in the Place Vendôme and had become a full-fledged couturière, she amused herself and her clients with the lighter side of Surrealism. Like Chanel, who under the tutelage of Misia Sert had taken to art and artists, Schiaparelli too became a patron of the arts, but in a more practical way, commissioning Dali, Bérard, Cocteau, Vertès, Drian to design her fabrics, buttons, scent bottles, advertisements... Her patronage undoubtedly helped them financially, but except that she chose her talents well and gave them their heads, the artistic influence was all in her direction. Although they were minor artists, the collaboration was enriching, and the thirties and forties were the last period in which artists worked creatively and closely with fashion. The only exception was in 1971 when Jules Crahay commissioned the sculptor, Eduardo Paolozzi, to design printed silks for his collection at Lanvin. Alas, this turned out to be a one-off shot.

In the fifties fashion instead of flirting or collaborating with art preyed upon it in a desperate search for ideas. The art of the past has always been a source of inspiration – Madge Garland conjectures whether Zuloaga's flamenco dancers were the origin of Lanvin's *robes de style*.[6] Castillo went to the Goyas at the Louvre. Helleu inspired Dessès and Balmain, as Winterhalter did Norman Hartnell. And so on. And each important exhibition at the Grand Palais in Paris was reflected in one or more of the Couture Collections. Perhaps the most absurd results came out of the Exhibition of African Art in 1967 which induced Marc Bohan at Dior to design a straw cloak in the shape of an African witch doctor's hut and to stretch his models' necks in Ubangi ringed collars.

In 1964 fashion had had a fling at Op Art, an eye-crossing phenomenon of which the British artist, Bridget Riley, was the leading exponent. Her dizzying calligraphic patterns translated easily into fabric designs, so easily that the art critic of *The New York Times*, John Canaday, was quoted as saying that Op Art had been 'prostituted by the dress and fabric industry'.[7] Happily the prostitution did not last long – perhaps people's eyes gave out.

In fashion Art Nouveau had a small resurgence in 1961 when Bill Poole of Liberty in London, rediscovering the original blocks from which the first Art Nouveau silks were printed, launched his Lotus range of fabrics. The range was appropriately introduced in Italy, for there Art Nouveau had been called the '*stile* Liberty', so closely was the store associated with the movement. This was however only a brief flowering – not a real revival.

More lasting and more devastating were two manifestations of the mid and late sixties: Pop Art which mushroomed into fashion in 1964, and two years later Art Deco, a so-called style ingeniously bred by Bevis Hillier out of the Exposition des Arts Decoratifs of 1925 by Art Nouveau.[8]

This exhumation had the strange result of sparking a new interest in Art Nouveau itself. Actually the first time Art Nouveau was revalued in this century was by the New York Museum of Modern Art in 1933 – in an exhibition of 'Objects: 1900 to Today' which concentrated on its purer aspects in architecture and objects contrasted with the products of the Bauhaus. In 1963 the Victoria and Albert Museum held an exhibition of Mucha posters, and in 1975 an exhibition to mark the centenary of Liberty & Co, naturally including the store's finest hours. In 1976 the Art Institute of Chicago rather belatedly awakened to the new appreciation of Art Nouveau by the followers of high camp, put on an ambitious exhibition of 'Art Nouveau: Belgium/France'. The influence on fashion is still, so far, nil.

Art Deco, whose success Mr Hillier somewhat puzzlingly attributes to the film, *Bonnie and Clyde*, was indeed a factor in the nostalgia for the twenties in so far as it fostered the fad for second-hand clothes, although the actual influence on fashion came primarily from the revivals of old films of the period. Art Deco mainly raised the market price of real or imitation Tiffany glass and bibelots in the horrible *style odéon*.

Pop Art has lasted longer, although the Pop Society it brought into being – a mixture of the Anglo-American meritocracy (hair dressers, fashion photographers, model girls) and pop celebrities like Baby Jane Holzer, creating a vortex whose twin centres were Andy Warhol and Mick Jagger

Overleaf left *Leon Bakst's costume designs for the Ballet Russe signposted a dramatic change in fashion direction. This sketch by Bakst is for the ballet,* Narcisse, *1911.*

Overleaf right *The relaxed elegance of this dress* evoked in Van Dongen an uncharacteristic mood of elegance. The perilously low vee-neck masked in the nick of time by a filler known variously as a 'modesty vest' or in the United States as a 'guimpe', the dangling ear-rings – and the chrysanthemums – place the dress, if not the painting, between 1911 and 1914.

and his Rolling Stones – has more or less quietly faded away but The Stones roll on.

One of the leading lights of this fugitive pop society was Nicholas Haslam. Mr Haslam, a premature swinging Londoner, went to New York in 1961 where he briefly became a switched-on art director and a member of the Warhol set.

In 1964 as art director of *Show* magazine (now defunct) he put Mrs Holzer on the cover. Mrs Holzer who had been nominated 'Girl of the Year' by the New York *Herald-Tribune* (also defunct), was photographed by David Bailey (alive and well and back in Britain) apparently wearing only a yachting cap, a pair of joke spectacles reflecting the World's Fair, and, held in her teeth, a souvenir-sized American flag. (This issue was also remarkable for containing the first appraisal of Warhol, as a serious artist, who up to then had been doing 'spots' – small drawings – for the back pages of *Vogue*.) Mrs Holzer's outstanding feature was her hair described by Tom Wolfe as 'an incredible mane . . . a vast tawny corona . . .', when he as the prime reporter of the 'cultural revolution' immortalized her in *The kandy-kolored tangerine-flake streamline baby*, published in 1965. That same year, Yves Saint Laurent, his ear to the underground as well as the ground, showed Pop Art dresses inspired by Andy Warhol. In 1971 Mr Warhol was apotheosized in a one-man exhibition at the Tate Gallery in London.

Mr Haslam, himself, is a one-man indication of the demise of high camp. Once the pioneer of ruffled shirts, black leather suits, suede trousers, boots and tiger skin waistcoats, he now wears conventional Savile Row suits and his hair is cut short (or fairly short) back and sides. Nothing kinky or far out there.

Unfortunately the Pop influence on folk fashion lingers on. T-shirts emblazoned with Pop phrases and slogans or ornamented with Pop idols' faces still top the inevitable jeans. And a few men, old enough to know better, still appear unsuitably attired à la Warhol at non-pop functions.

Chanel is given the Day-Glo super-realist treatment by Peter Blake in 1962, in a portrait painted from a photograph. It immortalizes the inimitable Coco in her imitable brass-buttoned blazer, and her stylist mannerisms: the flipped back white cuffs, the cigarette holder, the dead straight set of her hat, although the jazz spectacle frames are untypical.

Mondrian, like Art Nouveau, was revived as a fashion theme when, in 1966, Yves Saint Laurent discovered this pure abstract painter, it was said, in an art book given him by his mother. His Mondrian-inspired dresses were quickly and widely copied but all that was proved was that a Mondrian on the wall was worth two on the back.

At the moment the love affair between Art and Fashion has cooled. But anything can happen – and probably will.

Sculpture and fashion have never been the closest of friends, if one excludes Elie Nadelman as an eccentric exception. It was difficult to think why the Victoria and Albert Museum inserted into their exhibition of 'Fashion 1900–1939' a female figure in metal by the abstract sculptor, Oskar Schlemmer. It would have been far better to have taken a leaf from the Paris 1925 exhibition and commissioned formalized mannequins like André Vigneau's on which the clothes could have been put. But perhaps they were reaching into the future to presage the two years when sculpture and fashion did come together – sort of.

In 1966 Paco Rabanne had begun making dresses using pliers instead of needles and thread, and metal discs and chain mail instead of fabric. That year Quasar Khanh had made body sculptures of metal which his wife, Emmanuelle Khanh, used in her ready-to-wear collection. By July of 1968 the Couture in Rome and Paris had also discovered hardware – belts were hinged, fastenings latched, chains and bits of metal clanked and jingled. By February 1969 Courrèges, Féraud and especially Ungaro were thoroughly metal-minded, the last even putting his models into metal bras. By August of that year Ungaro was the leading metal merchant – with body sculptures (the metal mood having given birth to 'body jewellery') especially designed by the Italian sculptor, Gio Pomodori. That was the high point of the romance between these two 'disciplines' as the Colleges of Art would call them. After that it petered out, to the undoubted relief of the models who had had to wear them.

I have argued that fashion and interior decoration are closely allied. Architecture too has been a powerful influence. The days of the Louis xv *bergère*, an especially wide chair designed to accommodate panniers, of high-backed chairs to support wigs, and tall windows to permit their wearers to look out, are long before the period covered here, but as from 1919 with the formation of the Bauhaus and the beginning of what came to be christened in the thirties 'The International Style', rooms dwindled in size, and as dwelling space became increasingly minimal, as central heating became more widespread, clothes necessarily became lighter and skimpier, not only to fit into the living space but into the shrinking cupboard. The slim woman created by Poiret presaged the architecture of the future.

Science, too, has played an integral and vital part in the development of fashion. From nylon to the latest mixture of man-made and natural fibres, the test tube has been intimately involved with clothing. Drip-dry fabrics have had the same relentless impact on fashion as the invention of quick-drying acrylic paint has had on a whole area of painting.

1920
**TYPICAL VOTARIES OF TERPSICHORE, MOST GRACEFUL
OF THE MUSES**

Previous pages left *Otto Dix's cruel eye satirises the Jazz Age and incidentally the Jazz Age's dresses of 1927/8.*

Previous pages right *'Come Dancing' became a British television feature in the sixties and is still holding its audiences both in live performances and in dancehalls throughout the country and on the box. One of the features of these dancers is the costumes which by tradition are made by the performers themselves. They follow a pattern of innumerable tulle skirts, elaborately trimmed, like the chongsam, a uniform shape capable of a variety of individual permutations.*

6

The Dance and Fashion

The dance and fashion enjoy a curious relationship. Clothes have not always adapted themselves to this delightful pursuit. In fact pleasure in dancing can outweigh the inconvenience of unsuitable dress. For example, despite her vast ruffs, rigid elongated bodices and spreading farthingales, Queen Elizabeth I managed to enjoy country dances (nearly all kissing dances then) and the lively running *coranto*. According to Dr Roy Strong, she was 'a mistress of the art, having learnt in the Italian manner [Italy in the fifteenth century had been the scene of a renascence of dancing] to dance high.'[1]

Later and possibly less lusty performers found the stately paces of the minuet, pavane and gavotte more suited to the bum rolls, hoop skirts, panniers and towering wigs that were successively worn during the long life of these dances. In the nineteenth century, the light, high-waisted muslins, cambrics and lawns, reputedly brought to England when she fled the Terror in France by Rose Bertin, dressmaker to Marie Antoinette, were much-loved by Jane Austen's heroines, the perfect wear for jolly (but no longer kissing) country dances like the Sir Roger de Coverley in which Emma's friend Harriet Smith 'bounded higher than ever, flew farther down the middle and was in a continual course of smiles'.[2]

It was at the Assembly Rooms of Bath under the direction of Beau Nash, that balls were

On the occasion of the Prince of Wales' visit to Canada in 1908, a great ball was given in his honour at Parliament House by the Government of the province of Quebec. The Daily Sketch *sent an artist, F. Mataria, to cover the Royal progress and he rendered with fidelity the hour glass shapes, the marble expanse of monobosoms, the pompadoured hairdos, the alluring swirl of the skirts of the dancers as well as the graceful swooping gesture to gather their fullness when walking.*

inaugurated, and where sophisticated French dances supplanted the naive English country romps, that dancing really flourished. When the vogue made its way to London, London danced at Ranelagh, Vauxhall and most exclusively at Almack's, which was to become Brooks's Club.

It was at Almack's in 1816 that the waltz first won approval. Four years before, when it was first danced in English ballrooms it had aroused a storm of shocked disapproval. Even Lord Byron attacked in a poem, 'The Waltz: an Apostrophic Hymn', published in 1813 under the pseudonym of Horace Hornem Esq, its 'lewd grasp and lawless contact'.[3]

Dances had proliferated in the nineteenth century, which saw the introduction of the Galop, the Polka, the Lancers and the Cotillion with its figures and favours, but it was the Viennese waltz that first dramatically changed fashion.

'I'm going to Maxim's where fun and frolic gleams . . .' These lines from *The Merry Widow* according to Sir Osbert Sitwell, 'reflected the current ennui with the responsibilities of life . . .'[4] From where we sit seventy worried years later, it is hard to imagine what those boring responsibilities could have been. Affluence, security, luxury, self-indulgence, a close-knit social caste which enjoyed a happy licence freed from Victorian restrictions – none of these were yet objects of disapprobation. And the warnings of the *Daily Mail* and *John Bull* about Germany's aggressive intentions fell on ears attuned only to the lilting Lehar waltzes which Sir Osbert records 'served as a background to every meal in a restaurant, every dance and every garden party'.

MISS LILY ELSIE
FOULSHAM & BANFIELD

*The Merry Widow in 1907 had set
England waltzing and Lucile's dresses
for its star, Lily Elsie, changed fashion,
as did Miss Elsie's famous Merry
Widow hat.*

The dances and the balls were endless and the ballgowns magnificent. Vita Sackville-West describes Lady Roehampton dressed for a court ball, '. . . bare shoulders . . . oyster satin flowing out at her feet, pearls vanishing into the valley between her breasts, pearls looped round her wrists, a rosy scarf tossed round her shoulders' and again at the opera '. . . magnificent shoulders, emerging from clouds of tulle,' her head poised under a crown of diamonds.[5] But dancing with one of these dazzling beauties, corseted and heavily under-pinned, must have been like dancing with the Iron Maiden.

The Boston had been the exciting new dance of 1906, but although it was complicated enough to require ladies to take lessons in how to do it properly, it imposed no change in fashion. *The Merry Widow* did. The great plume-laden hats worn by its star, Lily Elsie, became as much *de rigueur* for the *demi-monde* as for the *monde* itself. These hats were worn at all hours of the day and night, indoors and out, Sonia Keppel describes her mother in a 'black velvet, low-cut evening dress with which she wore a high diamond and pearl dog collar, pearl ear-rings and a diamond drop – and above it all a huge, feathered hat'.[6] Suffragettes wore them, so did women strikers in New York. Some great ladies even wore them down to breakfast; they finally topped the heads of Pearlie Queens and Liza Doolittles. A similar fate awaited the once fashionable feather boa.

Miss Elsie's high-waisted dresses by Lucile of chiffon and crêpe de Chine, soft and pliant, sprinkled with beads, fine lace insertions, delicate ruffles, lover's knots of satin, replaced the stiff satins and brocades. Their most distinct hallmarks were the colours – the mauves, salmons and cyclamen

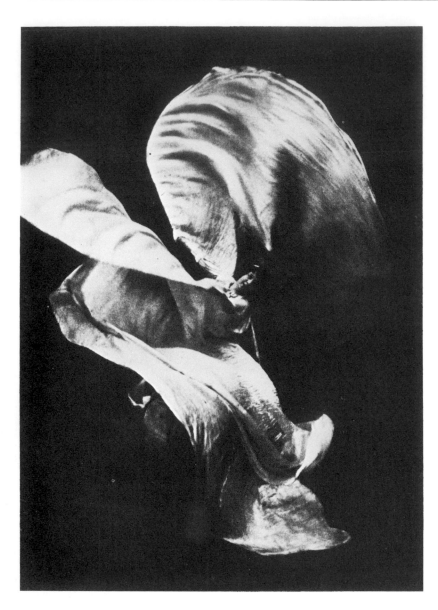

Loie Fuller who came to Europe from Illinois in 1890 was the precursor of another type of dancing – and another type of dancer. She scored a huge success swirling her gauzy draperies on which coloured lights were played. Her entranced audiences did not fail to note that her costumes were also diaphanous.

shades of the new varieties of sweet pea – 'a flower' which to Sir Osbert 'remains as typical of the age of *The Merry Widow* as does the camellia to the age of crinolines and muslins.'

In the last years of Queen Victoria's sober reign, a different sort of dancing from across the Atlantic made its appearance in England and on the Continent. The pioneer was Loie Fuller from Illinois, whose mild success floating around the stage in gauzy draperies, waving more filmy stuff attached to sticks, was transformed into a wild success when in 1890 she disovered the difference coloured lights would make on all this swirling. Next came Isadora Duncan from San Francisco in 1908. From the Tanagra figures at the British Museum she took the idea of dancing in bare feet and Greek chitons. Under the patronage of Mrs Pat Campbell, she gave performances at select private parties, where according to the *Encyclopaedia Britannica*, she 'enraptured' her audiences. She also shocked them deliciously with her uncorseted costumes and bare feet and bare legs.

The year before at Marienbad, Canadian Maud Allan whose repertoire was curiously similar to Isadora's (a nymph to Mendelssohn's 'Spring Song', a tragic mourner to Chopin's 'Funeral March'), and which, again like Isadora, she danced barefooted and barelegged, was invited to dance before the

Left *Maud Allan from Canada dispensed with tactful draperies and danced barefoot and barelegged. Royal approval helped her to her dazzling success climaxed in 1907 and marred only by a certain lack of understanding of her purely artistic motive in appearing as Salome clad mostly in beads.*

Above *Josephine Baker, 1926. Who thought full frontal nudity was new?*

Left *Isadora Duncan arrived in Europe from San Francisco in 1908. She is said to owe to the Tanagra figures at the British Museum the idea of dancing barefoot in brief Greek chitons. This gave an aura of artistic respectability to her bare-legged, uncorseted performances, and she rapidly became the idol not only of a titilated public but of other artists.*

King. Armed with royal approval, she obtained a licence from the Lord Chamberlain to perform in public. So successful was her season at the Palace Theatre that a special souvenir edition of her book *My Life and Dancing* was published in 1908 to commemorate her two-hundred-and-fiftieth performance. The high spot was when she danced before the King and Queen at a party given by Lord and Lady Dudley, after which she was received by the Queen. Later, Miss Allan found herself the centre of controversy when as Salomé, she wore above her beaded belt only some more beads and breast plates.

Miss Allan is supposed also to have danced at 10 Downing Street at the invitation of Margot Asquith, herself a noted performer of what was called 'skirt dancing'. Margot Asquith is commonly thought to be the original of E.F. Benson's *Dodo*, published in 1893, the year before she married. In it he describes her as dancing 'with unusual perfection ... Her figure, clad in its long, clinging folds of diaphanous, almost luminous texture, stood out like a radiant statue of dawn against the dark panelling of the room; her graceful figure bending this way and that, her wonderfully white arms now holding aside her long skirt, or clasped above her head ...' No Terpsichorean slouch, she, and clearly a forerunner of the so-called interpretative dancing.

Freed from the discipline of ballet technique, this free style of dancing caught on more violently in America, where Ruth St Denis and Ted Shawn carried on the Duncan tradition. In fact it became a sort of cult among middle-aged ladies, delightfully caricatured by Helen Hokinson in *The New Yorker* magazine and by Ruth Draper in one of her monologues where the invisible ladies were coyly invited by their teacher to change the invisible lambs which they were supposed to be leading for invisible lilies they were supposed to be holding aloft. In England society was titillated by all this bareness and corsetless abandon, but although they may have practised Dalcroze and eurhythmics in private, there is no record that they flung off their underpinnings or shed their footwear. In Paris, however, Madame Vionnet, in her seventy-ninth year, recalled proudly that in 1907 she had 'presented mannequins for the first time in bare feet and sandals, and in their own skins'.[7] Few seem to have followed her lead.

The Merry Widow waltzes were shortly to be superseded by the tango which was wafted to Europe from South America in 1911. Poiret had freed the body from its confining corsets, and instead of encasing it had lightly covered it in soft fabrics, emphasizing its new slenderness with swaying tunics, often edged in fur. The popularity of the tango forced him and his followers to split open the confines of the idiotic hobble skirt. Now draped or slit up the front, the ankle-length skirt revealed tango shoes, slippers laced from instep to ankle with satin ribbon. To match the sultry rhythms ladies took to sultry make-up, and flourished cigarettes in long holders. They were partnered by a new breed of otherwise unemployed young men, the gigolos who made a living being at the beck and call of these dancing ladies. In deference to the South American origin of the dance, they affected the long sideburns and patent leather hair which, when worn by Rudolph Valentino in *The Four Horsemen of the Apocalypse* in 1921 were to break millions of hearts. The main requirement for the job was that they were available from tea-time to dawn (for the tango craze produced the *thé dansant* and the nightclub), and could guide their partners through the intricate gyrations of the tango and the maxixe.

As these dances were difficult to learn and execute, their addicts needed instruction. America filled this need with a couple who soon became world-famous: Irene and Vernon Castle. Soon the Castles had added the syncopations of ragtime to their repertoire, and were expert interpreters of the one-step, two-step, fox trot, the Turkey Trot, the Bunny Hug and their own creation, the Castle

EXIT TANGO.

The Spirit of Dancing (*waking up*). "WELL, THANK HEAVEN THAT'S OVER; ONE OF THE DULLEST NIGHTMARES I EVER MET."

Punch's Spirit of Dancing in 1914 may not have known that she was bidding farewell not only to the tango but to the Poiret dress, which with its pagoda tunic and feather-crowned head-dress, is a kissing cousin of the real thing drawn for La Gazette du Bon Ton *in 1911. There is a touch of sour grapes in Punch's disapproval for the Spirit herself is far too stiffly corsetted to have attempted the dance she affects to despise.*

Walk. It was not only at nightclubs and parties that people danced. At home carpets were rolled up and victrolas blared as long as there were willing hands to wind them. All America and all Europe was dance-mad.

Everywhere everybody copied the Castles. Gigolos hurriedly transformed themselves into lounge lizards, emulating Vernon Castle's blonde slimness. Women slavishly copied Irene Castle's clothes, by Callot and Lucile, and her hair cut, known as the Castle Bob, unveiled in 1913. Although she may not have been the first to bob her hair (as with the invention of the brassière and the abolition of the corset at least as many have contested for this distinction as did 'towns contend for Homer dead'), she must have been the first to announce that her husband cut it for her.

The Castle's crisp, high-stepping gaiety was the healthy antithesis of the pseudo-sexiness of the

Irene Castle and her husband Vernon Castle, who became the first professional ballroom dancers, was a positive influence on fashion from 1913 when she first bobbed her hair. Although this photograph has been dated 1919/24, the long tunic overskirt and tango shoes seem to be earlier, perhaps 1914.

tango vamp and her, regrettably called, 'dago' partner. Mrs Castle's clothes were always in the latest fashion, but it was the leggy freedom and insouciance with which she wore them that made the impact.

The Castles had given birth to ballroom dancers, and they were succeeded in the twenties by other dancing teams, most successfully by Leonora Hughes who took over Florence Walton's partner and husband, Maurice. Miss Walton had been dressed, or to our eyes over-dressed, by Callot. Miss Hughes' dancing dresses were by Patou and her floating, ostrich-trimmed chiffons were the inspiration for Ginger Rogers' film costumes in the thirties. Although Miss Rogers partnered by Fred Astaire became the ideal for all dancers, as the Castles had been before them, Miss Rogers' clothes had little or no influence on fashion until the nostalgia era of the sixties.

The First World War didn't stop, it just interrupted, the dancing. When it resumed after the Armistice it was even more frenetic. Dixieland jazz, and the Blues which followed, intensified the passion. The Blackbirds had made Blacks fashionable: Florence Mills was the idol of London, and Josephine Baker was the toast of Paris, strutting in her golden skin and a few feathers. In the late twenties, New York discovered Harlem, where at nightspots like Connie's Inn, Small's Paradise and the Cotton Club, Duke Ellington and Cab Calloway tickled the ivories, Ethel Walters coon-shouted, and the long-legged, loose-limbed dancers elaborated on the Lindy Hop – said to have been invented by dancer Ray Bolger to commemorate Lindbergh's flight. Sensible whites in their low-waisted, flat chested wisps of dresses looked and listened only, for the jitterbugging was so

Ginger Rogers and Fred Astaire replaced the Castles as the ideal dancing pair. Miss Rogers' ostrich-trimmed dancing dresses, by Bernard Newman (who came to Hollywood from Bergdorf Goodman in New York) in films like Top Hat *made in 1935, were to start a wave of nostalgic dressing thirty years later.*

Gaby Deslys and her partner, Mr Harry Pilcer, posing in 1914, seem to be doing a premature Charleston. Miss Deslys' handkerchief-pointed underskirt was short enough for her to kick up her Louis-heeled shoes, but however did she balance all those feathers?

incredibly double-jointed, the gyrations so fast and furious, it was stupid to try to compete.

As the jazz, particularly the Charleston, made its way downtown, it commanded – and obtained – a change in fashion. Skirts lifted to the knees – and above. Underwear was now reduced to a single garment – the 'teddy', a combination of camisole and pantie. With nothing to hold them up, stockings were rolled or supported by the merest wisp of a suspender belt. Flaming youth was born and in *Dancing Daughters* Joan Crawford's brief fringed skirts by David Cox, and high-speed footwork flashed the Charleston message round the world.

The Charleston also spelled the doom of the statuesque beauty who was ousted by the skinny little flapper, just as the show girl (a breed of beautiful clothes-horse invented by Florenz Ziegfeld for his Follies and epitomized by Dolores, an English girl who had been one of Lucile's mannequins) was eclipsed by tiny, agile dancers like dimple-kneed Ann Pennington.

Another Follies dancer, Gilda Gray, introduced the shimmy, a dance in which the performer quivered like jelly. In fact puddings made of gelatine were occasionally called 'shimmy puddings', a more likely provenance than what the *Oxford English Dictionary* disapprovingly calls 'a corruption of chemise'. To accentuate her energetic shaking, Miss Gray wore brief dresses made of layers of fringe, a fashion which made its way to the French Couture.

As the twenties moved on to the thirties, the Charleston gave way to the Big Apple and the Black Bottom from Harlem, and the Shag from goodness knows where. The Charleston and its successors spelled the beginning of the end of what the Arthur Murray Dance Studio refers to as

Life

Teaching old Dogs new tricks

FEBRUARY 18, 1926

PRICE 15 CENTS

N

John Held Jr., the master cariacaturist of the Jazz Age, drew this cover for Life magazine in 1926. This witty weekly lost its life, so to speak, in 1936 when Henry Luce bought it up for its name, and for 85,000 dollars. Like all good cartoonists, Held had a precise eye for fashion, and the Charlestoning young lady is right from her shingled head to her Louis heel, from her long pearl necklace, and upper arm and many other bracelets, to her rolled and gartered stockings. If she had ever stood still, the flying side panel would have dropped well below her knee-length hem, a stylistic mannerism devised by Augustabernard.

*Any disco in 1965. In the darkness anything goes; in the crowded space
minimal dress is necessary.*

'touch' or 'smooch' dancing, (the sort which used to evoke cries of 'Get off that dime')
more politely known as 'cheek to cheek'. Today the young are now beginning to dance together
again.

The tango was supplanted by the Conga, the rhumba from Cuba and the Samba from Brazil.
The last, introduced by Carmen Miranda in Brazilian dress, laid its touch on fashion. In its shoulder
and bottom swaying wake came ruffled off-the-shoulder dresses, swathed behinds and flower-
topped Carmen Miranda turbans. With far sight it is possible to see in the last the genesis of the
terrible turban-type headgear that prevailed in England during the Second World War.

The late thirties and the beginning of the War saw a revival in England of country type dances –
the Lambeth Walk, Hands, Knees and Bumps-a-Daisy, the Hokey-Cokey, but these had no
influence on fashion – so soon to be restricted by coupons or uniforms. It was not until 1951 that a

rage for square dances popularized an amalgam of fashions, some started in America, some in Paris. 'Separates' had been a pre-war innovation of Schiaparelli. Working in her boutique was a talented young Frenchman, Hubert de Givenchy, who that year launched his first collection on his own – a collection of separates. His puffy-sleeved, cotton blouses were quickly copied. Teamed with wide Dior-type, ballerina length skirts puffed out even more by layers of petticoats, waists cinched with patent-leather belts and worn with the flat-heeled ballet slippers Claire McCardell had introduced, they became epidemic and rustled in offices and on the street as well as on the dance floor.

The be-petticoated dance dresses, exaggerated *ad absurdum*, became the costume for exhibition dancing which flourished in the provinces of England in the Sixties. These formation groups, mainly middle-aged, trained by competing teachers, prided themselves not only on their regimented performance but on their dress: the men in white tie and their partners in dresses they made themselves. With hair lacquered into towering beehive coiffures of a slightly earlier day at one end and teetering stiletto heels at the other, the often bespectacled ladies swayed and dipped through their set piece dances – dances rarely seen on dance floors, like the fast foxtrot and paso doble – in spangled costumes of multi-coloured layers of tulle. Fortunately this fashion (if it can be so called) remained safely on television screens in a weekly programme called *Come Dancing*, and in the dancehalls.

Rock 'n' roll started officially in 1956 when Bill Haley and his Comets hit the Number One spot with their record 'Rock Around the Clock'. In the same year Elvis Presley was being mobbed by squealing bobby soxers. How much the rock 'n' roll music and dancing contributed to the frightening Rockers uniforms – black leather jackets, nail-head studs, with their black-stockinged, tousle-headed female counterparts – is moot. By 1959 the Beat generation which had been born on the King's Road had its counterpart on the Left Bank and in Greenwich Village, and the next year the two combined influences persuaded Yves Saint Laurent to produce his ill-fated Beat Collection for the House of Dior. The Liverpool sound of the Beatles, who hit top billing in 1962, completed the revolution in fashion for the young – and made them, the mini skirt and Mary Quant, who took the latter to new heights, world famous.

At the beginning of the sixties Paris had invented a new kind of *boîte*, with canned, instead of real, music. These discothèques, small, dark, mini-nightclubs, upgraded the jukebox. To the jive and swing was added the Twist. The Couture responded to the discothèques by designing swinging little dance dresses, usually black, Guy Laroche scoring the most instantaneous success. In 1961 discos flew across the Channel to England, and their darkness encouraged, but did not inspire, the anything-goes attitude of the young who wore their hot pants and jeans with see-through blouses or sported see-through dresses or whatever they liked or had handy.

The music and the lonely gyrations of the jiving, frugging dancers and the clothes they wore to dance in were less an expression of fashion than of the frustrations of these angry years.

7
Chroniclers of Fashion

The brush, the camera and the pen – these are the tools of the chroniclers of fashion. To portrait artists fashion was a secondary consideration but we owe to them a glamourized vision of the fashion of their time. The artists served the Edwardian beauties well, giving them all the attributes that current taste demanded: swan necks, snowy shoulders, gleaming monobosoms above the silks and satins, long slender hands playing negligently with the strings of pearls.

To begin with the camera was less flattering to model and clothes alike. A true and disillusioning record is provided by the commercial photographic agencies – the most encylopaedic, the faithful documentation by the indefatigable Seeberger Frères of Paris of the Edwardian scene, high society and *mannequins de ville* alike, dressed to kill at the races and at the smart resorts. Fashion houses preferred pedestrian photographs (and still do), although often with grandiose and pretentious

The two Surrealist exhibitions in 1936 had a great influence on photographers'
props as well as on their ideas. Here Sir Cecil Beaton photographed Mlle Eve
Curie (now Mrs Henry Labouisse) as if, like a performing dog at the circus, she
had just broken through the paper ring.

backgrounds, for their aim is as exact a reproduction of the garment as possible.

But the photographers soon learned to please, and the Edwardians loved to display a vast framed array of the results of their exertions. In 1904, Howard Sturgis, an American living in the seclusion of Windsor catalogued these:

'Ladies looking over their shoulders with their hands behind their backs, ladies with sheaves of lilies and baskets of flowers, ladies looking out of paper-mullioned windows wreathed in sham ivy, ladies with children in lace frocks, ladies in ball dress, court dress, fancy dress, or simply what may be called photographic dress, consisting of the sitters' best low-necked gown and a hat, a combination which no one could be expected to believe was ever worn outside the studio.'[1]

No one in Windsor, perhaps.

The tradition of artificial décor was to persist well into the century, epitomized in the work of Baron de Meyer who perfected a cosmetic technique which became his hallmark. By a skilful use of backlighting and a soft focus lens, he gave his sitters an ethereal beauty, augmented by a profusion of props: satin pillows, sprays of blossom, ostrich fans, tapestry backgrounds, choice pieces of furniture. The origins of the Baron are as veiled in mystery as his work. Mrs Edna Woolman Chase, editor of *Vogue*, for whom he worked from 1913 to 1922, gives him a nicely assorted pedigree: forbears who lived in Finland, a German father and a French mother, name originally Adolphe von Meyer, surname changed to the French version, Christian name to Gayne, after having, as Mrs Chase says, 'met a numerologist'.[2] Valerie Lloyd puts him in the Almanack de Gotha. According to her his name was Demeyer Watson and his wife an illegitimate daughter of King Edward VII, which 'consequently' brought him a 'barony in his native Saxony'.[3] (Watson seems an odd name for a native of Saxony, and why 'consequently', but no matter.) Anyway both Mrs Chase and Sir Cecil Beaton[4] agree that in later life de Meyer's hair had turned bright blue. Sir Cecil's corroboration is needed, for Mrs Chase's view became somewhat acidulated when the Baron left *Vogue* to work for her arch-rival *Harper's Bazaar*. All three, however, are in accord that de Meyer was an innovator, a great technician and a profound influence.

Another powerful influence was Edward Steichen, who succeeding de Meyer in 1923, was brought into the *Vogue* net by Frank Crowninshield, the brilliant editor of *Vanity Fair*. Although born in Luxembourg, Steichen was very much a product of Milwaukee, Wisconsin, where he was taken by his parents when small. De Meyer had been a dilettante painter before he turned to the camera; Steichen also had his roots in painting, but his were deeper, and his association with art closer through Alfred Stieglitz, the first in America to understand and promote the importance of photography. This may have been responsible for the feeling that Steichen gave that although the importance of his work was indisputable, although he spent fifteen years as a fashion photographer, he looked down on fashion which he professed not to understand. In 1936 when he was offered a one-man exhibition of his work at the Museum of Modern Art (the first museum to found a Department of Photography of which Steichen was to become a director from 1947 until 1961), he proposed instead a show of his prize delphiniums. As a photographer he was an early exponent of

Erté considers this his favourite fashion design created for New York's Henri Bendel c.1916. Its lifted hemline dipping into a train at the back presages what became a Balenciaga hallmark forty years later.

Right *Baron Gayne de Meyer, 'the first artist in photography' according to Sir Cecil Beaton, is at his most typical in this portrait of the Hon Mrs Reginald Fellowes, in her version of the Eugénie hat. The diffused roundel of light against which the profile is delicately etched, the shimmer of pearls and fabric make one overlook the desperately artificial pose of hands and handbag. 1932/33.*

Above *A studio photograph of a fashion model has been superimposed on a drawn backdrop of a rainy day to fit the caption: 'A storm of complications: the Eternal Puzzle in Rainy, Windy, Muddy Weather. How to keep Umbrella up, Hold Hat on, and raise Skirt out of the Mud at one and the Same Time.' Photographer, alas, unknown, from* The Sketch, *9 March 1911.*

Right *Edward Steichen in 1911 chose a non-fashion background and non-fashion poses for his photograph of Poiret dresses for* Art et Decoration. *He considered these 'probably the first serious fashion photographs', according to Sir Cecil Beaton, 'quite mistakenly'.*

natural light, because, Mrs Chase thinks, the elaborate equipment of the *Vogue* studio scared him.[5] However he soon learned to harness it to his purposes. For a man who valued 'aliveness', his photographs are remarkably static, although his favourite model, Marion Morehouse, whom he made famous, gave them animation with her own special sparkle. It is a curious coincidence that Steichen's sister married the poet, Carl Sandburg, while his pet model, Miss Morehouse, married another poet, e.e.cummings. De Meyer and Steichen are the two struts on which fashion photography rested until the mid-thirties.

Sir Cecil Beaton followed the de Meyer line, adding a brilliance and invention all his own. As Hilton Kramer in *The New York Times* wrote in December 1975, Beaton's pictures bear 'the stamp of a highly individual sensibility – so practised and imperious in the ways of an extravagant and overripe artifice that it virtually dispenses with "nature" altogether . . .'

But with Beaton, as with de Meyer and Steichen, his great distinction as a photographer rests not on his fashion photographs but on his portraits and his vivid reportage. No one can forget his wartime photographs – the injured child, St Paul's amid the burning city, (1940) the bombed fire station in Tobruk (1942) nor his now famous portrait of Winston Churchill (1940). The *profil presque perdu* of de Meyer had made a great impression, and in 1927 Beaton outdid him in a photograph of Margot, Countess of Oxford and Asquith, in which her parrot profile was totally *perdu*, the photograph showing only her back against what seems to be a blow-up of a painting by Robert Delaunay.

Hoyningen-Huene, also a Baron, was on the Steichen trail. He occasionally took fashion out of the studio, but even in the sunlight on a beach his figures look as if they had been arranged into a formal composition.

Current fashions in art also influenced photographers and the late thirties saw an equally late wallow in Surrealism: Hoyningen-Huene, Horst P. Horst and even Beaton eventually succumbed to a change of props from swags of lace curtains, crystal chandeliers, butterfly-sprinkled tulle to de Chirico-type plaster casts of Greek gods, egg-beaters, bedsprings . . .[6] Horst photographed a corset à la Dali (1939), and both he and Man Ray (the latter in Paris closer to the fount of the Surrealist movement) toyed with distortion. Erwin Blumenfeld was a brilliant innovator to whose work that of Irving Penn shows an affinity.

While the mannerisms of fashion photography were adapting themselves to changing taste, the technique of photography itself was changing too. The breakthrough came in Germany when Oscar

Overleaf left The artists of La Gazette du Bon Ton often designed as well as drew the clothes they illustrated so brilliantly. Here in 1920 George Lepape imagines a tropical background for a strange safari costume, worn with a hood which he has topped with a solar topee.

Overleaf right When the enlightened Frank Pick was boss of the London Underground he set the pattern which still persists for the patronage of the arts by industry and business. Into his orbit he drew sculptors like Henry Moore and Sir Jacob Epstein to make the sculptures for the London Transport Building; architects like Charles Holden of Adams, Holden and Pearson, who designed that building as

well as many of the Underground stations that have become monuments to the thirties. Pick was not concerned only with architecture; in 1917 he commissioned the calligrapher Edward Johnson to design a new type for use on Underground posters – the genesis of the famous sans serif of Johnson's pupil, Eric Gill. For the posters themselves he went to artists like E. McKnight Kauffer whose work for the Underground and Shell was given an exhibition at the Museum of Modern Art in New York in 1937. Pick's eyes were everywhere and in 1931 he commissioned this poster by A. E. Marty, one of the original Gazette de Bon Ton team, which incidentally, and not unnaturally, includes a neat illustration of the fashionable dress of that year.

"Where runs the river? who can say
Who hath not followed all the way
By alders green and sedges grey
    And blossoms blue?"

By

George Hoyningen-Huene, born a Baltic Baron, gave rein to his baroque fancy
in 1931 for this group of dresses by Vionnet framed in a proscenium of
Sleeping Beauty flowers and trees.

Barnack, working for the firm of Leitz, hit upon the possibility of using 35 mm film in a still camera. The camera he constructed around the film, the Leica UR, small, easily carried, its wide aperture lenses permitting pictures to be taken in poor light, the 35 mm film allowing thirty-six exposures in comparatively rapid succession, was the first miniature precision camera – a major landmark in the development of photography. Barnack made this prototype in 1913 (a modified version of which was marketed in 1924) and with his last camera, the Leica 3A, made in 1935, the year before he died, he increased the shutter speed from 1/500 to 1/1000 of a second.[7]

Although the Leica has continued its development, as has the manufacture of film which now provides amongst other improvements increased sensitivity, it was Barnack's original camera which, by making action pictures not only possible but easy, brought fashion photography out of the studio into the great wide world.

Other cameras followed. Each quickly acquired its devotés. The German Rolleiflex (1928) with a fixed lens also accommodates larger film which produces larger negatives which in turn produce larger pictures with clearer definition. The Swedish Hasselblad (1947), developed from an aerial camera, can be fitted with wide-angle or telephoto lenses, and has the advantage of versatility giving the photographer variation of perspective and greater elasticity of composition.

While these innovations originated in the West, dramatic recent advances have come from the East. The Canon AE1, the Nikkormat EL, the Pentax K2, the Olympus OM2 (claimed to be one third smaller and thirty-five per cent lighter than other SLRs – and if anyone doesn't know that SLR stands for single lens reflex, they must be blind to advertisements), are all Japanese and incorporate built-in electronic brains. Not to be outdone, the latest Leica, the R3, has similar electronic shutter and exposure controls. With these devices the camera moves ever nearer the miraculous mechanism of the human eye, but the first and essential eye is still that of the photographer.

1935 was another key date. That was the year that Eastman Kodak introduced Kodachrome, a colour film, the invention of two young musicians, Leopold Mannes and Leopold Godowsky. The only drawback was that it could only be developed in Kodak laboratories which sometimes meant an inconvenient delay. To enable photographers to process their own film, in 1946 Kodak produced Ektachrome, first in sheet sizes and then, in 1947, in roll film. From 1955 to 1962 they continued to develop Ektachrome to increase the film speed. Until the fast film came into common use, colour processing was a laborious job involving three separations, and in the printing, the register could –

Richard Dormer, normally a shiny-paper photographer, took this photograph for the Daily Express *in 1951. The model is Barbara Goalen, the first English model to break out of the anonymity of fashion pictures – so much so that the* Express *featured the photograph as 'the first of the sensational new Barbara Goalen pictures . . .'; with the black velvet dress by Jacques Fath taking second place.*

Weegee, pseudonym of the Polish-born American photographer, Arthur H. Fellig, pointed the most candid of cameras at the more sordid aspects of metropolitan life. In this merciless shot of two bedizened New York matrons about to enter the Metropolitan Opera House in the full gold-diggers' regalia of the twenties, when they presumably snared their rich husbands (corsages of orchids, ermine cloaks, diamond tiaras, rivières and 'service stripe' bracelets), sublimely unaware of the disbelieving on-looker, one feels the lens had been washed in acid. Weegee entitled this press photograph 'The Critic' and the date is, unbelievably, 1943, in the middle of the War.

Les Petites Chocolatières

Hy. Tournier

and did – often go wrong. Early colour work looks stiff and self-conscious. With high speed film colour became lively and relaxed.

One of the first photographers to epitomize the aesthetic of the new mechanical freedom was Martin Munkasci. A Hungarian who was working in Germany where the high speed cameras were being developed, he was one of the first to venture out of the studio. Washed up on the shores of America in the early thirties by the rising tide of Nazism, he brought a gust of fresh air into fashion photography. His people didn't just smile; they laughed and breathed, ran and danced. He opened the skies for a whole generation of fashion photographers: Richard Avedon, Toni Frissell, Ken Heyman and in England, John Cowan.

It is easy to gain the impression that all the top photographers worked for American *Vogue*. Actually, although their early years were on *Vogue*, nearly all of them also worked for *Harper's Bazaar* after Carmel Snow had left *Vogue* to edit the other magazine. It was she and her brilliant art director, Alexey Brodovich, who were the first to perceive the special quality of Munkasci's work, and it was for Mrs Snow that Munkasci's lineal descendant, Richard Avedon, did his best work until her retirement when he followed her successor, Diana Vreeland, to *Vogue*.

Other *Harper's Bazaar* stalwarts have been Louise Dahl-Wolfe, Lillian Bassman, Horvath, Kubelin, Hiro, Sokolsky . . . whose photographs today spring from the page like Munkasci's, bursting with life and vitality, and in Dahl-Wolfe's case often with a lyric poetry.

Life magazine, during the years 1947 to 1969 when Sally Kirkland was fashion editor, created its own *Life*-style, lush in colour, punchy with action, eye-catching and always news. To be a *Life* photographer was status; to gain a *Life* cover was every designer's ambition. Mrs Kirkland could command – and did – top photographers, among them Mark Shaw, Gordon Park, Milton Greene, Howell Conant and Nina Leen.

In England John French and Norman Parkinson had begun working before the Second World War. John French, whose death in 1966 was a grave loss to fashion photography, was in the Steichen tradition of natural light, clean backgrounds and clear statements. He was one of the rare fashion photographers who understood the problems not only of shiny paper reproduction, but of newsprint as well. His studio was the training ground for many of the young British photographers who were to make their names – David Bailey and Terence Donovan among them. Parkinson goes on with ever-increasing strength. For years he was British *Vogue*'s mighty muscle, his ideas as fresh as if he had been given his first camera yesterday – one, however, suspects that, unlike the young Beaton, it would not have been a Kodak box Brownie.

In the sixties *Elle* magazine focussed fashion eyes on French fashion photographers, chief among them Peter Knapp, also *Elle*'s art director, perhaps more talented in the latter rôle. Others on the French front line are Jean-Loup Sieff, Alex Chatelain and Guy Bourdin. *Elle* also imported young English photographers like Brian Duffy and Terence Donovan, and English newspapers and magazines used the French (or Paris-based) photographers. Cross-Channel traffic was so heavy it was often hard to know who was where.

Chanel had made sun-tan, hitherto avoided, the height of fashion. By the mid-twenties it was on the way to becoming a cult but still new enough for 'La Vie Parisienne' to poke gentle fun at the sun-tanned, whom they called 'Les Petites Chocolatières', loosely translated as 'the little chocolate drops'. Drawing by Henry Fournier.

Left *Sarah Moon is an artist in ambiguous innocence, creating a dream-like beauty behind which lurks shadows of sexual implication. This photograph taken by her in 1971 was for an advertisement for Biba cosmetics.*

Opposite *Eleven years later Jean Shrimpton was on her way to becoming even more famous than Barbara Goalen. Here at the start of her career she is photographed by David Bailey (also at the start of his) in a swirl of lettuce green organza by Jules François Crahay, then at Nina Ricci.*

This was the decade when photographers went berserk. Blumenfeld had electrified his fellows in 1939 by posing a model on the dizzy edge of the Eiffel Tower. In the sixties Melvin Sokolsky for *Harper's Bazaar* had them flying through the Paris air in plastic bubbles or apparently simply by an act of levitation. Avedon photographed a society beauty naked to the waist. Bailey photographed a pregnant fashion editor totally naked. Others dangled models from helicopters, submerged them in water up to their painted eyes, nestled them into haystacks in evening clothes, made them walk horses in their nightdresses, lean against ladders, crouch like sphinxes. In Sokolsky's view 'anything that creates excitement is good': good for the photographer perhaps, but not so good for the clothes.

But that was all good clean fun. Worse was to follow. One unhappy aberration was a brutal distortion obtained by photographing models from above so that their heads were huge and unwieldy above tiny, wizened bodies. As this was at the height of the thalidomide horror, this objectionable mannerism was rightly dismissed as 'sick'. More enduring has been the mood of decadence which began toward the end of the sixties. The opening gun was, oddly enough, fired by British *Harper's Bazaar* (who also fired the fashion editor responsible), and was quickly taken up by *Nova* launched in 1965. Leading protagonists are Sarah Moon, Peccanotti, Eva Sereny, Deborah Turbeville and Helmut Newton. Pornography, having taken over films, the theatre and literature, took over fashion photography too. Its most sinister aspect is that the photographs are often inventive, imaginative and sometimes beautiful – but it's porn just the same. And it has little to do with fashion photography.

Today in England, Bailey and Barry Lategan have reverted to a straight Rolleiflex-tummy-view style. Perhaps that is the only way to cope with fashion as it has become. Gazing down the long perspective of seventy-six years, there seems no doubt that in the field of fashion photography, there

have been three masters of this elusive art in this century: the Hungarian Munkasci, the American Avedon and the British Parkinson. And of these, no one has excelled Richard Avedon in understanding fashion or in projecting it vividly, dramatically and memorably.

Editors and art directors, through opportunity, wise guidance and encouragement have wielded a powerful influence on the course of fashion photography. This is equally true of fashion illustration. Indeed one editor lifted fashion illustration to a new height. He was Lucien Vogel, who in 1912 founded *La Gazette du Bon Ton*. A legend has been propagated that it was his inspiration to persuade artists to turn their talents to fashion and to contribute illustrations to his elegant and elegantly produced journal, the plates hand-coloured and reproduced on handmade paper. This was not, as Geoffrey Squire of the Victoria and Albert Museum has pointed out, quite 'the stroke of genius' Vogel thought. The time was ripe for such luxurious frivolities. That same year *Le Journal des Dames et des Modes* appeared, almost pocket size (four and a half inches by nearly eight) containing one to five hand-coloured plates, some by Bernard Boutet de Monvel and Georges Barbier. Nor is it true that of the other six of the coterie of fashionable young artists who composed Vogel's original octet – Pierre Brissaud, Jean Besnard, A. E. Marty, Charles Martin, Paul Iribe and Georges Lepape – none had ventured into fashion illustration before. Paul Iribe had done drawings for a promotional brochure, *Les Robes de Poiret*, produced by Poiret in 1908, and Georges Lepape had contributed to its successor, *Les Choses de Poiret*, in 1911. Still, with the exception of the limited Poiret editions (*Robes* two hundred and fifty, *Choses* one thousand) and the expensive *Les Dames et des Modes* (annual subscription one thousand francs), until *La Gazette de Bon Ton* fashion illustrations had deteriorated until they were vapid as valentines, the backgrounds stereotyped and the figures, lifeless dressmakers' dummies.

The octet were all young men of fashion who endowed the garments they drew with an ineffable chic, and gave their vivacious figures delightful settings in which wit competed with sentiment. Indeed Mr Squire remarks that often the dress seems simply the excuse for a picture. Each was an individual stylist, but, so powerful must have been M. Vogel's taste and direction, their work has a group identity, easily recognizable. Inevitably they responded to the fashionable – and changing – taste in art: Japanese prints, the Ballet Russe, Picasso's cubist paintings, Modigliani's portraits, the Italian Futurists.

As *La Gazette* flourished, the octet was augmented by artists whose names have become equally famous: Etienne Drian (whose individual and contemporary style, derived from Helleu and Boldini, also appeared in *Les Dames et des Modes*), Pierre Morgue, Umberto Brunelleschi, Raoul Dufy, Georges Benda.

The members of the newly formed Chambre Syndicale de la Couture Parisienne, seven of whom (Cheruit, Doeuillet, Doucet, Lanvin, Redfern, Worth and Poiret) had been persuaded by the remarkable M. Vogel to back his quarterly, owe these artists a great debt of gratitude, as the photographs of their clothes as actually worn by large bulging ladies, their curves too exuberantly released from the discipline of their corsets, testify only too clearly. Inside all these fat ladies were thin Poiret ladies trying to get out. The *Bon Ton* artists not only fined down the ladies; they fined down the dresses as well.

Competing publications (*Femina* for one) imitated – or tried to – the format and style that M. Vogel had devised and coaxed many of his artists on to their pages as well, although none could approximate the *Gazette*'s taste and witty, perceptive expression of fashion. After the War Condé Nast took over *La Gazette* (and Lucien Vogel); its last issue appeared in 1925. But the *Bon Ton* artists continued to enrich the covers and pages of *Vogue* as did the later Luza and Benito. *Jardin des Modes*, another of Lucien Vogel's publications which Mr Nast also purchased, continued to be edited by M. Vogel until his death in 1954.

If the artists of *La Gazette du Bon Ton* were primarily artists who saw in fashion another facet of the brilliant world in which they shone, there were also fashion artists who simply illustrated fashion. American *Vogue* had a homegrown pair, Helen Dryden and George Plank, who provided highly stylized covers. From England came the young Cecil Beaton. Although Mrs Chase described his early drawings as 'spidery and fragile', it was the beginning of a long association with this remarkably gifted man who can turn his hand to drawing, photography, stage and film design, writing – all with distinction.

Above *Etienne Drian whose elegant line transformed portraits into fashion drawings and vice versa. For* La Gazette du Bon Ton *he often designed the clothes as well as drawing them, as in this sketch of 1914.*

Right *Harold Carlton followed in the pen tracks of Joe Eula, using in 1968 a few deft lines to synopsize Givenchy's see-through evening trousers of tiers of black organza, below a jewel-encrusted top.*

Other pearls on the *Vogue* string were the French Raoul Bouët-Willaumez who signed his work with his initials, and Carl August Erickson from Wisconsin who signed himself Eric. These two artists specialized in drawing people in fashionable settings, documenting not only the clothes but the mannerisms, the milieus, in fact the smart life of the time. Eric stayed on *Vogue*'s pages for twenty-five years until this type of snobbish conversation piece quietly slipped away. René Bouché was in the tradition of Drian. Jacques Demachy drawings had a quality of sophisticated flattery. Gruau using a bolder, more aggressive brush carried on into the fifties Drian's suave line, while in England Francis Marshall combined a style derived from Drian and Gruau with Eric-type conversation piece backgrounds.

Except for Gruau and Francis Marshall (whose drawings decorated the *Daily Mail*'s fashion pages), the other artists were shiny-paper stars. In the sixties Tod Draz for *The New York Times*, Kenneth Paul Block for *Women's Wear Daily* and Joe Eula for the New York and Paris *Herald Tribunes* and the London *Sunday Times*, combined brilliant reporting with incredible speed of production. Each used his pencil (or Pentel) in his own way: Draz and Block balancing button and seam accuracy with a clever parody of fashionable posture; Eula catching the essence of a garment in an explosive shorthand squiggle. Both Draz and Eula have turned to other fields. After Eula, the London *Sunday Times*'s Paris pages were ornamented by the French artist Christian Benais, very much in the tradition of the *Bon Ton* artists. Benais, too, has moved from illustrating, now designing men's clothes for Christian Dior. Block's drawings continue to appear on the pages of *Women's Wear*

Daily and *W*, but most other newspapers have moved from the pencil to the camera. Photographs have the virtue of verisimilitude, but the gaiety and sparkle of these talented pens are sadly missed.

Once the pattern of using artists as fashion illustrators had been established, a new and brilliant period opened for fashion. The tradition had been reinforced by Diaghilev for whom Picasso, Derain, Dufy and Laurencin designed sets and costumes. Condé Nast having taken over M. Vogel, *Vogue* had the original edge, but Hearst's *Harper's Bazaar* was soon on the trail and from the mid twenties such artists as Christian Bérard, Jean Cocteau, Pavel Tchelitchew, Eugène Berman, Jean Hugo, Salvador Dali, Vertès, Raoul Dufy and Giorgio di Chirico had all been cajoled on to the shiny pages of one or the other of these magazines. Bérard's witty, elliptical sketches made him a bone of contention at both *Vogue* and *Harper's Bazaar*. Although Mrs Chase disapproved of his opium-smoking Bohemian life-style, preferring the *Bon Ton* charm,[8] she continued to publish him 'because she knew that *Harper's Bazaar* would snatch him if *Vogue* let go for a minute'.[9] When *Harper's Bazaar* did get him, Mrs Snow had to battle Mr Hearst's equally conventional reaction which induced him to make Bérard the butt of one of the most-quoted unfunny jokes in journalism by dubbing him 'Faceless Freddie'.

If these two magazines shared these artists, even if unwillingly, Erté belonged to *Harper's Bazaar*. In fact, he had belonged too long, and Carmel Snow, when she took over, felt she should vary what she called 'the interminable series of Erté covers' with work by newer artists. Mrs Snow was perhaps right at the time but it would have been galling for her if she could have foreseen that these covers would become collectors' items in 1965 when a perceptive Paris art critic, Jacques Damase, rediscovered Erté and arranged exhibitions of his work. Erté, an acronym for Romain de Tirtoff, began his fashion life in 1913 working with Poiret. His first theatrical venture was designing costumes for Mata Hari; at seventy-five he costumed a Christmas programme for American television. In 1970 his costumes for a revue starring Zizi Jeanmaire at the Casino de Paris easily outshone those of Yves Saint Laurent. The Erté style echoes Beardsley and Art Nouveau, with essays into the lavish vulgarity of Art Deco, which he has salted with wit and illuminated with fantasy. Few other fashion illustrators can approximate the originality of his work or the invention of his lively brush.

Important not only to the development of fashion photography and illustration, but to the Couture itself were two American fashion magazines: *Vogue* and *Harper's Bazaar*. *Harper's Bazaar* dates from 1867 when as *Harper's Bazaar* it was launched as an adjunct of *Harper's Weekly*. After a brief period (1900 to 1907) in digest-size, it added an 'a' and became the magazine we know today. *Vogue* which was purchased by Condé Nast in 1909 had made its first appearance in 1892, also as a weekly. When Mr Nast acquired *Vogue* he also acquired a young Quaker, Edna Woolman Chase, who was to remain with Condé Nast publications for sixty years. Together they turned a dainty weekly into a powerful arbiter of taste and quality. In 1916 British *Vogue* was launched, in 1920 French *Vogue*. Thus a formidable triumvirate was created, to which were later added Australian, Italian and Spanish editions.

In 1932 Carmel Snow, who had been Mrs Chase's heir apparent, defected to the rival Hearst

Helmut Newton is a photographer of many styles; from witty pastiche to perversity, but here in 1969 against a set drawn in clever false perspective he takes a lively but straight fashion photograph of a coat and trousers by Cerutti in white double-faced cashmere.

Geoffrey Beene   Cathy Hardwick

Kenneth Paul Block has one of the most fluent pens in the business of fashion illustration. His drawings for Women's Wear Daily *and* W *catch not only the character of the clothes but the contemporary stance of the wearers, as in these beach clothes by Geoffrey Beene and Cathy Hardwick.*

publication *Harper's Bazaar*. Under the direction of this venturesome, strong-willed Irish woman, *Harper's* was soon competing with the *Vogues* in influence, exceeding it in excitement. Some of the power of these two women was based, it must be faced, on cupboard love, for between them they commanded the eyes and ears of the buyers for that vast, rich market which is America. That they so dominated the fashion scene was due not to the circulation of their publications which were never impressive, and in Mr Nast's time purposely so, but to the discernment, the reporting skill, and above all the dedication of their editors and fashion editors (Bettina Ballard for *Vogue* and Diana Vreeland for *Harper's Bazaar*) to the ideal of fashion.

Mrs Chase retired in 1952; Mrs Snow in 1957. Without these giants the magazines could not remain forever alone at the top. In 1956 Eugenia Sheppard of the now defunct New York *Herald Tribune* started a column she called 'Inside Fashion', a shrewd blend of fashion reporting and society gossip. She could be called the progenitor of the symbiotic relationship between designers of fashion and those who wear what they design – a relationship which created what John Fairchild of *Women's Wear Daily* was to christen 'the beautiful people'.

Reporting for the Paris *Herald Tribune* had been in the hands of Lucie Noel whose agitated pen never inscribed an unkind word. When Miss Sheppard arrived to cover the collections, her column was carried on the same page. Miss Sheppard's forthright comments soon resulted in Miss Noel being banned by Balenciaga. The paper loyally stood by her and made this item front-page news, but in due course Miss Noel's delicate comments were dropped in favour of Miss Sheppard's crisp copy. (Miss Sheppard also got herself banned but simply wrote up the sacred collection from buyers' reports.) Another *Herald-Tribune* resource is Tunisian-born Hébé Dorsey who contributes a regular fashion feature and shares the reporting of the Collections with Miss Sheppard. Miss Dorsey's recipe is similar to that of *Elle* magazine – a peculiary French combination of beaming in to the young ready-to-wear market while still respecting the traditions of the Couture.

Elle magazine, in the sixties, like *Vogue* and *Harper's*, attained a position quite incommensurate with its circulation which was never within spitting distance of that of *Marie Claire*. This was due to

Russian-born Hélène Gordon Lazareff's perception of the rising power of post-war French youth and the potential of the *pret-à-porter*. With her brilliant art director, Peter Knapp, they created a new and lively visual approach to fashion reporting.

John Fairchild, of *Women's Wear Daily*, heir to a solid publishing empire based on trade publications, has invented his own brand of fashion journalism. Starting from the original Sheppard formula, he has added more and more thorough fashion reporting (a necessity for a trade paper) and more, and more spicy, society gossip (brand-new for a trade paper). Working in *WWD*'s Paris bureau from 1955 to 1960, Fairchild became fascinated by the personalities and the politics of Couture, and on his return to home base he instituted a column, 'The Eye', which applied his new interest to the whole international spectrum of fashion and the fashionable. Readership extended far beyond the fashion trade for whom *WWD* was required reading, and in 1973 he hived off the gossip and the fashion highlights into *W*, a newspaper-size publication on heavier paper capable of fairly good colour reproduction. At first slim, *W* in three years is up to sixty-four pages, with a varied table of contents offering a kind of mixed salad of fashion and news, tossed together with Fairchild's own dressing, dedicated to the Beautiful (rich and successful) People – detailing not only what they wear and where they buy it, but also what they eat and where they eat it, what they do and where they do it. Power is heady stuff and in 1970 Fairchild attempted to play kingmaker with a rather threatening and premature promotion of the midi length, a disaster for stores and designers alike. Except for this unfortunate interlude, he has given the fashion industry in America a new and exciting image, although he is apt to be severe with those who, in his opinion, do not live up to his views.

In England, there was a halcyon period which began in the middle fifties when newspapers began to challenge the established magazines with the immediacy and vivacity of their reporting, the space their women's pages earned by attracting advertising, and the introduction of colour supplements. For many reasons, mainly economic, leadership has returned to the magazines with British *Vogue* well in the van. Its editor, Beatrix Miller, had been one of the triumvirate who made *Queen* such a fizzing success. In 1964 she left to become editor of *Vogue*. Miss Miller is more in the tradition of Carmel Snow than Mrs Chase, has a wide range of interests and is acutely aware of the world in which fashion functions as well as in fashion itself.

No longer a journalist, Diana Vreeland is still a chronicler of fashion. She had joined *Harper's Bazaar* before the last war where she stayed for twenty-five years, during which time a body of legend grew up about her positive and original personality. In 1963 she moved to American *Vogue* as editor, an appointment which was unhappily short-lived – Vogue simply did not have the muscle to cope with the impact of Mrs Vreeland's idiosyncratic conception of editing. She left in 1971, and reappeared as special consultant to the Costume Institute of the Metropolitan Museum of Art. Since then she has put on, with outstanding success, four exhibitions which *The New Yorker* found 'have had more influence on the attitude of New Yorkers toward fashion than the last thirty-six issues of any fashion magazine'. Mrs Vreeland will always be a power.

8
The Glamour of Fashion

The ultimate glamour of fashion rests in the beauties which it adorns – and nothing, including the wildest changes of taste in art, interior decoration, or fashion itself, is as unpredictable and inconstant as the changing taste in beauty. The glamour girls of today would not have caused a head to turn seventy-seven years ago, except in amazement, while the greatly acclaimed beauties of the Edwardian period, to catch a glimpse of whom lesser women stood on benches in the park, would be considered good candidates for Weight Watchers. The Edwardians subscribed to the Greek ideal of regularity of feature, while the new century preferred the Baconian principle that 'there is no excellent beauty that hath not some strangeness in the proportion'.

As Hardy Amies remarked, 'Many women and nearly all men forget how complicated a piece of

Miss Primrose Salt in 1933 softened her shingled hair-do with what were vulgarly called 'spit curls' or by the French, more prettily, croche cœurs *(heart-breakers). Miss Salt's dark red lipstick and plucked eyebrows are more typical of the late twenties, as is her shorn head.*

If you doubt the truism that beauty lies in the eyes of the beholder you have only to gaze at this photograph. Is this the top half of a wax dummy? A female impersonator in a wig? She is in fact the most famous beauty of her time whose lovers were legion and Royal, and to catch a glimpse of whom women stood on chairs as she drove by in Rotten Row. Lillie Langtry fared better with the brush of artists like G.F.Watts than with the camera, as this photograph taken in 1885 by Lafayette of Dublin, who advertised himself as 'Photographer to Their Royal Highnesses the Prince and Princess of Wales', attests.

design is a face.'[1] To embellish this piece of design women today have at their disposal a vast armoury not only of beauty aids but of experts dedicated to making them as beautiful as they would like to be. The most important of these are the merchants of hope who form the cosmetic industry. Besides the desire for embellishment, the beauty business has been helped by the strenuous search for youth which began when Poiret projected the thin woman. The Edwardian ideal had been mature, even matronly, for it is the admiration of men, not the envy of women, that puts the stamp of beauty on a type of looks, and the Edwardian code of morals made young girls sacrosanct and young married women equally so, anyway until they had filled a cradle with an indisputable heir – and preferably, a spare. Birth control – and *Lolita* – were light years away.

These large, imposing and not very young, ladies, for whom a surprising range of make-up was available, were forced by the dictates of society to employ them secretly and as unobtrusively as possible. Rouge was considered fast, and few respectable women would admit to its use, except with a very good excuse, like the heroine of *Young Visiters* who put 'red ruge' on her cheeks because 'she was very pale owing to the drains'.[2]

A white skin was an essential, and to simulate it, ladies enamelled. Enamelling was a hangover from the 1860s when it was popularized – and made notorious – by Madame Rachel after whom that shade of face powder was named. The enamel, a concoction of which the base was presumably alcohol, for one recipe calls for brandy and another white wine, was supposed to produce a fair and luminous complexion.[3] This it may have done, but as with any mask, the result was a rigidly impassive countenance, for any expression from a smile to a frown would cause cracks in the façade.

Whitening for the arms and neck was less drastic – simply a liquid powder sponged on and left to dry like shoe whitener. This was used with assiduity, and dancing partners and footmen alike ended the evening covered in a duststorm of powder.

Hair was dyed although surreptitiously and rather amateurishly. Elinor Glyn's observant heroine notes that her cousin's hair is 'dark as anything underneath, but all the outside is red'. She is then sent off to dress as the Countess begins to put 'red stuff on her lips'[4], for lip salves were unacceptable.

As early as 1903 there appeared a preparation that sounds like a contemporary foundation lotion, claiming to produce 'a dull finish' and leaving 'a sort of peach look'.[5] But by and large, especially for young women, cosmetics consisted of *papier poudré*, sheets of paper impregnated with dead white powder. For colour they had to rely on cheek-pinching and lip biting, but never, never, lip moistening. Vulgar. This puritanical attitude to make-up persisted in England up to the mid-thirties in the homes of backwoods Peers like Nancy Mitford's Uncle Matthew who considered that 'paint was for whores',[6] although by then the Prince of Wales' set was revelling in rouge, lipstick and scent. In the South in America, where English traditions were slow to die, the same was true. Scent was suspect there too, and ladies made little sachets of a powder called 'Azurea' which they tucked into their camisoles. The young were supposed just to smell clean.

It was the First World War that Elizabeth Arden said changed the beauty picture. An American war song that turned out to be powerfully true asked, 'How are you going to keep them down on the farm after they've seen Paree?' After the Yanks had seen 'Paree' and the *filles de joie*, they were ready to accept, indeed, according to Miss Arden, to demand, an equal liveliness of countenance from their wives and sweethearts. The beauty bonanza had begun.

Actually the pattern had been set, though timorously, in the early years of the century. Beauty editors even then were extolling their advertisers' products (beauty pages in women's magazines like city pages in newspapers tend to deal editorially in *quid pro quo*). The cult of personalities began, although it was not until the twenties that Pond's pioneered in persuading titled beauties to endorse their creams. Ladies of title did write books on beauty, but anonymously; professional beauties and idols of the stage and opera revealed their secrets and/or boosted products sold under their names. Gaby Deslys advertised her 'Secret Gaby Deslys' – an all-purpose preparation also purported to act as a deodorant. Sarah Bernhardt lent the lustre of her name to a Beauty Bath and, more prosaically, a wrinkle eradicator. Lillian Russell gave beauty advice. 1914, a date memorable for other reasons, also saw the publication of opera star Lina Cavalieri's book of her beauty secrets. In America, singer Anna Held's milk baths were front-page news.

After the War, in the twenties, actresses replaced the divas out of whose slippers admirers were reputed to have drunk champagne. In their turn they were ousted by film stars who were not only telling all in interviews but in the thirties some, like Mary Pickford, were entering the beauty business itself with their own range of cosmetics. By 1969 top fashion models like Penelope Tree and Verushka had become the oracles of beauty, while Zsa Zsa Gabor upheld the tradition of Lillian Russell.

The giant money-spinning beauty business based on powerful personalities was foreshadowed in the early years of the century. Harriet Hubbard Ayer had emerged as an authority on beauty in the 1890s, and by 1903 was marketing and advertising her own products.[7] It was Harriet Hubbard Ayer

Above *Marlene Dietrich's glamour triumphed over her habit of erasing her natural eyebrows, substituting an improbably pencilled higher line. Her red-varnished nails and ruched sleeves, still echoing in 1935 Adrian's 'Letty Lynton' sleeves invented for Joan Crawford in 1932, epitomize the period.*

Left *Ethel Barrymore, of America's Royal Family of the theatre, chose to wear her hair softly knotted low on her neck at a time when other women were padding, fringing and frizzing – and looks to today's eyes far more beautiful than they.*

Opposite *Garbo in 1932 – the pure face to beauty. Although inimitable, many copied her eye make-up, the brows plucked to follow the curve of the eye socket, the bold line emphasizing the top of the deep set lids, the heavily mascara'd lashes.*

who in 1910 helped a young Canadian, Florence Nightingale Graham, to plant her foot on the first step of a ladder which was to take her, as Elizabeth Arden, to world fame. Miss Arden stayed only briefly with Mrs Ayer, whom she left to start on her own. Mrs Ayer had called her range 'Grecian'; Miss Arden called her early range 'Venetian'. There the similarity ends. The rest is history.

Helena Rubinstein took her first steps in Australia. Always shy on dates (neither she nor Miss Arden although each had a shrewd eye for figures, cared much for those that pinpointed age), Madame Rubinstein is supposed to have arrived in Australia from Poland in 1902 and to have left there in either 1905[8] or 1909. Anyway, it was in 1908 that she opened her salon in London. Lord Salisbury, from whom she rented the handsome house in Grafton Street, told her she would lose her shirt. Instead she made her fortune. In 1915 she progressed to New York and began her conquest of

America. Both ladies spread their tentacles throughout the world, Miss Arden concentrating on Salons, Madame Rubinstein on sales of cosmetics and skin-care preparations.

The horizons of the beauty business were, and are, constantly being expanded. When Chanel displayed her suntan at the beginning of the twenties, she started a cult which has become almost a religion, certainly a rite, with its neophytes on beaches, in city parks, on penthouse terraces solemnly roasting themselves, often in hideously uncomfortable positions to insure the ultimate aim of an even brown. Suntanning provided another gusher for the beauty business with products to prevent tanning, products to stimulate it, products to simulate it. It soon became an industry on its own.

Ten years later attention was focussed on the finger tips. In 1930 Peggy Sage had launched dark red nails, and hands everywhere looked as if they had been dipped in blood. This varnish became such a fashionable necessity that Dorothy Parker satirized the effect of this preoccupation on a feather-brained New York lady:

'Miss Rose came about noon to do my nails . . . Didn't notice until after she had gone that the damn fool had put that *revolting* tangerine-colored polish on my nails. *Couldn't* have been more furious.

The pursuit of beauty began early in the United States. This photograph was taken in 1904 of the gymnasium at New York's Columbia University. Perhaps health not beauty was the object and the fully attired young woman being massaged modestly covered by a blanket may only have strained a ligament attempting to emulate her bloomered classmate.

Left *By 1925 make-up had come out into the open. Make-up was fun, the more so because it evoked the usual protests.*

Right *The compact had made its debut in 1930; by 1938 it had, along with a dark lipstick, found a home in every woman's handbag. The diminished eyebrows and the curly topped hair-do continued into the war years, the hair at the back dropping lower.*

Every time I look at my finger nails, I could *spit. Damn* Miss Rose. Wednesday. Made her take that *vile* tangerine polish off my nails and put on dark red. Didn't notice until after she had gone that it is practically *black* in the electric light; *couldn't* be in a worse state. *Damn* Miss Rose. Friday. Every time I look at those revolting *black* nails, I want to absolutely *yip . . . Damn* Miss Rose.'

In 1932 Charles Revson took a flying leap into this new arena, then a limited one of pale, medium and dark. Revlon's contribution was to expand the spectrum of shades. In 1939, Revlon added lipsticks in co-ordinated colours. That was just the beginning of a vast empire.

Of Miss Arden's salons the New York one was the most important, and to be summoned there was the equivalent of a provincial reporter being given a job on a great metropolitan daily. Like an editor, she kept a sharp lookout for talent, and in 1964 she brought to New York from her Rome salon a young Italian whose speciality was eye make-up. Pablo who had been discovered in 1957 by Princess Sciarra, director of the beautiful Salon on the Piazza di Spagna, was already well known to Italian beauties and foreign journalists. In New York Pablo was quick to capitalize on the ascendant interest in eyes, mainly evidenced until his arrival by massive sales of false eyelashes. His sequinned, feathered and flowery ocular (and sometimes jocular) fantasies won him a Coty Award the next year.

As the beauty business expanded with the ever-growing accent on youth and the increasingly bold use of cosmetics, others crowded into the field, but until death removed first Madame

Elizabeth Taylor at the end of the fifties, established as a Hollywood star, was wise enough to preserve her heavy eyebrows from the make-up man's tweezers. The strapless dresses of the time well-displayed her famous cleavage.

Rubinstein in 1965, and then Miss Arden in 1966 their ascendancy was never seriously challenged. They were famous rivals and this spirit of bitter competition was perpetuated by the two contenders for their crowns. Estée Lauder and, until his death in 1975, Charles Revson of Revlon. The pay dirt is worth competing for: in Britain alone, retail cosmetic sales reached £155,000,000 at the end of 1975. In the world-wide market the United States based company, Revlon, announced sales of $749,773,000 gross from products marketed to over one hundred countries.

In 1966 Mary Quant took a running jump into these shark-infested waters with her own range of cosmetics manufactured by the Gala Cosmetic Group. She was followed in 1970 by Biba. Both lines were bold, inventive and unconventional – and low-prices, aimed at a young market more interested in gimmicks and novelty in make-up than in skin care. Mary added the sparkle of irreverent names; Biba used Sarah Moon's sensuous photography to spread the message of her decadent thirties vamp look. Biba cosmetics have temporarily disappeared; but Mary has found happily insatiable markets in over sixty countries, besides the United Kingdom (the top ten being Japan, the United States, France, Italy, Hong Kong, Iran, Saudi Arabia, Denmark, Holland and Australia), which puts her in the big league. She is not yet real competition, but she is a trend-setter, and the giants keep a wary eye on her seemingly frivolous but always astute antics.

Part of keeping young is keeping slim. Major beauty salons had long included body massage.

Angus McBean, the dedicated theatrical photographer, enlarged this corner of Audrey Hepburn's face as Fred Astaire playing Richard Avedon was to do in Stanley Donen's 'Funny Face' of 1956. Miss Hepburn's soft-shadowed tilted eyes are the archetype of the 'doe-eyed look'.

Miss Arden's slimming exercises long famous, were immortalized in Clare Booth Luce's play *The Women*, made into a film in 1939. Continental spas and cures to which the Edwardians repaired to work off the effects of their gargantuan bouts of eating and drinking had been made fashionable by King Edward VII whose annual visits to Marienbad put the German spa on the world map. England responded after the War with its own health hydros; Tring, founded in 1925, being the oldest. Miss Arden had the brilliant idea of combining both beauty and banting, and opened her first health and beauty farm in 1934. She chose Maine for its venue and aptly christened the enterprise 'Maine Chance'. It proved so popular that she opened a second Maine Chance in Arizona in 1946, (now the only one for the original Maine Chance burned down).

By the sixties England had picked up the message. The message was the massage – and every other aid to achieve the body beautiful. Health farms proliferated offering saunas, steam cabinet baths, ultra-sonic sound waves, vibration, Faradism, and underwater massage as well as the manual kind. By 1970 even hair shops were adding massage and saunas to their usual curricula. Passive reducers and home-exercisers were selling like, well, not hot cakes which are fattening, but as fast. Instead of hot cakes, slimming breads and biscuits for confirmed nibblers flooded the market – United Kingdom sales peaked in 1973 at an estimated twenty-one to twenty-four million pounds. Soft drinks reduced their calories; best-selling and still selling hard, is Schweppes Slimline, introduced in 1965. In 1976 Philip Kleinman writing in *The Sunday Times* in London reported that research showed that in the past year 'twenty per cent of all women in Britain have tried to lose weight with the aid of special slimming products.' Diets were sure-fire circulation builders for newspapers and women's magazines, and in their first three years in the United Kingdom Weight Watchers claimed to have acquired 180,000 members. (By 1976 this figure had increased to 750,000.) For the not so disciplined and better-heeled, plastic surgery could remove extra poundage.

The body explosion was on, the inevitable result of the trend toward nudity: the ever-shrinking bikini, bare midriffs, see-through blouses, transparent dresses, cover-up but revealing cat-suits, exiguous bras and briefs. Lycra undercoverings like Warner's Birthday Suit (1962), the Body Stocking (1965) and the Shape Setter (1969) all combined to focus on the body.

The force of the explosion produced a vast increase in beauty products for the body and the bath. In 1970 Elizabeth Arden added a new range, *Seaqua*, which comprised eleven items including an 'aquaball' for exercising, to the twenty-one that she had already on the market. In England, Estée Lauder's 'Azurée' line had fourteen items, her 'Youth Dew' eight. Revlon's 'Borghese' line also offered eight. In America socialities were giving out bath, instead of beauty routines emphasizing besides the usual bath oils, bath salts and bath essences, body moisturising creams. Moisturisers are among the truly great advances in skin-care and were pioneered for the face by Charles of the Ritz in 1933 with 'Revenesence'. In 1971 they added 'Ritual' and 'Ritz' body lotions. The neck down was getting its full share of attention.

The Crowning Worry

The peak years for hair were the mid-sixties when hairdressers joined fashion photographers and models in the new meritocratic society. Hair had been through as many changes as the social scene itself. The first great change came when the shears replaced the curling tongs. The bob, popularized in 1913, not only spelt a new freedom; it meant a new source of income for hairdressers, for hair will grow and short hair must remain short. Hair continued to shrink: the Eton crop of 1924 and the shingle in 1925 demanded new hairdressing skills – the razor replacing the scissors.

Poor M. Marcel, who in 1888 had revolutionized hairstyling with his tongs, retreated into the shadows as finger waves, water waves and pin curls took over. The growing public acceptance of the permanent waving machine, invented in 1904, was the *coup de grâce*. The inventor was a German, Karl Nessler, who had moved to New York where he changed his name to Charles Nestlé. By 1907, after hefty advertising in women's magazines, his machines, Heath Robinson contraptions of wires and tubes suspended from the ceiling and heated by electricity, were installed in every hair shop in the USA that deemed itself worthy of the name. (Mr Nestlé also produced a home kit some forty years before the Toni.) The machines took most of a day to produce a mass of frizzy curls, usually smelling of scorch, and were distinctly chancey. There were indeed enough unfortunate incidents due to over-heating to inspire the American writer, Joseph Hergesheimer, to write a novel, *Linda Condon* published in 1929, in which the eponymous heroine's life was ruined by a disastrous permanent. As the machine itself and the time required were streamlined, the 'perm', as the English with their instinct for diminutives immediately called it, took hold, its popularity greatly increased by the introduction of the cold permanent in 1944/5 in the United States and 1947 in Europe, in which the wave is set with lotions instead of heat.

Left   *Helleu's sensitive pen could make even the cottage loaf hair style of 1906 look enchanting in this portrait of his wife which he presented to Madame Ida Rubinstein.*

Right   *In 1926 dangling ear-rings were needed to soften the harsh Eton crop which makes this unfortunate woman's head seem pitifully small compared to her patently unhappy feet. The long stole was to be revived in the fifties.*

As M. Marcel made do with his back seat, hairdressers themselves, rather than their implements, came into prominence. The creator of the sculptured head and the master of the razor cut and the pin curl, which it demanded, was Antoine who died in 1976 at the age of ninety-one. Willowy and languid, he was a master of publicity, first dyeing his poodle lilac to match his own tint, and later giving his borzoi the same blue rinse which he persuaded Lady Mendl to adopt in 1924, making her the first of a long line of blue-haired ladies.

Antoine began his career in the Edwardian years, but the twenties were his years of invention, the thirties his years of expansion. He, along with Poiret (later) and Irene Castle (later still) is credited with first cutting hair short in 1910, and he is said to have originated the upswept hairdo of the thirties.

The salon which Antoine had opened at Saks-Fifth Avenue in 1925 hatched an exotic chick. One of his hairdressers had become indispensable to a client who subsequently married a film producer. Unable to face life without those nimble fingers, she persuaded her husband to bring Sydney Guilaroff to the West Coast to dress the hair of the Metro-Goldwyn-Mayer stars as well as her own. He became the only hairdresser to achieve a film credit (the Westmore Brothers, although they rearranged the hair of stars like Claudette Colbert and Katharine Hepburn, were credited for make-up). As Mr Guilaroff's credits ran 'Hair styles by . . .', he may also have pioneered the title of hair stylist to 'hair dresser' what 'mortician' is to 'undertaker'. As one of Muriel Sparks' characters remarked about a similar euphemism, 'It brings lyricism to the concept'.

The next flashing star to join the hairdressing firmament was Alexandre, discovered by the

Begum Aga Khan and promoted by the Duchess of Windsor. Alexandre, like Antoine, understands the value of publicity and makes no effort in his luxurious Paris Salon to conceal his clients among whom are numbered Royalty and the reigning heads of Hollywood.

By creating the hair styles for the Couture Collections of Houses like Dior and Saint Laurent, Alexandre has rivalled Antoine in fashion publicity, but he has preferred travelling round the world at the behest of his illustrious clients to creating an empire, contenting himself with salons in smart European resorts. In 1966 he did, however, venture across the Channel to open a short-lived salon in London under Norman Hartnell's roof.

The Carita sisters bounced into the world spotlight when, in 1960, they triggered off the wig kick, although actually it took about two years before wigs came in to common use. For the first time since the early years of the century false hair was back, no longer concealed but flaunted. Hair pieces, long falls of hair and wigs became essential equipment and 'All your own work?' was a standard question when admiring someone's luxuriant locks. At first custom-made of real hair, and of the Occidental variety, wigs were expensive. As the demand grew, a hunt for cheaper hair ensued, and it was rumoured that Chinese and Japanese heads were as shorn as those of French collaborators in the War. But synthetic fibres took over and wigs were soon on sale off the peg at most large stores. More fashionable than whole wigs were the extra hair pieces, which by 1967 were being piled, like Ossa on Pelion, one on top of another. Heads grew larger and larger until in the seventies they began to shrink back to normal proportions.

The bouffant hair-do had started well before the Carita sisters launched the wig as a fashion and not a sad necessity. 'Teasing', the early way of accomplishing this amplitude had made the English hairdresser Raymond into a household word when under his nick-name of 'Teasy-Weasy' he became a television personality and surely the only hairdresser to own a Grand National winner, which, perhaps in deference to fashion, he had christened 'Rag Trade'. By the time teasing had been refined into 'backcombing' another revolution was under way – one which ranks with the Marcel wave, the permanent and the pin curl. This was the roller which was introduced in Italy and which by 1955 had spread to England and France.

The bouffant hair style achieved by rollers and backcombing was bad news for hats. Even petrified by lacquer it was still a fragile edifice. Just as Louis XIV's brother, Monsieur, would never wear a hat, even when he went into battle, for fear of flattening his wig,[9] so equally did ladies shy away from headgear. Milliners were to have a thin time, except for the fur hat, saved only by ceremonial occasions – weddings, funerals, Ascot, and the like – until 1970.

By 1965 rollers had become a way of life. *Time* magazine reported in April that in the States rollers had come out in the open and were seen in the streets, in the supermarkets, in the stores and in the cinemas. That same year in their April issue *Harper's Bazaar* published a photograph of a young woman in a nightdress, her hair in rollers. Rollers had come to stay.

Rollers changed the whole technique of hair setting; the comb-out became as important as the original set (by 1975 over £300,000,000 were being spent in hairdressing salons in Britain) and the aerosol hair spray introduced between 1951 and 1953 had become an integral accessory, as their sales show. (In 1974 the retail sales of hair sprays in the British Isles peaked at over £200,000,000.)

Twiggy, in 1968, veiled herself in a Lady Godiva wig. Her waif-like
thinness and look of lost innocence created a new type of androgynous
beauty, exactly suited to the mini – and generations away from the mature
curves of the beginning of the century.

Alas, not even hair spray manufacturers can win for winning. Beginning in 1971, the young turned away from the whole bouffant bit – hair pieces, backcombing, roller sets, hair spray, the lot – in favour of the 'blow-dry'. They have gone back to hair that looks like hair – not the kind of lacquered structure that inspired hairdresser Michael to advise a client to dust, not brush.

The ebullient techniques of the Italian hairdressers who invaded England and America encouraged young hairdressers to break away from conventional methods and styles and originate their own. Vidal Sasoon was an early innovator. Running counter to the rising taste for masses of hair, he returned to the scissors and brought back the bob. In 1961 Mary Quant bowed her head to his 'geometric cut', and in 1964 his 'five point' cut (strangely reminiscent of the shingle of 1926) became for him a landmark. Just as his young, uncompromising 'headlines' were in tune with Mary Quant's style, both personal and professional, they were also right for what used to be called 'far out' designers like Emmanuelle Khanh, Paco Rabanne and Ungaro, for whose first collection Vidal designed an asymmetrical cut, interesting rather than becoming. In Italy Vidal was the choice of Mila

In 1976 exaggeration was the keynote expressed in the mass of fuzzed out frizzy hair, while Biba's dark lipstick, eye shadow and nail varnish hark back to the past.

Schön; in the United States he was picked by Rudi Gernreich. No other British hairdresser has cracked the stony façades of foreign collections. And, so far, no other hairdresser has written two books (Alexandre wrote one – his memoirs in 1972). Vidal Sassoon's, both written with his wife, Beverley, are an autobiography, *Sorry I Kept You Waiting, Madame* in 1968, and *A Year of Beauty and Health* which in 1976 was on the American best seller list. The Sassoon hair shops multiply: his first shop on Bond Street opened in 1954, Vidal now has nine in the United Kingdom, three in Germany, six in the United States and one in Canada.

In Italy, in the sixties, hair was a work of art and artifice, the smart heads favouring different practitioners each season – from amongst those who hadn't emigrated to England. In America the hair scene was dominated by Kenneth Battelle. Kenneth (except for Vidal Sassoon most hairdressers seem to be referred to by their first names), according to Eleanor Lambert, 'established the fashionable coiffure of the 1960s',[10] with the large luxuriant shoulder-length hair-do he created for Mrs Onassis when she was First Lady. Kenneth began his New York career when he joined the beauty salon which milliner Lilly Daché, perhaps hedging her bets, opened to augment her hat business. Kenneth's hair-do's defied hats but won him a Coty Award in 1961. In 1963 he opened on his own in a luxurious Edwardian town house on East 54th Street in New York. His multi-floored Salon there is one of the very few business premises to be designed by ultra-fashionable decorator Billy Baldwin, who combined the fantasy of the Brighton Pavilion with twentieth-century luxury. In his capacity as vice-president of Glemby (Hair) Products, Kenneth opening a Glemby Salon in London in 1976, came out against backcombing and hair sprays. 'Hair', he pronounced, 'must bounce and move.' However, he reaffirmed his loyalty to volume and luxuriance, even though, at the end of the year, he was following Paris back to the chignon.

In and out of the mainstream of the longer-lasting styles like the Garbo shoulder-length bob of the end of the twenties, the page boy of the thirties, the long straight hair of the sixties (which replaced the pony-tail) there was a series of wild aberrations: the windswept and the upswept (both credited to Antoine) of the thirties, the bubble and the urchin cuts of the forties, the cottage loaf (a throwback to 1906, which was a throwback to 1898), the beehive of the late fifties, the 'fright wig' curly permanent, the flowing, frizzed Pre-Raphaelite locks, the Afro fuzz of the late sixties and early seventies. Rarely have hair styles been so much a matter of individual choice, rarely has hair been so paramount whether elaborately groomed or equally elaborately careless, and not since the eighteenth century have hairdressers themselves been so important.

Sweet Smell of Fashion

Scent has always been part of the accoutrement of glamour but the history of contemporary perfumes, if not shrouded in the mists of time, is glimpsed in a murky twilight out of which almost any date can be plucked depending on whose torch you are following.

The perfume business up to the mid twenties was dominated by long-established firms. Of the famous French names Houbigant and Guerlain can lay claim to the longest ancestry. Houbigant's shop is known to have been on the Faubourg St Honoré in 1775. Chardin, perfumer to Napoleon, in due course took over Houbigant, and by 1810 was supplying the Emperor, it is said, with one hundred and forty-four bottles of eau-de-Cologne a quarter. *Fougère Royale*, which still survives, one of their early successes before the turn of the century, was created by their perfumer, Paul Parquet, one of the first to use the synthetics which had been developed between 1850 and 1876. A later success in 1912 was *Quelques Fleurs*, the creation of another Houbigant perfumer, the charmingly named Robert Bienaimé.

Guerlain opened their first shop in 1828 and *their* star client was the Empress Eugénie for whom they created an Imperial eau-de-Cologne. Subsequent Guerlains have carried on the business and the Guerlain tradition, with scents whose names nostalgically span the decades: *Jicky* 1889, *L'Heure Bleue* 1912, *Mitsouko* 1919, *Shalimar* 1925 . . .

The third famous Paris perfumer, François Coty, is a comparative Johnny-come-lately. One story goes that in 1904 M. Coty, while trying unsuccessfully to persuade a Paris store to take even one sniff of his Rose Jacqueminot, accidentally on purpose broke the bottle. Attracted by the gorgeous smell, the customers flocked, and Coty's name was made. *L'Origan* (1905), *Chypre* (1917), and *L'Aimant* (1927) were the great Coty successes of the twenties.

In England, Floris, founded in 1720 and given a Royal Warrant by George IV in 1821, and Atkinson, founded in 1799, who received their Royal Warrant in 1828 two years before the King's death, have the longest lineage. (Yardley, although founded in 1770, did not get around to making their lavender water until 1817.)

To dip into the origins of eau-de-Cologne is to fish in troubled waters. Most historians of scent prudently hug the shore, and even two editions of the Encyclopaedia Britannica (those of 1910–11 and 1973) differ. Both, however, agree that the inventor of what came to be called eau-de-Cologne was one Johann Maria Farina, presumably christened Giovanni, born in Italy in 1685. In 1709 Farina moved to Cologne in Germany, taking with him his secret formula for 'flower-water' which by 1725 he had established under the name of 'Kölnisches Wasser'. As he prospered, Farina took on a nephew, whose grandson, another Johann Maria Farina, inherited the secret. Now onto the scene comes another claimant to the eau-de-Cologne crown – Paul de Feminis, a Milanese who had emigrated to Cologne in 1690. He called *his* product 'Eau Admirable', and he too bequeathed his secret to a nephew, also called Johann Maria Farina. In 1806 the first Johann Maria Farina moved to Paris, Frenchifying his name to Jean-Marie. To complicate matters the other Johann Maria (the descendant of Paul de Feminis) came to Paris at about the same time. As far as can be ascertained it was the first Farina who in 1840 sold his prosperous business to a M. Collas, the uncle of Messieurs Roger and Gallet who still produce 'the original' (attested by thirty-nine successful law suits) 'Eau-de-Cologne de Jean-Marie Farina'. Confusion is further compounded, for the Farinas were apparently a prolific lot (Roger et Gallet list thirteen) some of whom claim to use this process, and as the appellation, 'Kölnisches Wasser' was either unpatentable or never patented, it has been co-opted by other perfumers. One 'Kölnisch Wasser' has been given a romantic provenance. Its recipe, it is claimed in the lush prose of beauty products, written on 'an ancient scrap of paper', was given in 1792 as a wedding present by a Carthusian monk, whom the family had befriended, to a young Cologne banker called Muhlens. This formula, for what the Muhlens family called 'Aqua Mirabilis', made their fortune and is still sold under the name of *4711*, the street number given to the Muhlens' house in Cologne by Napoleon's billeting officer.

Like the beauty business, the scent business was a money-spinner and the Couture, ever looking for a sideline, began to invade the market. Chanel was the first in 1923[12] with her famous *Chanel No 5*, followed in 1927 by Lanvin with *Arpège*. Other great couturier perfumes are Shiaparelli's *Shocking*, Balmain's *Vent Vert* and *Jolie Madame*, Piguet's *Visa* and *Fracas*, Marcel Rochas' *Femme*, Balenciaga's *Fuite des Heures*, Madame Grès' *Cabochard*, Dior's *Diorrama*, Patou's *Joy* and *Moment Suprême*,

Worth's *Dans la Nuit* and *Je Reviens*, Saint Laurent's *YSL* and *Rive Gauche*, and from Barcelona Pertegas has thrown his hat into the ring with *Pertegas*, advertised as the passionate perfume from Spain. The list is as long as the list of top couturiers, for by the sixties it was par for the course of every couturier of stature to have a scent, or two or three – or more. Not all have been successful. Furriers too came into the game. Revillon launched their *Detchema* and *Carnet du Bal* shortly after the First World War, their *Crêpe de Chine* and *L'Insolent* in 1965. Weil have had a success with their appropriately named *Zibelene* (sable) and today with *Weil de Weil*. Farther north the Danish furrier Birger Christensen in 1968 came up with *Cheetah*. In America the ready-to-wear has followed this lead with *Norell* (launched in 1972 shortly before Norman Norell's death) and the recent *Halston*.

The beauty people naturally wanted a slice of the pie. Elizabeth Arden was one of the first with *Blue Grass*, launched in 1935, its name a tribute to Kentucky on whose blue grass some of the most famous racehorses stand, and horses, as everybody knows, were Miss Arden's second love. Revlon entered the fragrance market in 1960 when they purchased the famous Balmain scents, *Vent Vert* and *Jolie Madame*. *Norell* is another which they took under their banner. Estée Lauder made her debut in this field with her *Youth Dew*, introduced in the USA in 1953. In 1968 her *Estée Super Perfume* established her in this market. She followed this success in 1972 with *Alliage*.

There is a tendency to look down on synthetic scents as being a nasty modern substitute for natural products. It is true that the catalogue of the sources of the essential oils – peel, leaves, flowers, stems, roots, woods, barks, fruit, seeds – sounds more alluring than the chemical components of a synthetic perfume, but the results of the latter are often more interesting. It is commonly believed that *Chanel No 5* was the first synthetic scent. Actually it was rather the first sophisticated one. Previous synthetic perfumes had imitated the flower scents of the past. Chanel and her followers preferred subtlety to sweetness.

9

The Garnishes of Fashion

Skins

The turn of the century was also a turning point for furs and furriers. At the historic World's Fair of 1900 in Paris in which fashion was included for the first time, furriers, as well as couturiers exhibited. According to Mr Francis Weiss in an article from the German magazine *Marco*, the virtuoso performances of firms like the long-established Revillon, founded in 1723, put furs on a par with high fashion, and marked the debut of the fur coat as we know it today.

In the nineteenth century furs had mainly been used inside as lining. The 'fur outside' was an innovation. An early pioneer of the fur coat was Queen Victoria, whose watercolour portrait painted in 1823 when she was four years old by E.P.Denning, hangs in the Dulwich Museum where Mr Weiss spotted it. The fur was sealskin, the first great fashion fur, more usually made up into short capes or little fitted jackets known as 'sacques'. These also received the stamp of royal approval when

In 1960 Paris discovered a new fur: uncombed Mongolian lamb. Every couturier showed it, each in his own way. Balmain's was to use it in white to collar and line a coat of honeycomb knit and to make a hair-covering casquette.

Princess Alexandra brought several with her as part of her trousseau when she came to England in 1863. Another forerunner (but not a furrier) was Worth who by 1899 was showing an ankle-length princess fur coat, the skins intricately worked horizontally, vertically and into a chevron to mark the yoke. Doucet, too, was one of the first to handle fur like a fabric.

By 1900 the long fur coat and cape had arrived, worn mostly for evening, in ermine, sable, chinchilla, mink and seal. By 1903 motoring was becoming an increasingly fashionable form of exercise and as the early motors often lacked tops (although the British Standard had a folding one, making it look rather like a self-propelled pram, and the Daimler a fixed one, making it look a bit like a hearse), it is not surprising that long coats in tougher furs soon appeared. The long-haired furs favoured were bear, lynx, fox, wolf and even goat, to be followed by raccoon. Twenty years later the raccoon coat for both sexes had become the requisite motoring wear for American undergraduates. A coonskin coat and the favoured car, a Stutz Bearcat, became the symbols of the Roaring Twenties immortalized by the cartoonist, John Held Jr.

The smaller furs of the 1890s continued to be popular: a fox fur lightly carried over one arm, skinny little tippets (or neck pieces) and tiny round muffs in ermine, invariably trimmed with their tails. From 1903 wider stoles and larger, flatter muffs of black fox or chinchilla were adding richness to the dressy dresses of dressy ladies like actress Maxine Elliott. In 1905 the equally dressy Edith Wharton was photographed wearing a variation of the stole – an assemblage of multiple single skins –

Opposite Fox has had one of the most dramatic careers of any fur of this century. In 1905 the magic camera of Lartigue caught it in the Bois de Boulogne at its early height of elegance.

Right Mink is another success story. This so-called 'classic' treatment of the fur, stranding it from a narrow top (though shoulders are wide) to generous hem was made in 1948 by Calman Links who were then *buying* toiles from Christian Dior.

strung mouth to tail – of sable, mink, marten, kolinsky or fisher, which added a negligent touch of luxury to both day and late day wear. This fashion survived miraculously until the mid-thirties in America.

The skins came out of their mothballs in the early forties to be cannibalized into hats. This economy was not always appreciated as a *New Yorker* profile of John-Frederics, a pair of young Germans, who, with the French Lilly Daché, were then New York's reigning milliners, makes clear. A very rich matron who had come to them to have a hat made out of her own sables was to their minds rather meanly insistent on having the heads and feet returned to her. Her furs were handed to an attendant with the weary instructions, 'Save the giblets for Madam.'[1] In 1956 if anyone had thrown away the 'giblets' but saved the skin they would have been lucky, for that year Christian Dior revived the single skin neckpiece (headless and legless) as a little tie to tuck into the collar of a coat or jacket.

The shoulder cape, the stole, the neck-piece, the muff (which had grown by 1912 from looking like the barrel around a St Bernard dog's neck to a size resembling a flat pillow[2]) were to be staples that with inevitable variations persisted until the late fifties.

The mink shoulder cape, which in its natural state had long been a fixture abroad as a part of the survival kit in uncentrally-heated country houses, was given a boost by the new colour range produced by the cultivation of mutations. In 'silverblu', the mink cape became as essential a part of the travelling blue-haired American matron's luggage as her passport. The little cape, however useful, was never high fashion, nor was the hip-length jacket, beloved by the British, until the mid sixties when trousers became universal.

Mink is the great fur success story of our century. At the beginning when mink ran wild, it was not held in great esteem. Mink began to be successfully farmed in America in the mid-thirties,[3] according to J.G.Links, whose firm, Calman Links holds two Royal Warrants. There had been, he notes, earlier attempts to establish what were called 'minkeries'; these were unsuccessful, perhaps in part because of the name. Now over ninety per cent of all furs sold are ranch-bred.

The combination of ranching (or farming) and the breeding from mutations is responsible for the mink boom. Authorities differ on the colour and date of the first coat to be made up of mutation mink skins. Mr Links says the colour was grey and the date 1942. The *Fur Review* gives the colour as platinum and the date as 1943 when this pioneer garment was auctioned in the United States in aid of the Red Cross. Give or take a year, it was still an historic moment.

The breeding of minks has been encouraged, protected and promoted by associations dedicated to these premises, of which the most familiar are EMBA (an acronym for Mutation Mink Breeders Association of America), GLMA (another acronym, this time for Great Lakes Mink Association) and SAGA, which represents the four Scandinavian countries – Denmark, Finland, Norway and Sweden. Scientific cross-breeding and careful genetic control of mutations has resulted in a remarkable range of colours: besides white and as black as possible, there is a wide range from honey beige to dark brown, from palest grey to gunmetal. Nomenclature is tricky and best left to the furrier to translate. There are also dappled pelts and sprinkled pelts (with lighter or darker hairs than the under wool). Dark ranch mink has not been neglected; today it sells more than all the others put together. GLMA has a sub-division they call 'Blackglama' dedicated to what their advertisements call 'the world's finest natural dark ranch mink bred only in America by the Great Lakes mink men'.

Mink production has boomed. From six million minks ranched in 1956, the total twenty years later reached sixteen million. It seems inevitable that with such vast quantities, the status quality of the fur will be diluted. The name of the animal which Mr Links describes as 'a large weasel of extreme nervous energy and vicious character' has, as he points out, 'acquired a connotation far beyond that of a fur'. It has become a symbol – to some, of vulgar ostentation (earning Valentina's scornful 'Mink is for football'), to others, of the ultimate in luxury ('I got everything,' says the gangster's moll in *Born Yesterday*. 'I got two mink coats.') But the fact is that good mink is soft, light, and, above all, cosy. Katharine Hepburn was quoted as saying that she never knew what it was like to be warm until she had acquired her first mink coat.

Another fur which has had the benefit of intensive promotion is Persian lamb or karakul. This has had its ups and downs, but now with the help of energetic promotion by SWAKARA (still another acronym, this time for South West Africa Karakul) it, with mink, shares three-quarters of the world market in ranched furs. Persian lamb had gone through the doldrums when it was thought it looked middle-aged, and rather vulgarly prosperous, but by dint of powerful advertising and even more importantly by working with the fur designers, SWAKARA has returned it to favour.

Veruschka's bare skin was an invitation to the body painting fad of the late sixties. This six-foot-one German beauty, born Countess Vera von Lehndorff, is photographed here by Franco Rubartelli.

In 1926 fox was back again (this time red fox), still complete with head and tail, worn with paw clasped in mouth. Actually the point of this caricature from 'La Vie Parisienne' is the mannish tailored suit and bow-tied shirt, evoking the comment, 'With boys like that, one would pass up the girls.'

Above *In 1934 fox is still with us, in white as a summer fur.*

Right *E.O. Hoppé snapped this nadir of the silver fox in Regent Street. Only five years earlier the first silver fox skin had sold in the United States for twelve hundred dollars, but the story has a happy ending; fox made a giant comeback thirty years later and is still going strong.*

Another fashion outcast was fox. In 1910 a black fox fur sold at auction in London brought five hundred gold guineas; the first silver fox skin was purchased in 1929–30 by Marshall Field, the Chicago store, for twelve hundred dollars. (What the customer was charged, history does not relate.) From those splendid days in the late twenties when it was the necessary accessory, fox fell out of favour, and, in London during the Second World War, became the insignia of the tarts who braved the blackout on their Bond Street and Piccadilly beats during the Blitz. Best forgotten are the short, hump-shouldered fox coats of the thirties which Yves Saint Laurent tried to revive in 1971, succeeding only in creating a brief demand for them in second-hand shops. Still, you can't keep a good fur down.

Fox began a comeback in 1964 but the seemingly inexhaustible lure of ethnic dress which first beckoned in 1966 has put long-haired furs firmly back into fashion, and has made fox – with its natural range of colours: black, red, grey, blue, red and cross – now a runner-up to mink and Persian lamb, taking about ten per cent of the market. In the early days of fox supremacy, the skins worn always over one shoulder, were complete with heads and tails. As stoles they shed these, and, from

Overleaf left *Powder box by Jean Schlumberger for Tiffany & Co: a sea shell in 18 ct. gold inset with sapphires, emeralds and turquoises.*

Overleaf right *Brooch by Jeanne Toussaint for Cartier: a bird in platinum with sapphires and diamonds, 1933.*

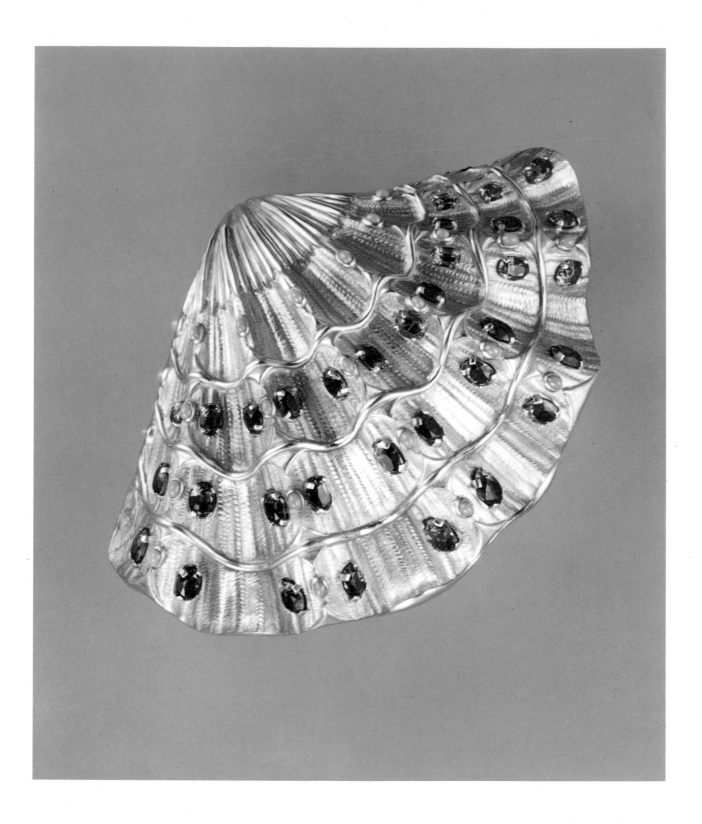

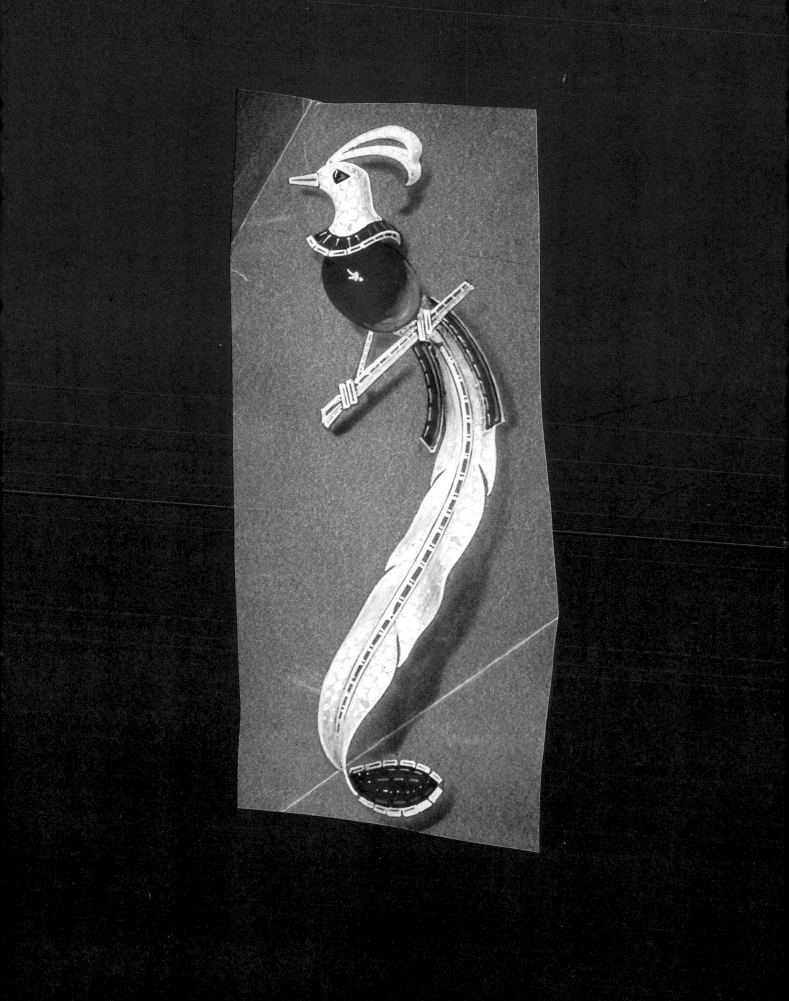

Revillon's 1976/77 way with fox – silver and blue – designed by Jean-Paul Avizou.

1966, the skins, which though bulky have the virtue of lightness, worked horizontally or vertically were used for full-length coats. In 1970 Oscar de la Renta in New York went to Outer Siberia for a peasant look to out-do all peasant looks which included a covering (it couldn't be called a coat) made of vertically slung separate silver fox skins, tails bobbing. In 1976 Bill Gibb handled his foxes in the same way.

In 1960 Paris discovered uncombed Mongolian lamb: Balmain showed his in white, the model accompanied by an equally tousled poodle to match; Balenciaga dyed his in colours no lamb, even a Mongolian one, could ever have been – sulphur yellow, candy pink, and gangster black – and used it to line coats in black leather or ciré, of brocade or sequins. Little did he know (or did he?) that he was leading a rout back to the nineteenth-century sheepskin pelisse, which the Bulgarian peasant wore skin out, fur inside. By 1967 this coat, the skin side brightly embroidered in Afghan style was *the* coat of the new gypsies (rich or less so), and shops specializing in these skins burgeoned where now the jeans shops bloom.

Because good furs like real jewellery stagger under the burden of expense the high fashion centres are where the money is: Paris, Rome and New York. And even Paris could show restraint, as Christian Dior noted when he introduced his fur-lined mackintosh in 1956 (anticipating Balenciaga by four years, though his fur inside was mink or beaver). 'You see', he explained to Joseph Links, 'not all my clients want a new fur coat *every* year.'

Each fur capital differs in character. In Paris the Couture Houses dominate the fur scene, and because the Couture furs are all made by Claude Wittelson, with the exception of Dior whose M. Manteau and his successor Frédéric Castet won fame in their own right as distinguished furriers, the only names known are those of the Fashion Houses. The specific quality of Paris furs is their combination of luxury and wit: Balmain's gold-buttoned ermine reefer and white mink trenchcoat, Cardin's spiral boa of intertwined black and white foxes, Saint Laurent's leopard jacket with knitted

Nieman–Marcus revive Christian Dior's fur-lined mack in poplin, heavily collared and cuffed in fox. The lining snaps out. 1976/77.

sleeves – these were landmarks of the sixties. Furriers Revillon and Chombert came into the fashion scene in 1966 when the former rejuvenated its image by taking on Fernando Sanchez from Nina Ricci and the latter for a clever caftan of stencilled rabbit. That year Paco Rabanne also scored with a variation of the 'fur inside', the skin cut in squares, the hairs puffing out between. This strange *tour de force* was executed by Simon Frères.

In Italy the names are Jole Veneziani and Fendi: their special quality is inventive innovation, like knitting strips of mink into light, soft fabric. In America, or rather New York, the furriers bask in their own limelight. The most creative have been Maximilian, Emeric Partos and Jacques Kaplan, and between them they command (or commanded) the ladies of unlimited purses – the kind who buy two or three furs at a time and who wouldn't be seen dead in last year's coat. Maximilian's styling in even the richest furs is so high that their fashion life is as brief as that of the mayfly, but each collection is sold out before the official opening show.

The firm of Maximilian, (he himself came to America in 1940 with a European reputation dating from 1918), has been run since his death in 1961 by his sister, Mrs Potok. It might be said that Maximilian and Jacques Kaplan bear the same relation to each other as do David Webb and Kenneth J. Lane in the field of jewellery. Maximilian made the skinny double-breasted black mink coat for Mrs Onassis when she was First Lady which became one of the most photographed coats ever. M. Kaplan translated the coat into Japanese mink at about one-tenth the price and made a killing from the many women who wanted to look like the then Mrs Kennedy.

Emeric Imre Partos became internationally famous when he made Barbra Streisand's trousseau including white mink knickers for her television spectacular in 1966. Partos, with the confidence bred of having worked for Christian Dior and Maximilian, and, until his death in 1975, as head fur designer for Bergdorf Goodman, had a daring and dramatic hand with luxurious furs. He shared with Maximilian America's highest fashion recognition, the Coty Award, and competed with him and M. Kaplan for the honour of bringing ermine back into fashion.

London's place in the sun, as far as fur is concerned, rests on its commanding position as the largest international centre for sales of raw furs. The doyen of fur auctions is the Hudson's Bay Company, which celebrated its tercentenary in 1970, and which operates under a Royal Charter. Hudson's Bay recently merged with Annings (formerly Annings, Chadwick & Kiver) who handle furs from the USSR. Another firm, of fur brokers, Eastwood and Holt, specializes in the sale of Southwest African karakul. In 1972 sales of raw furs in London totalled one hundred million pounds.

It is not the furriers' fault that London is not a pace-setter fashion-wise. It is just that the British are a conservative lot, and even if smart women could afford to, they probably would not wish to spend their money on the kind of extravagances which keep the top French, Italian and American furriers laughing all the way to the bank. British clients put a premium on good workmanship and fine quality skins but tend to prefer 'classic' styles that will not date too obviously. This imposes limits on imaginative design. There have been exceptions. When couturier Michael was designing furs for Bradley's at Debenham's, he produced some dazzling ideas – among them in 1965 a memorable coat of black and white fox, diagonally worked, and a bathrobe – belted white mink, collared in the white mink striped with black. Another exception is Furs Renée, whose owners, Mr and Mrs Bruno Stern, have the courage of their fashion convictions.

Rings by Elizabeth Gage for Annabel Jones.
Miss Gage was a winner of a de Beers Diamonds – International Award in 1972.

A virtue of this century has been its awakening awareness of the necessity of preserving the balance of nature. In 1948 the IUCN (International Union for the Conservation of Nature and Natural Resources) was founded. Not least among its supporters have been the furriers who have a natural interest in maintaining the animal population. They work closely with the IUCN: for example, the International Fur Trade Federation has financed conservation projects to protect the leopard in Africa and the ocelot in South America. The IUCN is less well known than the World Wildlife Fund (founded in 1961), which acts as the fund raising side of IUCN. A more emotional group is Beauty Without Cruelty, founded in 1959, which makes up in noise for what it lacks in logic.

Jewellery

Jewellery at the turn of the century luxuriated in royal patronage. Queen Alexandra set the fashion for display. Arrayed in her dog collars of many strands of pearls or diamonds, her swags of pearls, her tiaras, ear-rings, stomachers, bracelets and cascades of brooches, she looked a glittering icon. King Edward was also a great lover of jewels. It was at his invitation that Cartier started a branch in London, formally opened by the King himself in 1902. The next year, also at his invitation, Gustave Fabergé, the Russian creator of precious objects, also opened a shop in London. Boucheron had preceded both in 1901.

As in nearly every other area of fashion, the great firms whose names still sparkle today were founded in the affluent days of the last century, or even earlier: Collingwood in 1817, Mauboussin in 1827, Tiffany in 1837, Cartier in 1847, Boucheron in 1858, Benson in 1874, Bulgari in 1881, Van Cleef and Arpels 1893. Garrard who became Crown Jewellers in 1853 was actually founded in 1735, while Chaumet owes its origin to Napoleonic favour in 1780, although it did not take the name of Chaumet until 1875.

With a pause for the First World War these venerable jewellers were kept busy coping with the whims of fashion. Dog collars were re-strung into the pearls needed to fill in the new open necklines of 1908 (ladies who did not possess or could not afford the kind made by oysters were saved by Tecla who introduced their cultured pearls in 1913, followed by Ciro's in 1917). Platinum was introduced in 1910[4] to provide open-back claw settings for large stones (some probably prized out of no longer smart stomachers); other massive stones were set into wide bracelets *pavé* with diamonds. The twenties were happy years for them – stringing gems into yard-long necklaces, transforming brooches into clips for berets, skullcaps and the inevitable little black dress, creating tiaras that imitated the bandeaux that Suzanne Lenglen made famous, designing drop ear-rings to dangle below ear-covering bobs, button ear-rings for shorter hair, converting bracelets into chokers, sparkling Chinese lacquer with brilliants, producing the endless diamond bracelets for the gold-diggers to whom diamonds were a girl's best friend.

As these were all expensive jewellers, these were expensive whims. Following fashion too closely in fine jewellery is the prerogative of only a restricted clientele. Fashion by its nature dates quickly; an appreciable amount of time must pass before the fashions of yesterday become again the fashion of today. 'High' jewellery tends therefore toward the classic, the designer's skill directed to enhancing the importance and beauty of the great gem stones.

Some technical innovations have created their own fashions: the wristwatch invented by Louis Cartier in 1907 has become a permanent fixture, as have the emerald and baguette cuts of the thirties.

As the economy of the non-oil producing world totters, furs reach a luxury they have not attained since the beginning of the century. Then a full-length sable coat could be purchased for 300 guineas; it would cost somewhat more today. Furs Renée border a full-length cape of cerulean mink with Pearl fox, 1976.

(In 1976 an emerald cut diamond ring, flanked by two baguettes, platinum mounted, brought £512,048 at Sotheby Parke Bernet in New York.) The *minaudière*, the brainchild of Van Cleef and Arpels, much adapted and much copied, survives until today.

By and large these great Houses tended to be reticent about the identities of their designers. The knowledgeable, however, were aware of Jeanne Toussaint of Cartier. Madame Toussaint arrived at Cartier just before the end of the First World War and was to run Cartier's during the second one. She became Louis Cartier's assistant, and until her retirement in 1970 was regarded as one of the most distinguished jewellery designers in the world. She was early in realizing the great change that was to occur in this century, a change which was two-pronged: on the one hand an interest in great stones for their intrinsic value, on the other, a more lighthearted approach to jewellery itself. Madame Toussaint inaugurated in 1920 a department for 'small' gifts (which became 'les Must') and turned

The 'body jewellery' kick which had its brief life between 1966 and 1969 seemed breathlessly new at the time. But in 1901 'Femina' carried this story of a bolero worth 1,500,000 francs, designed by Hamel for a music hall 'divette', Mlle Fagette. The bolero was of silver scattered with diamonds, pearls, rubies, emeralds, sapphires and turquoises in motifs taken from the period of Louis XV. Yesterday's body jewellery wasn't in it.

The Ranee of Pudukota wore her tiara across her brow in the currently fashionable bandeau (or 'headache band') style at a Court Ball in 1921. The tiara was subsequently sold and purchased by England's Royal Family as a present for Princess Marina on the occasion of her marriage to the Duke of Kent in 1934. Princess Marina was photographed wearing the tiara on the back of her head with her wedding dress by Edward Molyneux.

her attention to semi-precious stones – amethysts, aquamarines, coral – which she handled in skilful and imaginative combinations. She even managed to give diamonds a frivolous look, setting them into swinging tassels or a delicate fringe falling from a single stone.

Two other women, Mesdames Belperron and Boivin, who flourished in Paris between the two wars, were also forerunners of the vogue for chic, original, rather than imposing, ornaments. As Fulco di Verdura, who was to become more enduringly famous, remarked: 'These ladies were very à la mode', especially in the thirties.

It was Chanel who was to father – or perhaps mother is the correct word – a new direction in jewellery, when she decided to reproduce copies of her own fabulous collection of rubies, emeralds, diamonds and pearls, said to have been given to her by Grand Duke Dmitri of Russia. She liked stones mixed in Byzantine splendour and worn in profusion with the simplest clothes – a sweater, a suit, a jersey dress. With Chanel jewellery, she once said, 'women can wear fortunes that aren't worth anything.' Although Chanel is universally given credit for being the originator of costume jewellery, it is hard to find a nice incontrovertible date, but by 1923 or 1924 Count Etienne de Beaumont was in charge of her jewellery department.

In 1932 De Beers invited Chanel to create a collection of diamond jewellery. Chanel turned the problem over to Paul Iribe, one of the artists of the *Gazette de Bon Ton*, and the designer of the Lanvin emblem – Madame Jeanne Lanvin and her daughter in ball-gowns – first used on the *Arpège*

Boule Noir bottle in 1927. As at this time Iribe was a very ill man, he commandeered the services of the young Sicilian Duca di Verdura who was then designing fabrics for Chanel. The Diamond Collection, which Chanel showed in her own house in rooms darkened except for lights trained on the diamonds, was a great success and Fulco di Verdura became her jewellery designer. 'We used topazes' he recalls, 'and badly flawed rubies and emeralds and very heavy gold.' It was he who designed the wide Chanel bracelet in white or black Chinese lacquer encrusted with a Maltese cross of multi-coloured stones. Verdura was to find his way to New York where after a few years with Paul Flato he set up on his own on Fifth Avenue in what had been Cartier's first shop in New York. (History relates that New York was bought for a string of beads; Cartier are said to have bought their shop, in 1907, for a string of pearls.) Verdura opened in 1939 on the day that war was declared

In 1929 Nancy Cunard was photographed wearing such a vast assemblage of painted wooden bracelets which she had found in Paris that The Sketch *dubbed her 'The Lady of the Brobdingnagian Bangles'. This fashionable addiction to polka dots can also be seen in Paul Tanqueray's photograph of Gertrude Lawrence.*

Right *Jeanne Toussaint of Cartier is considered one of the great jewellery designers of the century. This charming portrait shows the chic which was reflected in her designs. The simple cloche hat brightened by a diamond brooch in front, the short double string of pearls, the cheek-encroaching bob are clues to the date – 1927.*

Below *In 1928 Joan Blondell starred in Anita Loos' classic,* Gentlemen Prefer Blondes. *From her goo-goo eyes to her strapped shoes, she is a caricature of the twenties; the short dress with panels dropping to the floor, the jewels testifying to the gold-diggers' belief that 'diamonds are a girl's best friend'.*

Left *Pearls by the yard had become obligatory wear but with the arrival of Técla shortly after the War they were no longer restricted to those who could afford the kind that came from oysters. This advertisement of 1920 appeared in* La Gazette du Bon Ton. *In England these pearls were lightheartedly celebrated by a ditty which went:*

'*It may be only a Técla pearl,
But it was the gift of a belted earl.*

(one date, he says, he can't forget), and closed in 1973. In New York, he used the lacquer (nine layers) and gold cane on white or black morocco leather for cigarette cases; lapis lazuli, malachite and porphyry and the various colours of gold for jewellery.

Another distinguished artist-craftsman, as Graham Hughes terms them, of our time also came via costume jewellery. Schiaparelli had soon picked up Chanel's idea and she chose as her designer the Alsatian Jean Schlumberger. Schlumberger soon turned to real jewellery, opened on his own in Paris, and subsequently moved his Paris *cachet* to New York. In 1956, a year after Walter Hoving had taken over, he joined Tiffany & Co., as both star designer and vice-president. Schlumberger's forte is the bravura mixture of the real and the semi-precious, although he can handle the largest and most precious stones in a manner becoming to Tiffany. He can range from gold and enamel bangles to a diamond necklace enshrining the Tiffany canary diamond, supposedly the largest in the world, with equal ease. His – and Tiffany's – other asset was window designer Gene Moore, who diminished the windows with their priceless frontage on Fifth Avenue and 57th Street to miniature size, creating eye-stopping vignettes featuring the Schlumberger creations. Schlumberger, like Verdura, Jeanne Toussaint and the *á la mode* ladies understood that jewellery exists to adorn not obliterate the wearer. It takes an active effort of imagination to visualize one of René Lalique's spectacular Art Nouveau fancies in gold and glass, ivory, chrysoprase and *plique à jour* enamel being actually worn; in fact one would scarcely look at the wearer. These marvels of craft are far more suitably housed, as they are, in the Calouste Gulbenkian Museum in Lisbon. Much of so-called modern jewellery especially the German and Scandinavian seems similarly designed for its own sake, in their case as sculpture or as precious objects rather than human ornament.

David Webb was the youngest of the trio of fashion jewellers. A native American, from North Carolina, as soon as he opened the doors of his shop in 1963 he became an instant success. Webb is the opposite of New York's great stone-man, Harry Winston, who specializes in diamonds of size. Webb's flexible wrap-around bracelets in white and gold enamel, with coral knob ends, his jungle jewellery, his light dustings of diamonds all spell fashion. His pins, his bracelets, his ear-rings rapidly became status symbols – not of wealth but of fashionable awareness.

An off-shoot of Webb, or perhaps 'by-product' is a better word, and a direct descendant of Chanel, is Kenneth J. Lane. Like David Webb's and also in the sixties, his unashamedly junk jewellery became a badge of fashion know-how. Very much in the New York social scene, Lane noticed that the ear-lobes of the Beautiful People were being painfully tugged by the weight of the real stones in the chandelier ear-rings that were then the fashion. While working for Delman, the shoe company which the agglomerate Genesco was to take over, he saw that the lightweight plastic stones with which Delman embossed their evening shoes seemed to stick on quite well, and it occurred to him to use them for shoulder-grazing ear-rings. From then on he was in fakes – and in fashion. Lane has never pretended to originality. What his bright black olive eyes light upon he copies. The knock-off (trade for a cheap copy) is his speciality. He knocked off David Webb's supremely elegant jungle jewellery – in beads, cheap enamel, gilt and coloured stones. Oddly enough, the knock-offs simply stimulated an appetite for the Webb originals. Lane admits freely to his magpie habits. When a customer remarked 'I see you've knocked off the Cartier leopard,' he replied indignantly, 'I did not; I knocked off David Webb's knock-off of the Cartier leopard.' His success is partly due to his own fashionable personality and partly to the dramatic effectiveness of his great hunks of junk, with which, unless you are Elizabeth Taylor with that seventy-carat diamond for which Cartier paid $1,050,000, most real jewellery cannot compete, although some of his grandest customers amuse themselves by mixing his imitations with their own great pieces. Kenneth J. Lane picked up where Chanel left off.

In England the crippling post-war purchase tax on new jewellery, in 1947–8 it was one hundred and twenty-five per cent, which was not reduced until 1960, effectively stultified jewellery design. People either bought second-hand pieces which were free of tax, or great rocks to stash away in safety deposit boxes. Such investors had little interest in settings or design, only in the intrinsic value of the stones. Thus in this century, it is mainly since 1960 that contemporary jewellery design has come into its own in Great Britain. Its development has been greatly encouraged by the Worshipful Company of Goldsmiths who, kicking off in 1961 with the first International Exhibition of Jewellery from 1890 has given continuing support. De Beers too has been an important patron and their Diamonds – International Awards inaugurated in 1954 have made the world aware of the geographical extent of modern jewellery design. In 1976 the award attracted 1,113 entries from thirty countries.

In England one of the first of the new generation of British post-war jewellery designers to

In 1970 Andrew Grima, the Roman-born British jewellery designer was invited by the Omega Watch Company to design a collection of watches. The collection, which Grima called 'About Time', was exhibited that year at Goldsmith's Hall, the first exhibition of watches to be put on by the Worshipful Company of Goldsmiths. Typical of Grima's unconventional approach to a designing problem is this wristwatch. Grima received in 1966 the Queen's Award for Industry and the Duke of Edinburgh's Award for Design. His shop on Jermyn Street, opened in 1966, is as unlike most jewellery shops as his jewellery is unlike that of other jewellers.

In the sixties David Webb found himself fashion's pet when he launched his collection of jungle jewellery – in gold, enamel and brilliants. This amusing idea, beautifully executed by Webb was instantly copied, by makers of costume jewellery like Kenneth J. Lane and by Italian jewellers to whom working in enamel comes naturally and who were delighted to find a new theme. Mr Webb kept his jewellery in a middle price range, using semi-precious stones like coral, and jade, was sparing with diamonds, elaborate in enamel, simple in gold. The death of this charming North Carolinian in 1975 deprived America of an imaginative talent.

After Chanel costume jewellery ambled along until Kenneth J. Lane. His eye works at supersonic speed and what he sees he copies but he is engagingly frank about his magpie habits. Paulene Stone faced the New Year in 1967 wearing a large part of the current Lane collection commemorating the explosion of fashion jewellery (the only cheat is that her rings are really earrings) and the towering, turbulent falls of false hair that had been the major fashion themes of the past year.

make his mark was Italian-born Andrew Grima. His use of unpolished semi-precious stones – agate, quartz, tourmaline, lapis lazuli, rock crystal – in their natural shapes; his preference for baroque over regularly shaped pearls, his very personal handling of gold, has been a powerful influence. This affinity with natural shapes, matched with the increasing interest in ecology, is also seen in the work of the American Arthur King and the Swiss Gilbert Albert. Grima's most bravura effort was his collection of watches for Omega, designed in 1970. He is one of the master jewellers who has established his own style, a style that has nothing to do with fashion as such, but much to do with fashion in jewellery.

As the young began to bedizen themselves with rings (several to every finger), to jangle with bangles and clank with gilt or gold chain necklaces in the Chanel manner, jewellery shops sprouted in London to supply the need. And more serious designers like John Donald have found new markets in oil-rich countries.

10

Above, Below and Beneath

Above

If it was the numberless layers of outer clothing of the seventies, as well as the acceptance of central heating as the rule rather than the exception that transformed underclothing, it was hair more than any other influence that took hats over the bumpiest bumps of their roller-coaster ride.

The years until the Great War were the great years for hats. As dresses slimmed, they reached an apogee of amplitude, as large as tea trays, on which were piled flowers of the size seen only on seed packets, or curling plumes of ostrich feathers which South African success at ostrich farming had made plentiful. More exotic was the plumage of rare birds – like the osprey (or egret) which spouted like spume from the tops of Poiret's turbans. These massive, overladen objects could be perched upon pompadours, for the latter had a solid foundation of padding and frizzing to which the former

At Auteuil in 1912 an ambitious Parisienne topped her post-Poiret dress with a huge picture hat, in its turn topped with the plumage from a whole flock of egrets.

could be anchored, and from which they could be removed without too much disturbance of the elaborate hair-do beneath.

The year 1913 was a crucial one for hats. That year Irene Castle introduced the bob which, after the war, became the shorter shingle and even shorter Eton crop – no foundation for heavy outsize hats. And that year in America the Audubon Society, named after the great nineteenth-century naturalist John James Audubon, succeeded in introducing into the Tariff Act a ban on the importation of the plumage of such rare species as the egret and birds of paradise.

In England, the Royal Society for the Protection of Birds had been founded in 1889 when the slaughter of birds for their feathers was reaching truly horrifying proportions. From 1890 to 1911 sales at auction in London alone of rare birds – herons, egrets, sooty terns, lyre birds, kingfishers, hummingbirds, birds of paradise – came to over two million birds.[1] The RSPB had put a bill for the protection of these rare species before Parliament in 1904, but did not succeed in getting a Plumage Act, which like the American one banned the importation of these massacred innocents, passed until 1921.

Hats were stripped of their aviaries of feathers and changed in size dramatically. One must therefore conclude that it was short hair as well as conscience that was responsible for the diminution and simplification of headgear.

In the twenties hats, shorn of ornament, settled down firmly on the forehead. With their high crowns and narrow down-turned brims, their resemblance to the glass domes used for forcing plants gave them the name of cloches. Indeed, with their hats pulled down to their eyes, their short skirts and wrap-around coats above stem-like legs, women did look like orderly rows of identical plants in a well-kept garden. By 1928 hats had dwindled further into head-hugging brimless helmets, usually felt, cut like the hair they covered, their dullness alleviated by a jewelled clip. An alternative favoured by Chanel was a small beret worn to the side, similarly ornamented. The helmets had come down to the brows, the berets showed a bit of forehead, but it was still a rich thrill when hats slipped back off the face. America was first in 1927; on the other side of the Atlantic faces did not emerge until the early thirties.

After being content to look alike women wanted to look different. When they saw their exposed faces, they felt that their individual features needed individual attention. Millinery perked up again and a boost was given to made-to-order hat-making.

Adrian's slouch hat for Garbo in 1929 had swept America. His hat for her in *Romance* a year later, quickly known as the 'Eugènie' hat, was copied widely at all price levels, its original ostrich plumes dwindling to a single feather, and, as it plummeted to bargain basements, often plucked from lesser fowls. As we now know you can be too successful and by 1932 the Eugènie hat had become a joke. Before, however, its over-exposure had pushed it into limbo it appeared in 1934 on the other side of the Atlantic where it adorned the head of Princess Marina, just married to the Duke of Kent, whose resemblance to the Empress Eugènie it accentuated. Up to the Second World War a photograph of the Duchess, hat tipped over one beautiful eye, could be admired in the vitrine outside photographer Harlip's studio on Bond Street.

It must be remembered that short hair, like long hair today, was the prerogative of the young, so that the established 'hatty' hatters did not disappear overnight. The stately names of Reboux, who had been the millinery dictator at the end of the nineteenth century, Agnès and Legroux, with their impressive concoctions, continued to flourish through the thirties and forties. But to deal with the new demand for special hats for special faces a flood of new names appeared before the Second

Right *In 1900 Lady Ottoline Morrell displayed her well-known originality by adding to her ostrich feathers, black shadow lace, a bow of satin and binding on the lot with a chiffon scarf.*

Below *Edna Davis took time off from appearing in* Before Midnight *to pose: loyal to the London 1929 uniform of short-skirted tailored suit, fox fur and inevitable cloche hat headlighted with a diamond brooch.*

Above *The slouch hat designed by Adrian for Greta Garbo in* The Woman of Affairs (*the screen version of* The Green Hat) *had by 1928 changed the millinery picture in America.*

World War, to continue in strength long after: in Paris, Suzy, Maud Roser of Maud et Nano, Albouy, and the most distinguished of all, Paulette; in New York, Lilly Daché, John-Frederics and Sally Victor; in London, Aage Thaarup, Otto Lucas and Madame Vernier.

Hats tilted forward as hair grew to page-boy length at the back where it was sometimes caught in a snood of crocheted chenille (indeed the snood with a flat bow on the top sometimes superseded the hat, an ominous sign). In 1936, as hair was upswept to a fringe in front, hats became just top-knots of flowers and veiling. After the war there were as many hat shapes as there were milliners to invent them and women to wear them. There were high crowns, and low crowns, wide brims and no brims. Paris, as ever, was the fount of ideas. As the Couture spread its wings, pinioned during the dark years of the Occupation, they were at first content just to design clothes and let milliners design hats. 'Chapeaux par . . .' was a regular credit on the programmes of showings. Maud et Nano and then Maud Roser on her own did the hats for the first Christian Dior collections; Paulette's name cropped up all over the place. Some Houses had their own milliners, like Lanvin for whom Bernard Devaux, who had been previously with Cardin, created in 1960 memorable hats of soufflé lightness.

By then milliners were fighting a war on two fronts. The first was against hair – beehive or bouffant – whose owners were loath to have flattened by hats. The second was against the Couture itself, which, following the lead of Balenciaga who had always designed his own hats, embraced, like him, the concept of the total look which hats were to complete but not compete with. The

Madame Rochas in 1946 matched her pillbox by Legroux in straw veiled in black with lace gloves (by Rochas) of kid fingered in the same lace, a subtle advertisement for the new Rochas scent 'Femme' whose packaging repeated the black lace motif.

Above *Paulette's famous flower top knots (left) inspired gardens of hats like the one on the right designed by Graham Smith, both Easter bonnets for 1965.*

Left *The fur casquette in grey fox as shown by Mila Schön in 1968 with a grey maxi coat over a mini dress with black thigh high boots.*

mannequins' hair, too, had always been simplified – partly for practical reasons and partly, again, not to attract attention to itself. In 1960, another fateful year for hats, Cardin introduced the Carita Sisters' wigs; soon Alexandre was to be behind the scenes with his fleet of hairdressers busy adding postiche and falls as he created special hair-styles for favoured couturiers.

A great milliner like Paulette, who by jettisoning the stiff sparterie base had revolutionized the art of hat-making, managed to keep her salon busy with her steady clientele of Royalty and ambassadresses, avid for her light, draped, jersey turbans and flowery confections. Otherwise only a few modistes unconnected with Couture Houses were listed in the Chambre Syndicale's calendar. In New York by 1968, the year hair rose to a height and spread to an amplitude unprecedented in this century, two of New York's most successful milliners, Halston and Adolfo, turned to dress designing. In England, Royalty and Royal occasions kept milliners like Simone Mirman and Frederick Fox (who had inherited Madame Vernier's crown) going.

There have been occasional reprieves. Fur hats, not just the conventional sable, mink or beaver hat-shaped hats, but large caps of long-haired fur, which Christian Dior was the first to show in raccoon with a Cossack coat in 1947, saved the day, and still come out in the cold. Pill-boxes which Balenciaga introduced in 1946, and which were made standard headgear from 1960 by Mrs Onassis when she was the President's wife, were temporary life-savers.

But hats that needed a skilled milliner's hand were disappearing. Mrs Onassis (again) was photographed in a Spanish riding hat in 1967, and soon these along with sombreros and stetsons were parading the King's Road. Another fad that has nothing to do with the milliner's craft was the flat

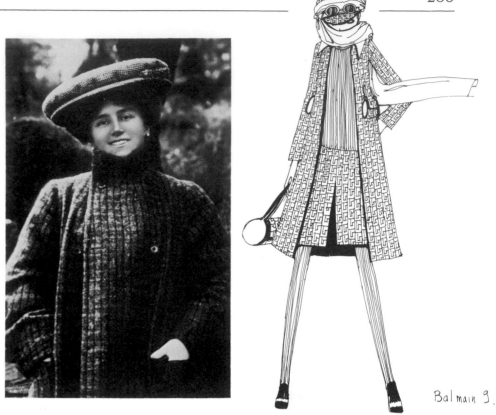

Balmain 9.

This boy's cap worn by actress Ellaline Terriss as early motoring gear in 1903/4 was to make periodic reappearances: in 1961 when Jeanne Moreau wore one in Jules et Jim, *in 1971 when Balmain showed one complete with goggles and veil with shorts for a motoring outfit (right), and again in 1976/77.*

working man's cap as worn by Jeanne Moreau in *Jules et Jim* (1961). This cap has a strange provenance: it first appears wider and flatter, in the first decade of the century for motoring, next in 1948 as high fashion by Schiaparelli, and in 1976 when the London *Sunday Times* magazine was the first to resuscitate it. Another film, *Bonnie and Clyde*, temporarily resuscitated the beret in 1967. The die had, however, been cast in 1960 when Yves Saint Laurent in his last collection for Dior showed for the first time the rib-knit, forehead-covering skating cap which he revived in 1971 for his Rive Gauche shops. This, with the latest version of the headscarf epidemic since the War, a kerchief tied straight across the brows, ends the sad tale of the hat – and takes us back fifty years to the bandeau'd days.

Below

A shoe, an object necessarily of limited size, offers limited scope, and as in clothes ideas of the past are bound to recur. What are called today wedge-heels are of Elizabethan origin,[2] square toes and flat heels, Napoleonic.[3] The exaggeratedly pointed toe of the sixties harks back to the thirteenth century, while the Louis heel, associated with the glamorous lady loves of Louis xv, has reappeared with monotonous regularity since it made its debut in the eighteenth century.

As long as skirts were long, shoes and stockings were inevitably of minor interest. The tango shoe, a Louis-heeled slipper tied on with criss-crossed satin ribbon, was the first to be revealed when

Opposite *The plume-laden hats are delicately ridiculed for* La Gazette
du Bon Ton, *1922.*

The Coronation of King George V and Queen Mary in 1911 brought out a curious rash of fantasy in stockings and shoes: stockings embroidered or painted with lovebirds, storks and spiders; hand-painted and jewel encrusted shoes, here illustrated in a special Coronation supplement of The Sketch.

Roger Vivier's exquisitely embroidered and bead-encrusted shoe recalls the elaboration of 1911, although, fifty years later, in 1961, he has transformed the shape with the subtle elegance of his chisel toe and high 'comma' heel.

the pre-First World War craze for dancing forced an opening in the hobble skirt, and was the first to leave its footprint on our time. By 1908, according to Ada Leverson, 'little boots with cloth tops' like built-in spats were the thing to wear with 'tailor-mades'.[4]

As skirts rose in the twenties, whether their brevity was broken by godets or handkerchief points, softened with fringe or dipped at the back, shoes were inevitably more in evidence. It is sad that they were so dreary with their long pointed vamps, their T-straps and stumpy Louis heels. The thirties brought in a rash of novelties: platform soles and peep-toes, evening sandals, short vamps and high straight heels, ankle-straps and sling-backs, wedge-heels and ankle boots, most of which carried on into the forties, many to be revived at discreet intervals since.

The second item of footwear to make its mark (literally this time) was created in 1951 by a little Parisian bootmaker called Jordan. M.Jordan, striving for an ever slenderer high heel, impossible with wood alone, hit upon the idea of combining wood (for the top half) with steel (for the bottom). His invention turned out to be one of the most ruinous in fashion history, for these heels, taken up and honed to an even finer point by the Italians (hence their name, 'stiletto') pockmarked parquet, dangerously perforated aircraft floors, punctured rugs and carpets. So damaging were these three to four inch spikes that by 1965 the stiletto-heeled could only gain admission to the Louvre Museum by purchasing protective heel-caps. By 1957 the heels became allied to exaggeratedly long, pointed toes, (said to have been the invention of American shoe designer, Beth Levine in 1956) in England these toes, which the Italians had also put on men's shoes, were dubbed 'winklepickers'. As worn by

Overleaf left John Hassall was quick on the draw in 1904 to use the new-fangled horseless carriage for a poster intended to advertise what? The new motor car? Motor fashions? Motoring safety – 'your little boy will love it'? We shall never know.

Overleaf right In 1965 Mary Quant entered the field of underwear and hosiery. Underwear had been approaching a minimum but Mary managed to make the maximum impact on a limited area with red and white stripes and matching 'joy' socks for wearing under jeans. By 1976 the last were seriously threatening the tights market.

women, winklepickers became a chiropodist's dream, and in 1961, worn by the Teddy Boys and hoods, a murderous weapon.

Dangerous, distorting and irrational, shoes so equipped swept the markets of the world at all price levels, and survived despite discouragement. Three happenings contributed to their final defeat. One was Roger Vivier's low (two inch) stacked-leather-heeled, chisel-toed shoe which he first showed for Dior in 1957. By 1961 it was influencing shoes at the top and middle of the price spectrum in England, and by 1963 was in such popular demand that Sir Charles Clore blamed it for the poor showing of his shoe empire still teetering on stiletto heels. The second event was the cold winter of 1962 and the freeze of 1963 when all England took to boots which quickly made their way across the Channel to end up surprisingly on Balenciaga's sacred carpet. The third was Courrège's shorter skirt of 1964 for which he provided calf-high boots with low baby's shoe heels and olive toes; by 1965 the rise of the mini clinched the low heel and blunt toe.

Except in America, inexpensive off-the-peg shoes were pretty awful until after the Second World War. Any resemblance between shoes and feet seemed purely coincidental. An American writing about England in the thirties, said that English shoes must have been made by people who had heard of shoes but never seen one.[5] (That was generally true although there was an exception.) French and Italian cheap shoes were if anything worse. Those who wanted pretty shoes had the choice of having them made or going to an expensive shop. The exception was the London branch of Delman which led with its unique last and its high quality chic. Saks-Fifth Avenue and I. Miller had their devotees too. Paris had Pinet, Italy Ferrogamo. Pre-First Word War fashionables knew of Yanturni and Perugia, but until the fifties shoes were mostly known only by the names of the firms that manufactured them. As with clothes, it took time for the designers to become known in their own right.

The shoe designer to reach the greatest fame is the Frenchman Roger Vivier. Slender, fair, blue-eyed and soft-voiced, Vivier began his career working for Schiaparelli for whom he invented the modern wedge heel. He went on to design for a German shoe firm, then opened on his own and soon attracted a large clientele, among them Delman with whom he signed a contract in 1935. In 1941 he went to Delman in New York where he stayed until 1944. In 1945 M. Boussac the cotton magnate, had persuaded Christian Dior to leave Lelong where he had worked, as he said, for ten happy years and they were engaged in founding the House of Dior. By 1947 when the House opened with the first collection, Dior had concluded a deal with Delman to make Dior shoes under Roger Vivier's direction to be called Dior-Delman. Vivier designed not only the shoes for the collections but special made-to-order shoes for special customers, and special they were: aristocrats like the Comtesse de Paris and the Duchess of Devonshire, actresses like Edwige Feuillère, film stars like Marlene Dietrich, dancers like Margot Fonteyn and Zizi Jeanmaire. His fantastic bead-embroidered shoes soon became collectors' items. In fact all Vivier's shoes, for day or evening, whether from his couture collections, or, later when he set up on his own in 1963 from his ready-to-wear, have been status symbols. Indeed his widely copied shoe of 1966 with its eighteenth-century buckle in mother-of-pearl or tortoiseshell as well as the traditional silver, was the most instantly identified status symbol in footwear. (Actually he had first shown this buckle, which became known in the trade as the 'status' buckle, with a pointed toe and stiletto heel in 1957.)

In 1966, however, the Italian leather firm of Gucci who had recently expanded from handbags and belts into shoes, first for men, then for women, produced a rival status symbol in their reverse calf mocassin, its tongue caught by a gilt bit. The Gucci mocassin was a sophisticated version of the

Right *In 1963 boots came out of the cold into high fashion – and have stayed there ever since: thick and thin, then thick again; knee high, calf high, thigh high and back to knee high; flat heeled and high heeled. These, in navy rubber, were by Russell and Bromley in 1971.*

Above *Perugia is a great shoe name, celebrated in this drawing in* La Gazette du Bon Ton *displaying his T-strapped shoe of 1924/25, as the title says, 'A dear little shoe'.*

Right *Manolo Blahnik came to London in 1970 via the Canary Islands, Geneva (where he went to the University) and Paris (where he studied art). Before opening his Zapata shop in Chelsea he showed his shoes in New York to critical acclaim. He has designed shoes for Saint Laurent and Ungaro in Paris, for Ossie Clark, Zandra Rhodes and Jean Muir in London. This shoe from his 1977/78 Collection is of silk satin, the print designed by Blahnik and executed by Sartor, soled in natural leather.*

pre-war Joyce Casual launched in California – a low wedge-heeled style which swept the world. Its latest incarnation is the city espadrille, its rope sole rising at the back in sixteenth-century style, with patent instead of canvas top, introduced by Givenchy in the early seventies, now also made by Ferrogamo.

Although England has produced no shoe designers of the calibre of Vivier or the American Joyces, Beth Levene or David Evins; Edward Rayne, shoemaker to the Queen, has done his best to divert designing talent into his pretty shops designed by stage designers, Oliver Messel and Carl Toms. The first to introduce Vivier, Evins and Faie Joyce to Great Britain, Mr Rayne was also the first (in 1957) to invite couturiers Hardy Amies, Digby Morton, Norman Hartnell and John Cavanagh to design shoes, and in 1964 to go to Jean Muir, Roger Nelson, Gerald McCann, and Moya Bowler (the only specialist in shoe design) for a young collection. Mary Quant had designed shoes for the Miss Rayne collections of 1961 and 1962 but was soon to produce her own.

The rest of the shoe story is sad. In 1971 Saint Laurent, in his back-to-the-thirties collection. showed black patent pumps with four-inch heels. As bad news is said to travel fast, so does bad fashion, and in England in no time Biba and Mr Freedom were exaggerating these already high heel to the height of tarts' taste. Mary Quant, the Chelsea Cobbler and Biba between them produced footwear, the most ungainly being the thick-soled clogs of 1974 and 1975, which merited Mrs Simon's remarks of thirty years before. It is curious that a nation of women whose feet are not their best points have an apparently irresistible urge to make them as conspicuous as possible.

The footwear that looks like being near permanent is the boot. Ankle boots which had come in toward the end of the Second World War, reappeared in Paris in 1961, but it was the great freeze of 1963 that inspired the whole of Paris to follow the English lead. That year Vivier made thigh-high boots for Saint Laurent. That year Cardin showed high stocking boots. Balenciaga stuck to gumboots. In 1964 Courrèges produced his white baby boots, copied into quick obscurity, but not before an unhappy lot of fat calves had been painfully pinched. By 1966 the *Zhivago* kick had firmly established boots. Now they seem to be a permanent fixture – for as gap-fillers they have become as necessary to the midi as they were to the mini. The only changes have been that the boot top has got heavier and as wrinkled as elephants' legs while the heels have been raised.

Gazing at these footprints on the sands of our time, one cannot help but be struck by the absurdity of some, the ugliness of many, the ingenuity of others. Of them all, Vivier's shoe of the early sixties, with its high slender heel curved into a graceful comma, its toe delicately blunted, remains the most beautiful object – its impracticality recalling Théophile Gautier's dictum that 'nothing is truly beautiful unless it is also useless.'[6]

In the early years of the century stockings were a dazzling rainbow of colour – a fashion which was not to return for over half a century. D.H.Lawrence was riveted by them and lists the colours lovingly over and over again: dark green, grass green, emerald green, canary yellow, bright rose, pink silk, yellow wool, dark grey, thick scarlet, royal blue, and finally 'thick silk stockings, vermilion, cornflower blue and grey, bought in Paris'.[7] How delicious they sound and how sad that

In 1941 The British Board of Trade inaugurated 'Utility' clothes, which had to be made to strict specifications in order to conserve fabric and man-power. To make the idea of regulated clothes more palatable leading couturiers were invited to design them. These are by Sir Norman Hartnell for Berkertex in 1943.

they were soon to be replaced by sober shades enlivened only by embroidered clocks – cotton on cotton, silk on silk. By 1902, Mrs Eric Pritchard was firm that 'a "gay" [sic] stocking may be excusable in some instances, but it is not to be catalogued in the really fashionable hosiery of the hour.'[8] She recommends bronze or black, with self-coloured clocks, prefers lace insertions 'right up the instep and sometimes up the leg' to openwork stockings which she finds 'a bit at a discount'. Still there are those still alive who remember the excitement of a glimpse of purple- or green-stockinged legs as late as 1908 and 1909.[9]

Mrs Pritchard did admit that some women would persist in matching their stockings to their shoes which may explain why white became the unflattering alternative. Sober colours – taupe, gunmetal, brown and the perennial black – held sway for a remarkably long time, forming the backbone of the market until 1938 in America, although long before then flesh and skin tones had been introduced. Geography and the gap between high and mass fashions may account for the differing dates authorities give for the debut of these new shades: Elizabeth Ewing writes that 'flesh-coloured stockings began to be fashionable and popular among all classes in lisle, silk and, above all, the new artificial silk' in 1922.[10] Madge Garland records the appearance of flesh stockings in the Paris collections of 1924,[11] while the American trade magazine *Hosiery and Underwear* in its fiftieth anniversary number (1967) which was made available to me by the Hosiery and Allied Trade Research Association, and from which I have shamelessly culled, reports that same year that Fifth Avenue buyers were noting 'a decline of skin tones and preference for browns, blacks and grays'. Two years later, after a trip to Paris, the head of a well-known Fifth Avenue store made news by bringing back from Paris 'a new idea' – matching hosiery to the customer's skin. It was not however until 1938 that warm, bright degrees of suntan actually took over.

The 'new artificial silk' to which Miss Ewing refers was rayon which had not yet been christened in 1924 when duPont havered between 'Rayon' and 'Glos'. In 1925 rayon (with a small 'r') had pushed glos into the shade.

The hosiery world was a seething arena where fully-fashioned (i.e. shaped) stockings, which had

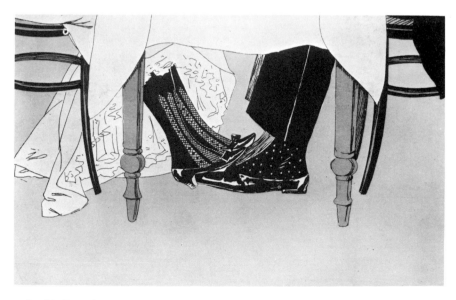

In this French postcard of about 1905 the lady playing footsie beneath the table displays the beguiling charm of lace-inset black silk stockings when set off by frilly white petticoats.

Boldini's delightfully gartered lady in her black silk stockings, stooping to put on the voluminous skirts of the 1900s which will effectively conceal them is demonstrably more alluring than the twenties miss with her flagrantly exposed rolled stockings as depicted in 'La Vie Parisienne' in 1926.

fought for recognition since 1910 and had begun to achieve it in 1921, joined battle with seamless stockings in 1923 ; where silk contested with rayon, the sheerness of the former compensating for its fragility and higher cost ($2.75 to $17.50 a pair). Although the depression brought the price of silk stockings down to seventy-nine cents in 1932, fragility was still a problem and in 1936 Best & Co. advertised 'the ultimate in sheer hosiery' with the slogan, 'They won't wear well, but she'll adore them.'

Both silk and rayon were to meet their Waterloo in 1938 when duPont began experimenting with their new yarn, nylon. Nylon stockings were put tentatively on the market in 1939, just as raw silk prices began to mount. By 1940 nylon had won its war, somewhat ahead of the real one, and in 1941 its victory had become a boom, a short-lived one for 7 December and Pearl Harbor brought America into the War. The next year the Government took over all nylon for military purposes, and it became patriotic to wear rayon, which in its turn was to become rationed for civilian use in 1943. 'Buyers', reported *Hosiery and Underwear*, 'have little on the shelf.' This shortage was painfully familiar to women in Great Britain and on the Continent. The American troops who had been lucky or clever enough to equip themselves with a few pairs of nylons before the ban, found them as good as, if not better, than currency when they were sent abroad. Considering their rarity and their desirability, it is to America's credit that a black market in nylons did not spring up until 1945 when

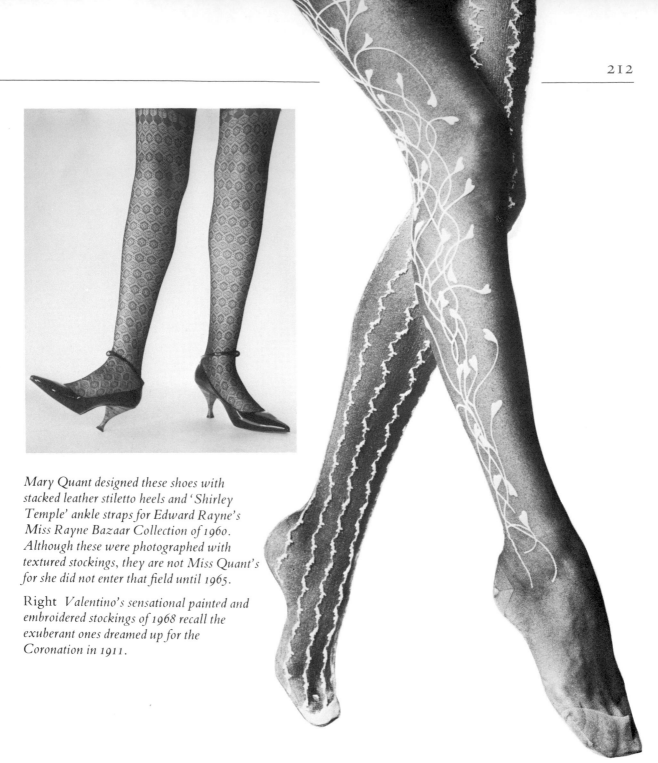

Mary Quant designed these shoes with stacked leather stiletto heels and 'Shirley Temple' ankle straps for Edward Rayne's Miss Rayne Bazaar Collection of 1960. Although these were photographed with textured stockings, they are not Miss Quant's for she did not enter that field until 1965.

Right *Valentino's sensational painted and embroidered stockings of 1968 recall the exuberant ones dreamed up for the Coronation in 1911.*

this precious commodity sold for ten or twelve dollars a pair. By 1946 the industry reluctantly admitted that nylon had come to stay.

Nylon was the second great revolution in legwear. Sheerness as with silk and rayon was the ideal, and 'denier', a technical word defined by the *Oxford Concise Dictionary* as 'a unit of weight by which silk or rayon yarn is weighed' (and of course nylon yarn as well) came into fashion language just as 'thread' and 'gauge' had with silk.

In 1944 teenagers had made ankle socks into a badge for bobby soxers. In the late fifties black or white stockings proclaimed the Beat Generation. In Paris the Couture was infiltrating the stocking scene. By and large they were content to lend the lustre of their names and made no great innovations, although Jackques Fath in 1956 did add deep lace tops. As the problem of keeping up such fragile wisps was left unsolved, they were probably intended only for the purpose they achieved – publicity.

Hosiery seemed to amble along until 1960. That year in the United States seamless stockings which had been fighting to upgrade themselves finally made it, and ended the dominance of the seamed variety. Other innovations were revivals of past American novelties which suddenly exploded in England in 1962. There were the seamless stockings, now called 'seam-free', stretch stockings (new in 1955) now in crepe, nylon or Helanca, knee socks (new in 1954), tights (new in 1958), a variety of textures (new in 1959), weaves reviving the meshes of the thirties – diamond mesh, lace mesh, lattice mesh, fish net – a hark back to even earlier days with fancy rib knits, and a full spectrum of colour (in England, Wolsey was offering a range of ten). This focus on legs changed the whole hosiery scene. Of these excitements tights turned out to be the third revolution, relegating stockings – and girdles – to a poor second place.

All this was fun, but there was more fun to come. In 1962 Balenciaga had introduced black tights, harlequin patterned in lozenges of bright colours. Tights and stockings became so lively, and as skirts rose, so conspicuous that *The Sunday Times* magazine reported in 1963 that legs had never had it so good. Every leg that wasn't hidden by a boot flashed a new message. D.H. Lawrence would have loved it. The stocking manufacturers certainly did, for 1963 was only the beginning. Those poor millionaires, having gone about as far as they could go with built-in obsolescence, as far towards sheerness as machines could take them, had been reduced to extolling new shades of beige and new shapes of heels. Under auspices so eminently distinguished as Balenciaga, anything went: mad patterns, wild stripes, vivid colours, in crochet or heavy rib knit as well as nylon. England was a medley of colours; the Italians brought back white; Paris brought back black; Valentino brought back clocks. In 1964 John Bates had shown stockings scattered with appliqué rose petals. In 1966 Mary Quant was making white tights patterned in her daisy logo. In 1968 Valentino was showing lace-encrusted stockings (shades of Mrs Pritchard), stockings embroidered in feathers, embossed in chains, flocked with flower fronds. In 1971 Saint Laurent unsuccessfully tried to bring back seams.

The curtain had gone up on legs with the mini; it came down with the midi – and the leg kick was over. Actually, it was not just the midi; it was the combination of long skirts and boots and the alternate and inevitable jeans which pulled the market in tights in Britain alone down from fifty-two million dozen pairs in 1972 to twenty-one million dozen in the first six months of 1976. The decline in the hosiery market throughout Europe has been serious enough to become a concern of the EEC which in 1976 formulated a policy to try to cope with the over-production of women's stockings and tights. The most conspicuous result in Britain was the closure by Courtauld's, one of the major fibre companies, of two factories. Philosophically, Courtauld's bow to the power of fashion which having produced a lively market unwittingly reduced it.

Beneath

The story of underwear in the twentieth century is a tale of a disappearing act. In the Edwardian years it had played, if not a star part, at least a strong supporting role. Dozens and dozens of chemises, corset covers, camisoles, drawers, petticoats and nightdresses plus the Iron Maiden corsets were the mainstays of every lady's wardrobe. To conceal the hair until it was properly dressed, there were adorably becoming so-called 'boudoir' caps (eventually, alas, to become the bedraggled symbol of slatternly housewives) and little *peignoirs* to wear while the hair was being combed. All of this finery was made by hand in fine lawn, batiste, silk and even flannel. Flannel petticoats were scalloped and

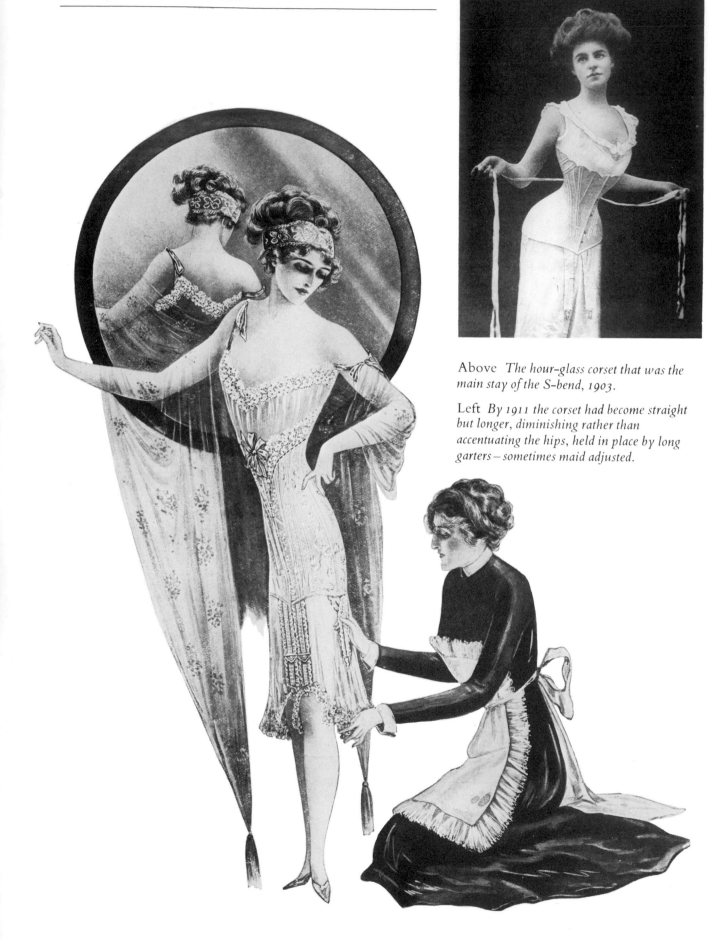

Above *The hour-glass corset that was the main stay of the S-bend, 1903.*

Left *By 1911 the corset had become straight but longer, diminishing rather than accentuating the hips, held in place by long garters – sometimes maid adjusted.*

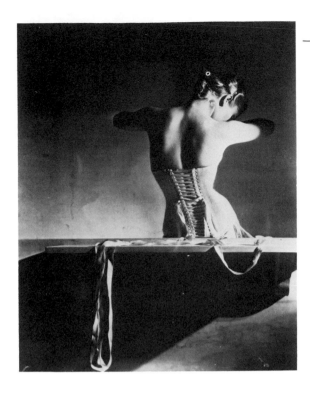

In 1959 Mainbocher attempted to revive the hourglass corset, its longer laces inspiring Horst P. Horst to parody Dali's limp watches in his 'Persistence of Memory' painted in 1931 and given to the Museum of Modern Art in New York in 1934. It has been suggested that Mainbocher's corset was the forerunner of Dior's guepière. It was in time, but bore no relation to Dior's tiny waist-pincher.

eyelet-embroidered, the others frilled and pin-tucked, exquisitely monogrammed, or trimmed with Binche or Valenciennes lace (the latter known familiarly as 'Val') for edging and insertions threaded with the narrowest pale pink or blue satin ribbon. The effect of these frothy frills glimpsed when the covering skirts were gracefully gathered to one side while mounting steps or crossing streets, their snowy whiteness accentuated by black silk stockings, was titillating, and, when skirts were lifted even higher by the can-can dancers, positively electrifying.

But underwear was not limited strictly to white, as this lyric of 1907 saucily testifies:

> I've a little pink petty from Peter
> And a little blue petty from John
> And I've one green and yellow
> From some other fellow
> And one that I haven't got on.
> I've one made of lovely red flannel
> That came from an Amsterdam store
> But the point that I'm at
> Is that underneath that
> Well, I haven't got on any more.

Even black was permitted, though not recommended, for it was considered a bit exotic.

After the demise of the terrifying whale-boned, steel-busked corset, sometimes as long as two feet at the back, in favour of the pull-on girdle, lingerie, although reduced in quantity to a slip and matching wide-legged panties (still called French panties and now being revived) was equally feminine in silk or satin, usually peach or pink (black was still considered naughty) bordered and appliquéd in ecru Alençon lace. Negligées were of satin, maribou- or ostrich-trimmed. They, like the slips and nightdresses, reflected the influence of Vionnet in their bias clinging cut. These were the undergarments of the twenties, to be replaced by the variously-named step-in, cami-knicker or teddy – a single garment which doubled as slip and panty.

As contradiction is the soul of fashion, while bodies were left as free as short skirts and scanties could make them, bosoms were ruthlessly flattened. Bras existed to minimize rather than to accentuate; the most popular one in America was called the 'Boyshform', while in England some desperate young things bandaged themselves with wide ribbon. This lunatic suppression did actual harm and was perhaps even more deleterious than the tight lacing of earlier years.

Bosoms gradualy reasserted themselves, greatly assisted by Hollywood where breastworks were considered a measure of talent. Bosoms, if not in, were certainly out. The motto of the makers of a pre-Hughes bra was 'What God has forgotten, we fill with cotton.' The almost lethal bosoms such contraptions produced were cariacatured in *The New Yorker* magazine when the famous 'little king', having invited one of these well-endowed damsels to dance, found at the end that he had acquired two cone-shaped holes in his chest.

By the mid fifties the American woman was so inflexibly curved that a French fashion photographer was moved to say 'I think they put on their dresses, and then are blown up by bicycle pumps.' These bras killed the British Kestos which relied only on clever seaming to achieve the desired shape, and they in turn were killed by the trend towards nudity which started in 1964, carried to absurdity by Californian Rudi Gernreich's topless swim suit, but more soberly giving birth to the body stocking and the same Mr Gernreich's no-bra bra. The days when Hollywood measured talent

Above *In 1905/6 Kees van Dongen foreshadowed the teddy of the twenties in this painting of what was then called a chemise.*

Right *In 1977 Janet Reger echoes the van Dongen chemise in her revival of the teddy.*

By 1965 Rudi Gernreich had launched the 'no-bra' bra, totally transparent. In 1968, moving toward modesty, Emmanuelle Khanh designed this white tulle bra, with its strategically placed white lace flowers, for Erys.

by projection were over. By 1968 when Yves Saint Laurent showed his totally transparent shirt not even no-bra bras were worn. Just no bras at all.

Petticoats which had disappeared with the advent of Poiret's slim woman, were brought back in 1947 by Christian Dior made of stiffened nylon net to hold out the billowing skirts of his New Look. They burgeoned on into the fifties under the puffy skirts worn for barn dancing, and to sustain the full, mid-calf length skirts of the short evening dress. Called 'ballerina', these skirts were actually mid-calf, an unbecoming length long since abandoned by the ballet.

The greatest change in underwear had come in the fifties with the imaginative and inventive use of man-made fibres in which America's Sylvia Pedlar was a pioneer. Underwear no longer needed to be hand-made to be pretty. There was a vast variety of drip-dry fabrics; there was nylon lace, nylon ribbon, as well as permanent pleats. But underwear continued to shrink. The influence of the film *Baby Doll* in 1966 reduced nightgowns to babydoll brevity. By the sixties the trend to nudity along with Women's Lib finally restored a natural shape and underpinnings dwindled to a minute, often transparent bra and equally minute briefs – in fact underwear for a weekend nowadays can fit into a pocket without altering its shape a whit. From the teens to the grave these two items plus a pair of tights compose the great undress. It may be cheap, some may find it sexy, but no one can say it's seductive.

11
Fashion in Movement

'Faster, faster' cried the Red Queen: in *Alice Through the Looking Glass*, published in 1898, Lewis Carroll gave Alice a foretaste of the pattern of the years that lay ahead. The combustion engine ushered in the age of speed, but it was just one aspect of a disease which rapidly became epidemic. Motoring moved on from unhurried touring with its pleasures of discovery and exploration to become simply the means of getting from here to there in the shortest time on anonymous autobahns and speedways. Leisurely ocean crossings have been abandoned for streaking through the skies stuffed into super-sonic aircraft. Sport is no longer an amateur pastime; it is fast, strenuous, competitive and professional. Allied to this acceleration of speed and intensity has been an increase of comfort in both passive and active recreation. Clothes for movement, as in other areas of fashion,

The Talmadge sisters, Constance (left) and Norma (right) in the mid-twenties at the height of their film fame posed in their one-piece bathing dresses at Norma's Santa Monica beach house. Talkies brought Norma Talmadge's career to a close in 1930. After seeing the reviews, Constance, who had already retired, telegraphed her, 'Leave them while you're looking good . . .'.

*Although the motor car was the latest mode of transport in 1905, bicycling was
still fun. The gentlemen here are sensibly clad in knickbockers and caps; the
ladies are still in hampering skirts, the one on the left in a proper hat,
the one on the right sensibly wearing her motoring cap and veil.*

have diminished, and, curiously, the market for sportswear has expanded as the amount of coverage
has decreased.

The sheer ruggedness of early motoring is hard to believe in these days of cars that are heated or
air-conditioned, of cars that start with a turn of an ignition key, of cars with spare wheels.

> . . . He'd have to get un-der,
> Get out and get un-der
> To fix his little machine . . .

was not only a topical song in 1914 but a true picture of those early days of crank starters and easily-
punctured tyres that had to be blown up by tyre pumps. Open to the elements, at best with only
draughty isinglass screens to ward off rain or snow, motoring imposed protective clothing on the
early aficionados. As seen by Sir Osbert Sitwell, ladies arrayed for winter motoring, 'were clad in
caps and furs and capes and mufflers and many veils and thick fur gloves as though equipped for
arctic exploration.'[1] In summer Ada Leverson saw them 'in little "cottage bonnets", blue motor
veils and large white coats with high collars.'[2] The goggles had a peculiarly home-made look with
their heavy rims and mica lenses, held on to the head by elastic bands. As for the veils they ranged
from the becoming to the dotty, if one goes by advertisements of the time. These give the impression
of fevered imaginations at work. Who can have worn Burberry's veil with a mica window or their
'adjustable' veil which when closed made the wearer look like a bird cage covered for the night,
except few bird-cage covers are tied below in winsome bows, ensuring, one would have thought,

ultimate suffocation? As cars improved in passenger comfort, special clothes became unnecessary. Except for the short car coat, it is hard to think of any contemporary fashion specifically designed for motoring.

Similarly, in the early daredevil days of flying in open cockpits of biplanes, helmets and goggles were essential, and pants useful for scrambling up and in, but as air travel became commonplace, and as the airlines compete with each other in providing greater creature comforts, the main effect on fashion has been to stimulate the demand for drip-dry and uncrushable clothes (and for light-weight luggage to pack them in). The habit, of the sixties, of flying in trouser suits is an inscrutable one, given the constricting accommodation of aircraft lavatories.

The noble days of ocean liners, of huge Vuitton steamer trunks and 'wanted in cabin' stickers, produced only one uniform: the oatmeal tweed coat, collared and faced in lynx, as necessary as a first

Left Ski-ing in 1910 was sporting though skirted, as outfitted by Dickens and Jones. The 'club' cap, says the advertisement, 'can be worn as a Helmet completely covering the head and neck'. For 2s 11d one couldn't expect to see.

Below Nearly sixty years on, in 1969, ski-ing clothes had become pretty as well as practical.

class ticket. Yachting inspired Chanel to take over sailors' bell-bottomed pants as more practical and decent than skirts for negotiating the accommodation ladder of a ducal yacht. Thus a lasting fashion was started.

As the pioneer motoring days arouse stupefied admiration, the early athletes arouse admiring stupefaction. What iron determination they must have had even to contemplate playing, not only croquet, but tennis and golf, bundled up in long skirts and hampered by large elaborate hats.

Burberry's, who issued their first catalogue of sports equipment in 1904, did suggest for golf a sort of tam o'shanter – a salute, no doubt, to the the 'Royal and Ancient' but it could equally well have been a Dutch bonnet for the encyclopaedia suggests that the game was played in Holland before it was introduced in to Scotland. (Burberry more usefully also devised for golfing ladies an adjustable skirt which could be hiked up to clear the green.) Even in 1910 Miss Coles played tennis in a straw boater, and Suzanne Lenglen wore a hat for play until she substituted her famous bandeau in 1919. Cyclists wore hats, so did skiers. Fedoras or boaters were worn with bloomers by smart French cyclists, giving the Allés de Vélos in the Bois de Boulogne a delightfully comic air as recorded by artist Jean Beraud in 1900. Although bloomers immortalized the name of dress reformer, Amelia Bloomer, they did not really catch on in England where skirts (sometimes divided) were preferred, worn with a trim tailored jacket. Even in Mrs Bloomer's native America her namesakes were soon relegated to school gymnasiums. For grown-ups, the 'tailor-made' and the bicycle symbolized a new freedom for women, although out shooting in her Norfolk jacket and pheasant-feathered hat, the New Woman's skirt still swept the moors.

Skiers in St Moritz in 1926 wore modish town hats with bulky sweaters or short fur coats over riding breeches and heavy knee socks. In 1923 in England Aquascutum had suggested a military look for the slopes with puttees and a neat, long jacket with strapped cuffs and pouch pockets. As, beginning in 1960, skiing became more widely popular, no longer limited to the smart mountain resorts, ski wear became the object of concentrated attention. After the Second World War, it had gained, thermally speaking, from the experiments of the Royal Air Force in clothing to protect their pilots and crews against the cold. These wind-cheaters, developed from the RAF flying jackets of nylon stuffed with nylon fibre, were bulky. The adoption of the Eskimo's anorak or parka, in 1952, the outside fabric quilted, was probably a watershed, figuratively as well as literally. A later alternative to the nylon fibre filling is down, also bulky, but the latest, an aluminium lining as used by the astronauts, is not only light in weight, but acts as an air-conditioner against both heat and cold. The first truly chic skiing outfit was the one Emilio Pucci designed for himself just after the war which caught photographer Toni Frissell's eye and 'schussed' him into a career in fashion.

Bathing – which was really just taking a dip for which skirted bathing dresses were worn – eventually gave way to swimming. In 1900 Annette Kellerman, the aquatic star, introduced a one-piece swimsuit but it did not replace the dainty, soggy dresses until ten years later. The original Annette Kellerman was a desperately unbecoming garment. Still it led the way to the minimal swimwear of today. A truly appalling innovation was dreamed up by the French in the sixties – swimsuits with built-in bras of concrete intransigence. Designed to help, they succeeded in hindering, coming as they did in arbitrary sizes, rarely congruent to the anatomy beneath. By contrast, the bikini which changed the view on beaches throughout the world is a challenge to the wearer's personal equipment. The bikini was launched in Paris by a little known designer called Louis Reard in 1946, four days after the atomic explosion at Bikini Atoll. M.Reard explained that for him the name symbolised 'the ultimate'.[3] M.Reard's extraordinary tastelessness has met its just

Left *In 1910 bathing dresses were really dresses, worn complete with shoes and hats.*

Below *In 1976 the bathing dress had shrunk to near invisibility, although probably few would go as far as this minimal covering designed by Marielle Bolier.*

desert, for most people think the minimal garments got their name from Bikini Beach. The bikini did not appear in Great Britain until 1950 and it was not until 1959 that it became a top seller. Unfortunately not all of its wearers seem to realise that it is better to conceal what cannot be controlled. Although the rubber skin diving suit is a total cover-up, it can be equally revealing.

By and large the direction has been toward freedom of movement, as well as exposure. Golf is played in whatever are the most comfortable and practical clothes, depending on personal taste. Tennis, on the other hand, perhaps because of Forest Hills, Wimbledon *et al.*, has enjoyed a special limelight, and ever since Mlle Lenglen tennis clothes have been news. From her mid-calf pleats by Patou in 1919 to Alice Marble's shorts, glimpsed under her button-through dress, in 1933, to Christine Evert's abbreviated neatness of today, each step along the way to brevity has been chronicled in the Press. The Lenglen mid-calf length was for starters. Ten years before, in 1909, Mrs

Opposite left *Miss Camille Clifford, when she wasn't being the Gibson Girl, was an accomplished equestrienne. Here she wears the proper riding habit of about 1905, substituting a bowler hat for the formal silk topper.*

Opposite right *In 1961 riding had by-passed the formality of Hyde Park for the ease of the Western ranch-style – cotton shirt and cowboy pants, rodeo boots and Stetson.*

Above *Suzanne Lenglen playing at Cannes in 1920 was elegantly gowned by Patou. The skirt seems a fairly practical length above her white stockings and shoes, but those long sleeves . . . No wonder she wore her 'headache band'. Although retaining the bandeau, she was soon to appear on the court in a sleeveless jumper, setting a pattern followed today.*

Right *Chris Evert, in 1972, plays barelegged, as well as bare-armed, in a shift brief enough to show a glimpse of lace panties, like those by Teddy Tinling which made Gussy Moran famous in 1948.*

Sterry had worn what looks like a nurse's uniform with black stockings and black ankle-tied shoes just showing beneath; in 1910 Miss Coles' long skirt revealed white stockings and shoes as did Mlle Lenglen's shorter one. Today it's bare legs and ankle socks or sun-tan tights.

The once demure skating dress – fitted basque jacket, long graceful skirt, flattering fur trim, tiny, flirtatious muff, gliding to the strains of *Les Patineurs* – gained its impetus toward brevity from the films. When Sonja Henie became Hollywood's skating star in 1939 she wore skirts lifted to what was later to become known as mini height.

It was not films but the First World War that changed the look of formal riding clothes. The super-elegant habit in black melton, the perfectly fitting coat collared in black velvet, the apron skirt

gracefully masking the breeches, the white stock and the shining top hat – have vanished along with the side saddle, to be seen now at only a few exclusive hunts in England and America. After the War which had brought a new freedom to women, riding breeches came out into the open as their owners preferred to ride astride. Soon the breeches were exchanged for jodhpurs which eliminated the need for polished riding boots, the formal coat was replaced by a hacking jacket, while the neat man-tailored shirt and four-in-hand tie gave way in due course to the poloneck sweater. So far what is left of Rotten Row hasn't seen many jeans but they are acceptable in the land of ranches and rodeos.

With the delightful illogicality which is the essence of fashion, as tennis and swimwear contract, as ski clothes become ever more streamlined, and as riding pants are about to be 'modified' still further, the craze for jogging has brought in the shapeless, covered-up track suit – loose, drawstring-tied top and baggy pants, but no longer the dingy institutional grey, a rainbow of colours for those that want them.

But really good riding kit should be made to order. Clothes for most other recreations make the fortunes of the sports manufacturers, especially in America. Other exceptions are the social sporting events – Ascot, Longchamps, the Kentucky Derby and the like still act as showcases for expensive clothes. One activity perhaps not to be catalogued as sport but ever gaining popularity is gardening. It is said that Mrs Paul Mellon's gardening aprons are made for her by Givenchy. The beautiful ex-Countess Bismarck wore for gardening, shirts and shorts by Balenciaga in cinnamon colour to match her hair and the walls of her Capri villa. In general, however, this is one area that the bright boys seem to have overlooked.

12

Wars, Revolution and Turbulence

The year 1900, the dawn of the new century, also saw the celebrations that marked the relief of Mafeking. From then on it is hard to find a time or place where there is no fighting.

Wars have only a tangential effect on fashion; they change the pattern of life, and fashion reflects that change. In the First World War, it was as if a tidily completed jigsaw puzzle had been blown apart, and when it was put together there were some pieces that were forever missing. The horror of its terrible cost in human life is still haunting, reawakened by plays like *Oh! What a Lovely War*, by revivals like *Journey's End* and by the recent flood of biographies of the period. The reaction to the slaughter of a generation shaped the twenties. It was said that nothing was the same after the First World War; it was even more true of the next one. With its new and formidable machines of destruction it left indelible scars on the fabric of the countries involved as well as on the lives of those who survived, and cast the shadow of nuclear warfare over the world. The war in Vietnam,

In 1942 women were really in the War. Manning anti-aircraft guns meant taking no shelter during air raids. Still, the ATS (Auxiliary Territorial Service) cocked their snooks at bombs and their tin hats at a becoming angle.

remote though it may have seemed to Europe at the time is the third upheaval to dislocate conventional thinking and destroy accepted axioms. Quentin Bell[1] suggests that revolutions influence fashion more than wars. In revolutions the mode of dress becomes a badge of political affiliation. The Puritans proclaimed their convictions which culminated in the Revolution of 1642 by a conscious emphasis in their clothes on modesty, sobriety and simplicity in contrast to what they considered the extravagance, elaboration and impropriety of the Cavaliers. After the French Revolution of 1789 any ostentation with its implication of wealth and privilege was fraught with danger. The result of this restraint was anything but puritanical. Infected with what James Laver called 'the licentious notions of the Directoire',[2] women stressed only too literally the outward and visible signs of their loyalty to the new Republic by wearing transparent versions of the costumes of ancient Greece on whose ideal of democracy the Republic was supposedly based, achieving an acme of indecent exposure not to be seen again until the middle 1960s.

'Congleton War-Working Party' painted by John B.Gibbs now in the Imperial War Museum gives a strangely formal impression of these splendid volunteer workers cutting out and sewing away in their neat hats and tidy coats and skirts.

This still from a wartime film made in 1942 might be an illustration for Miss Do and Miss Don't. After several distressing accidents the Government had urged women in factories to bind their hair to avoid the risk to being scalped if their locks became entangled in the machinery. Although Miss Patricia Roc, playing the heroine, has tucked her hair back into the fashionable and, protective, snood, her curly fringe constituted a possible danger. The girl on the right with her hair in a bandanna would have been the Government's pin-up girl.

The so-called bloodless revolution which has been steadily eroding the social structure of Great Britain with its sweeping re-distribution of wealth and the concomitant creation of a classless society has powerfully affected every aspect of life – including inevitably fashion. The universal addiction to jeans – basically a work garment – cannot be explained entirely by their alleged comfort and convenience.

The Great War, as the First World War is still called, accelerated the advance of female emancipation, but in England women did not gain the vote until 1928, trailing their American counterparts by eight years. Women of all backgrounds played their part in the War effort. They joined the VAD and served as volunteer nurses in hospitals; they drove ambulances and vans, enlisted in the services, worked in munitions factories, went on the land. The munition workers became the new rich. Well-paid by the standards of the time, for many of them it was the first time they had had the opportunity and means to discover fashion, although at work they wore protective baggy boiler suits. The only uniform which was, however, to have a positive effect on the dress of the future was that of the 'land girls', then called 'women-on-the-land', who wore breeches and boots. A genealogical family tree can be drawn from these breeches to the omnipresent trousers of today. One unexpected result of what she described as 'the unaccustomed freedom of breeches and gaiters' was felt by Vita Sackville-West who had helped to organize the Women's Land Army and whose history she wrote. Miss Sackville-West recorded that on wearing them for the first time 'everything changed suddenly – changed far more than I foresaw at the time; changed my whole life'.[3] It was they which awakened her to her 'duality' and inspired her to dress as a boy and pursue her love affairs with her own sex. There is, however, no evidence that her reaction to what was not a very attractive uniform was a general one.

This strange War, near enough for soldiers to go back and forth to the Front, did not discourage fashion. Advertisements continued to feature Paris fashions, although in 1918 according to James Laver an attempt was made to introduce a 'National Standard Dress',[4] a forerunner of the utility clothes of the Second World War. The aim was to make the soldiers' leaves happy ones, and after a day at war work as Alison Settle put it 'the tunic dresses still moved to syncopated music . . .'[5] Actually these tunic dresses soon lost their hobble skirts, by 1915 they had elongated themselves and women found their feet.

The most important effect of the War was on the clothing industry itself which was more or less commandeered by the Government to produce the uniforms for the Forces. This resulted in a vast improvement in its machinery and methods of production, and a new recognition of its importance. By 1915 the first step toward its organization came with the setting up of the Tailors and Garment Workers Union, a union organized on an industrial instead of a craft basis. The modern needle trade is the child of that War.[6]

In Paris, Poiret had closed his salon and joined his regiment; Doeuillet had joined the volunteers, but Madame Cheruit decided to continue to keep open. 'Women must have clothes, war or no war' she is quoted as saying, 'and those who make them must have a way of earning their living.' Edith Wharton living in Paris was also concerned with unemployment in this luxury trade. She found that it had become fashionable in the Faubourg to sew for the troops. Unfortunately the zeal of these smart ladies was putting real seamstresses, who had no other means of subsistence, out of work. With her accustomed energy Mrs Wharton, within a fortnight of the outbreak of War, had established a workroom which eventually employed up to a hundred women at a time. Besides pay, they were given free lunch, medical care, and, in winter, an allowance of coal. Mrs Wharton raised the funds and obtained orders for the lingerie, dresses, handkerchiefs and children's clothes which her workers were turning out through her network of friends in France and America.

The War did not really come home to Americans until the sinking of the *Lusitania* brought their country into the conflict. Before that one of the main concerns of those who dealt in fashion was the fate of the Paris Couture, both as a fount of inspiration and the stuff from which fashion pages are made. To Edna Woolman Chase, editor of *Vogue*, it was an inexpressible relief to find 'that after the first frightening months the French Couture would resume virtually normal production and that throughout the War, *Vogue* would be able to publish Paris models . . .' Indigenous talent had to await recognition until the next war. As in England, throughout the First World War, American fashion remained Paris-orientated.

The air raids of the Second World War brought the whole population of England into the firing line. For the first time women were actually called up into the services or directed into some other form of war work. The field was vast, for the blitz opened up new areas where help was needed. Besides the to-be-expected ones – the land, hospitals, factories – there were jobs as air raid wardens, fire watchers, ambulance drivers. Women replaced men in offices, penetrated the masculine preserves of government ministries. Others ran canteens or joined Lady Reading's Women's Voluntary Services. Those in uniform were lucky, for the Government in this war was successful in controlling fashion and in 1941 brought in clothes rationing. A thin book of coupons whose meagre contents had to cover all the essentials of a wardrobe, except hats, was issued twice a year. The introduction that same year of 'Utility' (quickly dubbed 'Futility') clothes regimented the clothing industry, for specifications were tightly drawn. To conserve fabric, width, length and even pleats were controlled, to conserve man-power,trimmings were reduced. It would be nice to be able to say that the designers whom the Government called in to produce prototypes were inspired by the restrictions to a new concept of clothes; the fact is that they simply perpetuated more skimpily the Schiaparelli silhouette – squared, coathanger shoulders, nipped-in waists, narrow skirts – that had prevailed in 1939. Fashion everywhere was frozen in this outline until 1947 when Christian Dior's New Look electrified a fashion-starved world.

The two most enduring fashions that came out of the War in Britain were due to necessity rather than design. Because of the cold – bomb-blasted windows were often just papered over – women lived in trousers or boiler suits. Because keeping hair tidy was a problem – bombs could cut off water supply or an air raid siren could sound in the middle of a shampoo and set sending the whole hair shop to shelter – women covered their heads in a variety of different ways with kerchiefs. Actually this latter was encouraged for factory workers by the Government for the prevailing hair style with its frizzy fringe carried with it the danger of being scalped.

Jewellery was also a casualty of the War as many of the craftsmen turned their special skills from creating exquisite baubles to the production of high precision tools – gauges, micrometers, gun aligning instruments, aircraft parts. They, especially the watchmakers, played such a vital part in the development of radar and the automatic pilot for aircraft that at the urging of the austere Sir Stafford Cripps after the War the Government gave one million pounds to back the peacetime recovery of the jewellery trade.

The fall of France isolated America as well as Great Britain from Paris. Chanel and Schiaparelli closed their doors. Mainbocher returned to his native soil as did Molyneux to his. The conquerors were deflected from their plan to transport the remaining Couture Houses bodily to Berlin or Vienna by Lucien Lelong, then president of the Chambre Syndicale de la Couture Parisienne, and

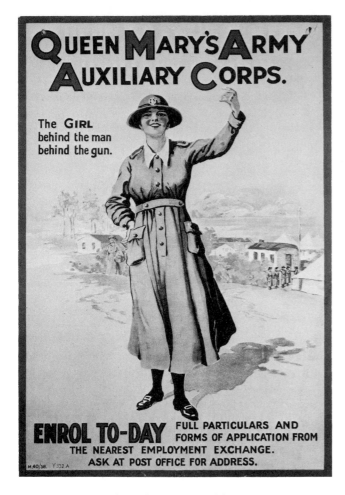

Women's role in the First World War was seen differently in Great Britain and the United States. This war was the first in which women were called to the colours, but for Queen Mary's Army Auxiliary Corps (formed in 1918) in their distressingly unbecoming uniforms, although they can be seen drilling in the background, they were, as this recruiting poster says, "behind the man behind the gun", and presumably behind the Front. That same year the poster for The Motor Corps of America by illustrator Howard Chandler Christy shows a much more martially uniformed young woman actually shouldering a somewhat ambiguous weapon and the implication is a call to arms.

although their clients were fraus and frauleins, the Couture was able to survive even under the dark shadow of Occupation. Parisian women overcame their shortages with characteristic gaiety creating a fashion of defiance: towering turbans at one end, clogs with thick wooden soles at the other.

In America, first nylon (in 1942) and then rayon (in 1943) went to War, but the Government waited until 1943 to impose price controls and restrictions on use of fabric and superfluous trimming. American designers responded to the restrictions with more ingenuity than their British opposite numbers, and showed themselves cleverer at reheating Paris left-overs. Although there were gestures, in order to step up recruitment, toward making the uniforms of the British women's services more becoming, the slickly designed and tailored uniforms of the American women's services were a source of envy and admiration. Mainbocher's uniforms for the WAVES may have been one of the reasons why most of the upper crust young Americans tried to get on the high seas. At home, cut off abruptly from Paris, America was forced to find its own designers. Decentralization of production brought Dallas and Los Angeles to enrich the fashion scene, previously dominated by New York. This mining of native ore brought rich returns.

Looking back, the comparatively quiet Aldermaston March (a Ban the Bomb walk from Aldermaston in Berkshire to London [about forty-eight miles] organized by the Campaign for

*As a gesture of defiance during the Occupation, Parisiennes denied the
amenities of milliners and couturiers devised towering turbans of whatever
fabrics they could lay their hands on, achieving a puzzling (to the Germans)
smartness; this one decorated the Christmas cover of* La Femme Chic *in 1945.*

The members of the Women's Land Army looked not much different in the Second World War than they did in the First, although slacks had replaced the exciting breeches and puttees for jobs like mucking out the pigs.

Nuclear Disarmament) in 1958 was the genesis of the demonstrations of protest that were to erupt regularly throughout the next decade and more. The marchers, mostly in ponchos, duffle-coats and jeans with prams or papoose slings filled as accessories, had not yet devised a uniform. The student 'demos' in Paris that began in 1963 eventually made an impact on Yves Saint Laurent who in his winter collection of 1968 used the protest indenti-kit Red Indian headband which along with Red Indian fringes became the badge of those participating in anti-Vietnam demonstrations. Both headbands and suede fringes continued to turn up in the Paris Haute Couture collections – one complete with Indian bead embroidery making its appearance on Louis Féraud's runway in 1970.

The classless society in Britain began to manifest itself in fashion in 1959 when the catch phrase was 'You can't tell the deb from the shop girl'. By the time the mini reached its height and when jeans took over this was indeed all too true. What's more one could not tell a long-haired girl from a long-haired boy. There were a mass of amusing and inexpensive clothes, as the ready-to-wear adjusted to the situation, but as in everything else, this was a process of levelling down rather than upgrading. The truth is that as taxes mount for the deb-type families, wages rise for the shop girl. The spiralling cost of labour is changing the pattern of retail trade. More pay means less staff, and middle market shoppers may have to adjust themselves to the impersonal self-service of the hypermarket sort instead of the individual attention of salespeople.

The sharp decline of the pound, however, has opened new markets in London. Not only for the oil-rich countries but as far as Germany, from where the inhabitants come in bus loads, London has become a shopping centre. This has been a bonanza for the top end of the ready-to-wear which can now produce clothes of higher cost and quality than ever before.

Epilogue

As I began this book with a quotation from Lord Melbourne it is fitting (and irresistible) that I should end it with another. 'Human affairs,' he said, '... never stand still ... they are always moving, forward, backward, laterally, up, down, straight, crooked, in some direction or other.' If for 'human affairs' you read 'fashion', you will find it equally true. Before the First World War, fashion, in the wake of Poiret moved sharply forward. In the twenties fashion moved up and down as skirts rose and fell, but Vionnet and Chanel carried on the forward thrust, as did Schiaparelli in the thirties. The New Look of 1947, which introduced Christian Dior as one of the greatest designers of the century, could be considered a step back, for after nearly forty years of corsetless freedom Dior restored constriction with his *guepières*, his architecturally constructed clothes and multiple petticoats. Dior had found his inspiration in the peasant dress of his native Normandy, but so adroitly did he assimilate its essential character that the result was completely contemporary with no hint of costume or fancy dress.

   In the fifties the main direction under Balenciaga's influence was toward shapelessness, culminating in the Sack and Saint Laurent's Trapeze. Anarchy was a word often used for the sixties as fashion swung wildly from one extreme to another. Jet travel brought the most remote countries

Epilogue

Below *At the opening of the exhibition, 'The Glory of Russian Costume' arranged by Diana Vreeland at the Metropolitan Museum of Art in New York, Mrs Onassis made news in her strapless dress by Mary McFadden, its two-tiered pleats reminiscent in 1976 of the Fortuny dresses of the early years of the century.*

Above *As Paris lifted skirts to new heights, so did London. In his 1977 collection Bill Gibb, one of Great Britain's strongest and most inventive talents, returned to his native Scotland for a way few native Scots would probably dress. With ingenuity and wit he has interpreted traditional Scottish themes in a completely contemporary idiom, transforming the kilt into the skirt of a brief, kimona-sleeved jacket, outlined in silver braid, the neck embroidered in the roses of England and the thistles of Scotland. From one shoulder drops his version of the plaid, the ends pleated. The feather jutting from hairdresser Leonard's tight little chignon recalls the feather in the traditional tam o' shanter; the socks boast the traditional moiré 'flashes' and the shoes by Bally are a modern interpretation of a brogue.*

Yves Saint Laurent established his 'rich peasant' look in his Spring/Summer Collection of 1977, bringing back the rustle of taffeta, perpetuating fashion's love affair with ancient Russia.

into easy reach and designers hungry for ideas fell upon ethnic dress from Eskimos' to gypsies' with such enthusiasm that collections seemed to have walked straight out of the pages of the *National Geographic* magazine. Television and late night movies brought the past within pushbutton reach, and started the apparently permanent wave of nostalgia. What young designers have failed to realize is that, as veteran Hollywood designer Edith Head has pointed out, the clothes that so seduce them were seldom fashion in the real sense but costumes designed to suit the character the star was playing, and, not least, the star's own whim of iron. Still, while many were wallowing in the near past, others like Courrèges with his hard-edged discipline, Cardin with his Space Age clothes and Mary Quant with her mini skirts were in tune with the time. At the risk of belabouring Lord Melbourne's aphorism, unisex ('Loonisex' to *Private Eye*), the passion for exposure, for the uniforms of violence and protest, for second-hand clothes, were crooked paths leading nowhere. Through the sixties and dominating the beginning of the seventies are the anti-fashions: the denims, the jeans, the work clothes of cowboys and lumber jacks worn out of context, serious play clothes – sailing and fishing gear, jogging suits – worn in city streets, a direction not conceived by Lord Melbourne. These were counterpointed by the opters-out – the Flower People and the Hippies whose trailing disarray was distilled into poetic fantasies by England's Zandra Rhodes and Bill Gibb.

Ethnic dress was not merely a source of fresh inspiration to designers running out of ideas. As early as 1962 the American writer, John Updike, noted in the artistic efforts of the Iron Curtain countries a strong and recurrent ethnic theme which he saw as a 'retreat from the difficult and disappointing present' into folklore and peasant costume. Four years later, the film *Dr Zhivago* provided the same escape hatch for the West and put fashion firmly on the steppes of nineteenth-century Russia. Top Russophile Yves Saint Laurent's 'rich peasant' collection of 1976 was, as Diana Vreeland's exhibition, The Glory of Russian Costume, at the Metropolitan Museum of Art in New York later in the same year showed, a close reproduction of the real 'rich peasant' clothes. As *The New Yorker* magazine pointed out these 'rich peasants' were 'actually free farmers or craftsmen or manufacturers or merchants' who 'dressed their women with surprising luxury',[1] as does Saint Laurent (one of whose dresses can cost nearly £3,000). Saint Laurent makes little effort to re-cycle his sources of inspiration but this seems to enhance rather than detract from his present position at the top of the fashion tree.

Another resuscitation of the past is the strapless evening dress which Christian Dior engineered to safe wearability in 1947 and which survived until 1963. Where his imitators nervously boned their tops so heavily that quite often when the wearer turned the dress remained stubbornly stationary, Dior relied on cut and a firm but invisible vertical support from the diaphragm above his nipped-in waists. This gave his strapless dresses a dangerous seductiveness of the sort which inspired the famous exchange between singer Mary Garden and one of America's elder statesman, Chauncey Depew. Mr Depew frostily surveying Miss Garden's decolletage asked if she would tell him what held her dress up, to which Miss Garden replied, 'Only your age, Sir.' Now rising above straight-falling soft fabrics, a new generation of collarbones is on display.

Jean Cocteau said of fashion, 'il faut tout lui pardonner; elle meurt si jeune (one must forgive fashion everything; it dies so young). Die fashions do. Announcing the demise of jeans, the *Daily Express* announced on 3 January 1976 that 'the bottom's falling out of the jeans market.' Although the phrasing is less felicitous than Cocteau's, it proves his point.

Fashion in the early years of this century luxuriated in what Evelyn Waugh called 'great healing draughts from the well of Edwardian certainty';[2] more than three-quarters of the way through all is confusion and disorder – inevitable, for fashion reflects the world in which it lives – and dies. It has been noted, however, that fashion tends to change (for the better) mid-decade. Although two years behind schedule, it is still too soon for total pessimism. In what James Stevenson calls 'the patois of hip bureaucracy',[3] we may be facing an ongoing situation and we don't want to discourage any incoming talents; rather let us maintain an overview and hope that they will outreach themselves and that there will at last be an end to carry-on motifs – like those old Russian steppes. We don't want to make a mistake in issue identification, do we?

Reference Notes

N.B. All publishers and dates of publication of the books listed below are included in the Bibliography on page 243.

Beginnings
1 *Times Literary Supplement* 29 October, 1976

The Lotus Years
1 *Lytton Strachey: A Biography* Michael Holroyd p. 568
2 *A Concise History of Costume* James Laver
3 *Edward VII and his Circle* Virginia Cowles p. 267
4 *The Glass of Fashion* Cecil Beaton p. 127
5 *Swann in Love* Marcel Proust
6 *Within a Budding Grove* Marcel Proust
7 *Paris Fashion* ed. Ruth Lynam p. 61
8 *Victoria R.I.* Elizabeth Longford p. 86
9 *The Scarlet Tree* Osbert Sitwell p. 193
10 *The Theory of the Leisure Class* Thorstein Veblen
11 *On Human Finery* Quentin Bell p. 127
12 *The Glass of Fashion* p. 232
13 *Victoria R.I.* p. 246
14 *A History of Fashion* J. Anderson Black and Madge Garland p. 293
15 *The Cult of Chiffon* Mrs Eric Pritchard p. 118
16 *Within a Budding Grove*
17 *Women in Love* D.H.Lawrence

When Paris Ruled
1 *Within a Budding Grove*
2 *The Cult of Chiffon* p. 7
3 *Glimpses of the Moon* Edith Wharton

Where America Leads
1 *The Wheels of Fashion* Phyllis Lee Levin p. 54
2 *Always in Vogue* Edna Woolman Chase and Ilka Chase p. 98 ff
3 *The Movies* Richard Griffith and Arthur Mayer p. 227
4 *Harper's Bazaar – 100 Years of the American Female* ed. Jane Trahey p. 118
5 *World of Fashion* Eleanor Lambert p. 258
6 *In My Fashion* Bettina Ballard p. 166
7 *American Fashion* ed. Sarah Tomerlin Lee p. 211

When London Swung
1 *Silver and Gold* Norman Hartnell p. 24
2 *Vile Bodies* Evelyn Waugh
3 *Silver and Gold* p. 94
4 *Silver and Gold* p. 96
5 *In My Fashion* p. 250
6 *Just So Far* Hardy Amies p. 54
7 *In My Fashion* p. 247

The Arts and Fashion
1 *The Rainbow Picnic* Daphne Fielding p. 52
2 *Pioneers of Modern Design* Nikolaus Pevsner
3 *Homes, Sweet Homes* Osbert Lancaster p. 56
4 *Edwardian Daughter* Sonia Keppel
5 *Masters of Modern Art* The Museum of Modern Art, New York p. 76
6 *Fashion* Madge Garland p. 128
7 *The Beautiful People* Marylin Bender p. 70
8 *Art Deco* Bevis Hillier pp 96, 107

The Dance and Fashion
1 *Elizabeth R* Roy Strong and Julia Trevelyan Oman p. 29
2 *Emma* Jane Austen
3 *The Waltz Emperors* Joseph Wechsberg p. 50
4 *The Scarlet Tree* p. 275
5 *The Edwardians* Vita Sackville-West p. 155–156
6 *Edwardian Daughter*
7 *Paris à la Mode* Celia Bertin p. 169.

Chroniclers of Fashion
1 *Belchamber* Howard Sturgis p. 124–125
2 *Always in Vogue* p. 144
3 *Fashion 1900–1939* Idea Books International in association with the Scottish Arts Council and Victoria & Albert Museum 1975 p. 23
4 *The Glass of Fashion* p. 80
5 *Always in Vogue* p. 151
6 *Photobiography* Cecil Beaton p. 70

7 *Leica – The First Fifty Years* G. Rogliatti
8 *Always in Vogue* p. 232
9 *In My Fashion* p. 127

The Glamour of Fashion

1 *ABC of Men's Fashion* Hardy Amies p. 79
2 *The Young Visiters* Daisy Ashford p. 9
3 *Fashions in Make-up* Richard Corson
4 *The Visits of Elizabeth* Elinor Glyn
5 *Fashions in Make-up* p. 404
6 *The Pursuit of Love* Nancy Mitford p. 51
7 *Fashions in Make-up* pp. 365–366 and 415–416
8 *Madame* Patrick O'Higgins p. 85
9 *The Sun King* Nancy Mitford p. 33
10 *World of Fashion* p. 230
11 *History of Perfume* Francis Kennet p. 161
12 *A History of Scent* Ray Genders p. 204

The Garnishes of Fashion

1 *Take Them Up Tenderly* Margaret Case Harriman
   p. 205
2 *The Mode in Furs* R. T. Wilcox p. 156
3 *The Book of Furs* J. G. Links p. 149
4 *The Art of Jewellery* Graham Hughes

Above, Below and Beneath

1 *Fashions in Feathers* Robin Doughty
2 *A History of Fashion* p. 164
3 *A Brief History of the Shoe* Wilhelm Sulser p. 6

4 *The Limit* Ada Leverson
5 *With Malice Toward Some* Margaret Simon
6 Introduction to *Mademoiselle Maupin* Théophile
   Gautier
7 *Women in Love*
8 *The Cult of Chiffon* p. 191
9 *La Belle Epoque* published by the Costume Society p. 69
10 *History of Twentieth Century Fashion* Elizabeth Ewing
   p. 90–91
11 *A History of Fashion* p. 319

Fashion in Movement

1 *The Scarlet Tree* p. 196
2 *The Limit* p. 245
3 *The Shell Book of Firsts* Patrick Robertson p. 24

Wars, Revolution and Turbulence

1 *On Human Finery* 74 ff
2 *Taste and Fashion* James Laver p. 198
3 *Portrait of a Marriage* Nigel Nicolson p. 105
4 *A Concise History of Costume*
5 *Paris Fashion* p. 74
6 *History of Twentieth Century Fashion* p. 86

Epilogue

1 *The New Yorker* 20 December 1976
2 *Vile Bodies*
3 'A Reporter at Large', *The New Yorker* 27 December
   1976

Bibliography

Allan, Maud, *My Life and Dancing* (Everett, London, 1908)

Amies, Hardy, *Just So Far* (Collins, London, 1954)
ABC of Men's Fashion (Newnes, London, 1964)

Ashford, Daisy, *The Young Visiters* (Chatto & Windus, London, 1957)

Aswell, Mary Louise, *Carmel* (McGraw Hill, New York, 1962)

Austen, Jane, *Emma* (Collins, London, 1973; W.W. Norton, New York, 1972)
Pride and Prejudice (MacDonald, London, 1974; Dutton, New York, 1976)

Baillen, Claude, *Chanel Solitaire* (Collins, London, 1973; Quadrangle/New York Times, 1974)

Ballard, Bettina, *In My Fashion* (Secker & Warburg, London, 1960)

Balmain, Pierre, *Balmain* (Cassells, London, 1964; Doubleday, New York, 1965)

Beaton, Cecil, *The Glass of Fashion* (Weidenfeld & Nicolson 1954; Doubleday, New York, 1954)
Photobiography (Odhams Books, London, 1951; Doubleday, New York, 1951)
The Wandering Years (Weidenfeld & Nicolson, London, 1961; Little, Brown and Company, Boston, 1962)
The Years Between (Weidenfeld & Nicolson, London, 1965; Holt Rinehart & Winston, New York, 1965)

Bell, Quentin, *On Human Finery* (Hogarth Press, London, 1947; Schocken Books, New York, 1976)

Bender, Marylin, *The Beautiful People* (Coward-McCann, New York, 1967)

Benson, E.F., *Dodo* (Methuen, London, 1893)

Bertin, Celia, *Paris a la Mode* (Gollancz, London, 1956; Harper & Row, New York, 1957)

Black, Anderson and Madge Garland, *A History of Fashion* (Orbis Publications, London, 1975; Morrow, New York, 1975)

Carter, Ernestine, *With Tongue in Chic* (Michael Joseph, London, 1977)

20th Century Fashion: A Scrapbook 1900 to Today (Eyre Methuen, London, 1975)

Chase, Edna Woolman and Ilka Chase, *Always in Vogue* (Gollancz, London, 1954; Doubleday, New York, 1954)

Chierichetti, David, *Hollywood Costume* (Studio Vista, London, 1977; Crown Publishers, New York 1976)

Contini, Mila, *Fashion* (Paul Hamlyn, London, 1965; Odyssey, Indianapolis, 1965)

Cooper, Duff, *Tallyrand* (Jonathan Cape, London, 1932; Stanford University Press, Stanford, 1932)

Corson, Richard, *Fashions in Make-up* (Peter Owen, London, 1972; Universe, New York, 1973)

Cowles, Virginia, *Edward VII and his Circle* (Hamish Hamilton, London, 1956)

de Courtois, Georgine, *Women's Headdress and Hair Styles in England* (Batsford, London, 1973; Rowman, New Jersey, 1973)

Dior, Christian, *Dior by Dior* (Weidenfeld & Nicolson, London, 1957; Ambassador, New York, 1957)

Doughty, Robin, *Fashions in Feathers* (University of California Press, 1975)

Ewing, Elizabeth, *History of Twentieth Century Fashion* (Batsford, London, 1973; Scribner's, New York, 1975)

Fielding, Daphne, *The Rainbow Picnic* (Eyre Methuen, London, 1974)

Forbes-Robertson, Diana, *Maxine* (Hamish Hamilton, London, 1964; Viking Press, New York, 1964)

Garland, Madge, *Fashion* (Penguin Books, London and New York, 1962)
The Indecisive Decade (Macdonald, London, 1968)

Genders, Roy, *A History of Scent* (Hamish Hamilton, London, 1972; Putnams, New York, 1972)

Glyn, Elinor, *Visits of Elizabeth* (Duckworth, London, 1922)

Green, Martin, *Children of the Sun* (Basic Books, New York, 1976; Constable, London, 1977)

Griffith, Richard and Arthur Mayer, *The Movies* (Spring Books, London, 1963; Simon & Schuster, New York, 1957)

Haedrich, Marcel, *Coco Chanel* (Robert Hale, London, 1972; Little, Brown and Company, Boston, 1972)

Harriman, Margaret Case, *Take Them Up Tenderly* (Knopf, New York, 1944)

Hartnell, Norman, *Silver and Gold* (Evans Brothers, London, 1955; Pitman, New York, 1956)
Royal Courts of Fashion (Cassell's, London, 1971; International Publications Service, New York, 1971)

Hawes, Elizabeth, *Fashion is Spinach* (Random House, New York, 1933)

Hillier, Bevis, *Art Deco* (Studio Vista, London, 1968)

Holroyd, Michael, *Lytton Strachey: A Biography* (William Heinemann, London, 1967; Holt, Rinehart & Winston, New York, 1968)

Hughes, Graham, *The Art of Jewellery* (Studio Vista, London, 1972)
Modern Jewellery (Studio Vista, London, 1963; Crown Publishers, New York, 1963)

Ironside, Janey, *Janey* (Michael Joseph, London, 1973)

Kennett, Frances, *History of Perfume* (Harrap, London, 1975)

Keppel, Sonia, *Edwardian Daughter* (Hamish Hamilton, London, 1958)

Lambert, Eleanor, *World of Fashion* (Bowker, New York, 1976)

Lancaster, Osbert, *Homes Sweet Homes* (John Murray, London, 1939; Transatlantic Arts, New York, 1939)

Laver, James, *A Concise History of Costume* (Thames & Hudson, London, 1969; Scribner, New York, 1974)
Taste and Fashion (Harrap, London, 1973, Dodd, Mead, New York, 1938)

Lawrence, D.H. *Women in Love* (Penguin, London, 1969, Modern Library, New York, 1937)

Leslie, Anita *Edwardians in Love* (Arrow Books, London, 1974; Doubleday, New York, 1973)

Leverson, Ada, *The Limit*

Levin, Phyllis Lee, *The Wheels of Fashion* (Doubleday, New York, 1965)

Lewis R.W.B., *Edith Wharton* (Constable, London, 1975; Harper & Row, New York, 1975)

Links, J.G., *The Book of Fur* (James Barrie, London, 1956; Ambassador, New York, 1956)

Longford, Elizabeth, *Victoria RI* (Weidenfeld & Nicolson, London, 1973)

Mitford, Nancy, *The Pursuit of Love* (Hamish Hamilton, London, 1945; Random House, New York, 1946)
Love in a Cold Climate (Hamish Hamilton, London, 1949; Random House, New York, 1949)
The Blessing (Hamish Hamilton, London, 1951, Randon House, New York, 1957)
The Sun King (Sphere Books, London, 1966; Harper & Row, New York, 1966)

Moore, Doris Langley, *Fashion Through Fashion Plates 1771–1970* (Ward Lock, London, 1971; C.N. Potter, New York, 1972)

Nicolson, Nigel, *Portrait of a Marriage* (Weidenfeld & Nicolson, London 1973; Atheneum Press, New York, 1973)

Nicholson, T.R., *Passenger Cars 1863–1904* (Blandford Books, London, 1970; American Heritage, 1970)
Passenger Cars 1905–1912 (Blandford Books, London, 1971; Macmillan, New York, 1971)

O'Higgins, Patrick, *Madame* (Weidenfeld & Nicolson, London, 1971; Viking Press, New York, 1971)

Pevsner, Nikolaus, *Pioneers of Modern Design* (Penguin, London, 1960; Penguin, New York, 1964)

Priestley, J.B., *The Edwardians* (Heinemann, London, 1970; Harper & Row, New York, 1970)

Pritchard, Mrs Eric, *The Cult of Chiffon* (Grant Richards, New York, 1902)

Proust, Marcel, *Swann's Way* (Chatto & Windus, London, 1966; Random House, New York, 1970)
Within a Budding Grove (Chatto & Windus, London, 1967; Random House, New York, 1934)

Read, Donald, *Edwardian England* (Historical Association 1972)

Robertson, Patrick, *Shell Book of Facts* (Ebury Press, London, 1974)

Rogliatti, G., *Leica – The First Fifty Years*

Schiaparelli, Elsa, *Shocking Life* (Dent, London, 1954, Dutton, New York, 1954)

Sedgwick, Michael, *Passenger Cars 1924–1942* (Blandford Books, London, 1975; Macmillan, New York, 1976)

Simon, Margaret, *With Malace Towards Some* (Simon & Schuster, New York, 1930)

Sitwell, Osbert, *The Scarlet Tree* (Macmillan, London, 1946; Little, Brown and Company, Boston, 1946)

Smith, Cecil Woodham, *Queen Victoria* (Hamish Hamilton, London, 1972; Knopf, New York, 1972)

Strong, Roy and Julia Trevelyan Oman, *Elizabeth R* (Secker & Warburg, London, 1971; Stein & Day, New York, 1972)

Sturgis, Howard, *Belchamber* (Constable, London, 1904)

Sulser, Wilhelm, *Shoes*

Sykes, Christopher, *Evelyn Waugh* (Collins, London, 1975, Little, Brown & Company, Boston, 1975)

Taylor, Deems, Bryant Hale, Marcelene Peterson, *A Pictorial History of the Films* (Allen & Unwin, London, 1949; Simon & Schuster, New York, 1949)

Veblen, Thorstein, *The Theory of the Leisure Class* (Allen & Unwin, London, 1925; Houghton Mifflin, Boston, 1973)

Veronesi, Guilia, *Into the Twenties* (Thames & Hudson, London, 1968; Braziller, New York, 1968)

Waugh, Evelyn, *Vile Bodies* (Penguin, London, 1970; Farrar, Straus & Giroux, New York, 1930)

Wechsberg, Joseph, *Waltz Emperors* (Weidenfeld & Nicolson, London, 1973; Putnams, New York, 1973)

West, Vita Sackville, *The Edwardians* (Hogarth Press, London, 1930; Doubleday, New York, 1930)

Wharton, Edith, *Glimpses of the Moon* (Appleton, London; 1923, Appleton, New York, 1922)

    A Backward Glance (Constable, London, 1972; Appleton, New York, 1934)

    The Age of Innocence (Penguin, London, 1974; Appleton, New York, 1920)

Wilcox, R. Turner, *The Mode in Footwear* (Scribner, New York, 1948)

    The Mode in Costume (Scribner, New York, 1949)

    The Mode in Furs (Scribner, New York, 1951)

Wolfe, Tom, *The kandy-kolored tangerine flake streamline baby* (Jonathan Cape, London, 1965; Farrar, Straus & Giroux, New York, 1965)

Ziegler, Philip, *Melbourne* (Collins, London, 1976, Knopf, New York, 1976)

Other Sources of Reference

American Fashion, edited by Sarah Tomerlin Lee

Catalogues of the Costume Institute of the Metropolitan Museum of Art, The 10s, The 20s, the 30s; Romantic and Glamorous Design 1974; The World of Balenciaga 1973; American Women of Style, 1975

Costume, The Journal of the Costume Society

Gilbert Albert, Jacques & Pierre Chaumet, Alexandre Grassy, Andrew Grima, Rene Kern, Harry Winston

Fashion from Ancient Egypt to the Present Day, edited by James Laver (Paul Hamlyn, 1965)

Harper's Bazaar – 100 years of the American Female, edited by Jane Trahey (Random House, New York)

In Vogue, edited by Georgina Howell (Allen Lane Penguin Books, 1975)

Fashion 1900–1939 (Idea Books International in association with the Scottish Arts Council and the Victoria & Albert Museum, 1975)

La Belle Epoque (The Costume Society, 1967)

Paris Fashion, edited by Ruth Lynam (Michael Joseph, London, 1972)

The Art and Craft of Hairdressing, edited by Gilbert A. Foan

The New Yorker Magazine

The Saturday Book, 21, Hutchinson of London, 1961

The Saturday Book, 31, Hutchinson, 1971

The Sunday Times 1955–1972

Time Magazine

W, published by Fairchild Publications

Picture Acknowledgments

The author and publisher would like to thank the following museums, collections and private individuals by whose kind permission the illustrations are reproduced. Numbers are page numbers. Sources without parentheses indicate the owners of photographs and paintings; those within parentheses refer to illustration sources only.

12 Bibliothèque Nationale, Paris. (Snark International, Paris)

14 The Costume Research Centre, Bath.

15 The Mansell Collection, London.

17 Courtesy of Mrs Doris Langley Moore, London.

18 Photograph by Baron de Meyer. The Metropolitan Museum of Art, New York – Gift of Polaire Weissman.

19 left Radio Times Hulton Picture Library, London.

19 right Radio Times Hulton Picture Library, London.

20 Fashion plate by Robert Dammy for *La Gazette du Bon Ton*. (Snark International, Paris)

21 Fashion plate by Georges Barbier for *La Gazette du Bon Ton*. (Mary Evans Picture Library, London)

22 Royal Photographic Society, London.

23 (The Mansell Collection, London)

24 Fashion plate by Paul Meras for *La Gazette du Bon Ton*. (Mary Evans Picture Library, London)

26 Gerveux: 'Five o'clock chez Paquin'. Worth Collection, London. (Snark International, Paris)

27 left From *The Queen*, *The Lady's Newspaper*. Courtesy of Mrs Doris Langley Moore, London.

27 right Photograph by Desoye. Copyright S.P.A.D.E.M., Paris. (Author's collection, London)

28 The Mander and Mitchenson Theatre Collection, London.

29 Photograph by E.O. Hoppé. The Mansell Collection, London.

30 above Lepape: 'Robe de Madame Poiret'. Paul Poiret Collection, Paris. Copyright S.P.A.D.E.M., Paris. (Snark International, Paris)

30 below left Drawing by Georges Lepape. Copyright S.P.A.D.E.M., Paris. (Bulloz, Paris)

30 below right Radio Times Hulton Picture Library, London.

31 Fashion plate by Valentine Gross for *La Gazette du*

Bon Ton. Copyright S.P.A.D.E.M., Paris. (Mary Evans Picture Library, London)

32 From British *Harper's Bazaar*. (Author's Collection, London)

34 above left The Costume Research Centre, Bath.

34 above right The Costume Research Centre, Bath.

34 below left Photograph by David Bailey for *The Sunday Times*. (Costume Research Centre, Bath)

34 below right Photograph by Foto Relang. (Camera Press, London)

36 Photograph by Sir Cecil Beaton. Sotheby's Belgravia, London.

37 left Radio Times Hulton Picture Library, London.

37 right Photograph by Alec Murray for *The Sunday Times*. (Alec Murray, London)

38 Photograph by Sir Cecil Beaton. Sotheby's Belgravia, London.

39 Photograph by Sir Cecil Beaton. Sotheby's Belgravia, London.

40 (Weidenfeld & Nicolson Archives, London)

41 Photograph by Bob Greene. (Camera Press, London)

42 Fashion plate from *La Gazette du Bon Ton*. (Mary Evans Picture Library, London)

43 Sketch by Jean Patou. Courtesy of The House of Jean Patou, Paris.

44 Photograph by Sir Cecil Beaton. Sotheby's Belgravia, London.

46 Photograph by Norman Parkinson. (Camera Press, London)

47 Courtesy of The House of Nina Ricci, Paris.

48 Drawing by Christian Benais for *The Sunday Times*. (The Costume Research Centre, Bath)

49 Transworld Feature Syndicate. (The Costume Research Centre, Bath).

51 above Photograph by Carlo Orsi for *The Sunday Times*. (The Costume Research Centre, Bath)

51 left Courtesy of Emmanuel Ungaro, Paris.

51 right Drawing by Eula for *The Sunday Times*. (The Costume Research Centre, Bath)

51 below Drawing by Christian Benais for *The Sunday Times*. (The Costume Research Centre, Bath)

52 Photograph by Foto Relang. (Camera Press, London)

53 Courtesy of The House of Dior, Paris.

54 Photograph by Giancarlo Botti. (SYGMA/John Hillelson Agency)

56 Photograph by Norman Eales for *The Sunday Times*. (The Costume Research Centre, Bath)

59 From the *Illustrated London News*. Courtesy of Mrs Doris Langley Moore, London.

60 left Courtesy of Geoffrey Beene, New York.

60 right Courtesy of Adolfo, New York.

61 Photograph by Chris von Wangenheim. Courtesy of the *New York Times* Magazine. (The Costume Research Centre, Bath)

62 Photograph by Ormond Gigli. (Camera Press, London)

63 Courtesy of Calvin Klein, New York.

65 Courtesy of Pierre Cardin, Paris.

66 M.G.M. Studios. (The National Film Archive, London)

67 20th Century Fox Studios. (The National Film Archive, London)

68 Courtesy of Oscar de la Renta, New York.

69 Photograph by Ormond Gigli. (Camera Press, London)

70 left (The National Film Archive, London)

70 right R.K.O. Studios. (The National Film Archive, London)

72 Courtesy of Bill Blass, New York.

74 Drawing by Eric for French *Vogue*. (The Costume Research Centre, Bath)

75 Photograph by Sir Cecil Beaton. Sotheby's Belgravia, London.

76 Photograph by Mark Shaw. From *Fashion* by Madge Garland, Penguin, London, 1962.

78 Photograph by Norman Eales for *The Sunday Times*. (The Costume Research Centre, Bath)

81 Photograph by John Cowan for *The Sunday Times*. (The Costume Research Centre, Bath)

82 The Costume Research Centre, Bath.

83 left Radio Times Hulton Picture Library, London.

83 right Radio Times Hulton Picture Library, London.

85 Photograph by Paul Tanqueray. Paul Tanqueray, London.

86 left Cartoon by C. Hildyard for the Cambridge Univ. Footlights Review Programme, 1921. (The Mander and Mitchenson Theatre Collection, London)

86 right Radio Times Hulton Picture Library, London.

88 Sketch by Sir Norman Hartnell. Courtesy of Sir Norman Hartnell, London.

89 Courtesy of Sir Norman Hartnell, London.

90 Photograph by John Cowan for *The Sunday Times*. (The Costume Research Centre, Bath)

92 Photograph by Clive Boursnell. Clive Boursnell, London.

93 Photograph by Clive Boursnell. Clive Boursnell, London.

94 Photograph by John Hedgecoe for *The Sunday Times*. (The Costume Research Centre, Bath)

95 left Keystone Press Agency, London.

95 right Photograph by John Adriaan for *The Sunday Times*. (The Costume Research Centre, Bath)

96 Courtesy of Laura Ashley, London.

99 Photograph by Annette Green for *The Sunday Times*. (The Costume Research Centre, Bath)

100 Photograph by Richard Dormer. (Author's Collection, London)

101 left Photograph by Tim White for *The Sunday Times*. (The Costume Research Centre, Bath)

101 right Photograph by Karl Stoecker for *The Sunday Times*. (The Costume Research Centre, Bath)

102 Photograph by Stuart MacLeod. Stuart MacLeod, London.

105 Boldini: 'Consuelo, Duchess of Marlborough'. The Metropolitan Museum of Art, New York. Gift of Consuelo Vanderbilt Balsan, 1946. Copyright S.P.A.D.E.M., Paris.

106 C. Dana Gibson: 'Of course you can tell fortunes with cards'. The Mander and Mitchenson Theatre Collection, London.

106 Camille Clifford and Leslie Styles. The Mander and Mitchenson Theatre Collection, London.

108 H. Thiriet: 'Exposition de Blanc'. (Weidenfeld & Nicolson Archives, London)

109 Fashion plate for *La Gazette du Bon Ton*. (Mary Evans Picture Library, London)

110 left Madame Arp Collection, France. (Weidenfeld & Nicolson Archive, London)

110 right Photograph by Curtis Moffat. (Weidenfeld & Nicolson Archive, London)

111 left J.S. Sargent: 'Study for a portrait of Madame Gautreau'. The Tate Gallery, London.

111 right Osbert Lancaster cartoon. From *Tableaux Vivants*, Gryphon Books, London, 1955.

112 Photograph by Sir Cecil Beaton. Sotheby's Belgravia, London.

114 Sketch by Bakst. Fine Art Society, London. (Cooper-Bridgeman Library, London)

115 Van Dongen: 'Lady with Chrysanthemums'. Musée d'Art Moderne, Paris. Copyright S.P.A.D.E.M., Paris. (Bulloz, Paris)

116 Peter Blake: 'Coco Chanel'. Private Collection, London. (Snark International, Paris)

118 Otto Dix: 'Les Noctambules'. Centre panel of triptych. Pont Collection, Essen. (Snark International, Paris)

119 Copyright B.B.C., London.

120 Cartoon from *Punch*. (Brown Collection, London)

122 Drawing by F. Matania for *The Sketch*. Courtesy of Mrs Doris Langley Moore, London.

123 The Mansell Collection, London.

124 (Weidenfeld & Nicolson Archives, London)

125 above left The Mansell Collection, London.

125 below left Abraham Walkowitz: 'Isadora Duncan' Zabriskie Gallery, USA. (Weidenfeld & Nicolson Archives, London)

125 right Roger-Viollet, Paris.

127 Cartoon from *Punch*. (Mary Evans Picture Library London)

128 The Mansell Collection, London.

129 Still from *Top Hat*. R.K.O. Studios. (The National Film Archive, London)

130 Gaby Deslys and Harry Pilcer. The Mansell Collection, London.

131 Cover of *Life* magazine. Drawing by John Held Jr. Benjamin Franklin Centre, Paris. (Snark International, Paris)

132 Photographed for *The Sunday Times*. (The Costume Research Centre, Bath)

134 Photograph by Sir Cecil Beaton. Sotheby's Belgravia, London.

137 Erte: 'Splendours'. Private Collection (Charles Spencer, London).

138 left From *The Sketch*. Courtesy of Mrs Doris Langley Moore, London.

138 above right Photograph by Baron de Meyer. (Weidenfeld & Nicolson Archives, London)

138 below right From *Art et Decoration*. Photograph by Steichen. (Weidenfeld & Nicolson Archives, London)

140 Fashion plate by Georges Lepape for *La Gazette du Bon Ton*. Copyright S.P.A.D.E.M., Paris. (Snark International, Paris)

141 Poster by A.E. Marty for London Transport. Lords Gallery, London. (Weidenfeld & Nicolson Archives, London)

142 Photograph by Hoyningen Huene for French *Vogue*. (Weidenfeld & Nicolson Archives, London)

143 left Photograph by Richard Dormer for the *Daily Express*. (Weidenfeld & Nicolson Archives, London)

143 right Photograph by Weegee. Collection, The Museum of Modern Art, New York.

144 Henry Fournier: 'Les Petites Chocolatières'. From *La Vie Parisienne*. (Mary Evans Picture Library, London)

146 Photograph by Sarah Moon. (The Costume Research Centre, Bath)

147 Photograph by David Bailey for *The Sunday Times*. (The Costume Research Centre, Bath)

149 left Fashion plate by Etienne Drian for *La Gazette du Bon Ton*. (Mary Evans Picture Library, London)

149 right Drawing by Harold Carlton for *The Sunday Times*. (The Costume Research Centre, Bath)

150 Photograph by Helmut Newton for *The Sunday Times*. (The Costume Research Centre, Bath)

152 Drawing by Kenneth Paul Block for *W. W*, New York.

155 Photograph by Paul Tanqueray. Paul Tanqueray, London.

156 The Mander and Mitchenson Theatre Collection, London.

158 M.G.M. Studios. (The National Film Archive, London)

159 left (Weidenfeld & Nicolson Archives, London)

159 right Photograph by Sir Cecil Beaton. Sotheby's Belgravia, London.

160 (Snark International, Paris)

161 left Photograph by E.O. Hoppé. The Mansell Collection, London.

161 right The Mansell Collection, London.

162 Photograph by Sir Cecil Beaton. (Weidenfeld & Nicolson Archives, London)

163 Photograph by Angus McBean. Gruber Collection. (Weidenfeld & Nicolson Archives, London)

165 left Helleu: 'Portrait of Madame Helleu'. Lumley Cazalet Gallery, London. Copyright S.P.A.D.E.M., Paris. (Weidenfeld & Nicolson Archives, London)

165 right Photograph by E.O. Hoppé. The Mansell Collection, London.

167 Photograph by Justin de Villeneuve for *The Sunday Times*. (The Costume Research Centre, Bath)

168 Courtesy of Biba Cosmetics Ltd., London.

173 Photograph by Norman Eales for *The Sunday Times*. (The Costume Research Centre, Bath)

174 Photograph by Lartigue. (John Hillelson Agency, London)

175 Courtesy of J.G. Links Collection, London.

177 Photograph by Franco Rubartelli for French *Vogue*. (Weidenfeld & Nicolson Archives, London)

178 From *La Vie Parisienne*. (Mary Evans Picture Library)

179 left The Mansell Collection, London.

179 right Photograph by E.O. Hoppé. The Mansell Collection, London.

180 Courtesy of Tiffany & Co., New York.

181 Courtesy of Cartier, Paris.

182 Courtesy of Revillon, Paris.

183 Courtesy of Neiman-Marcus, Dallas.

184 Photograph by John Blackburn & Partners, London. Courtesy of Jones of Knightsbridge, London.

187 Photograph by David Charles. Courtesy of Furs Renée, London.
188 left (The Mansell Collection, London)
188 right The Costume Research Centre, Bath.
189 Photograph by Sir Cecil Beaton. Sotheby's Belgravia, London.
190 above left Courtesy of Cartier, Paris.
190 below left From *La Gazette du Bon Ton*. (Batsford Archives, London)
190 right Radio Times Hulton Picture Library.
192 left Courtesy of Andrew Grima, London.
192 right Courtesy of David Webb, New York.
193 Photograph by Norman Eales for *The Sunday Times*. (Costume Research Centre, Bath)
194 Roger-Viollet, Paris.
197 above Radio Times Hulton Picture Library.
197 below left Radio Times Hulton Picture Library.
197 below right M.G.M. Studios. (The National Film Archive, London)
198 From *Album de la Mode du Figaro*, 1946. (Mary Evans Picture Library, London)
199 left Photograph by Carlo Orsi for *The Sunday Times*. (The Costume Research Centre, Bath)
199 right Photograph by Richard Dormer for *The Sunday Times*. (The Costume Research Centre, Bath)
200 left The Mander and Mitchenson Theatre Collection, London.
200 right Sketched for *The Sunday Times*. (The Costume Research Centre, Bath)
201 Fashion plate from *La Gazette du Bon Ton*. (Mary Evans Picture Library, London)
202 From *The Sketch*. Courtesy of Mrs Doris Langley Moore, London
203 Courtesy of Edward Rayne, London.
204 Courtesy of Mary Quant/The Nylon Hosiery Co. Ltd., London.
205 Poster by John Hassall. (Weidenfeld & Nicolson Archives, London)
207 left From *La Gazette du Bon Ton*. (Mary Evans Picture Library, London)
207 above right Photograph by Patrick Lichfield for *The Sunday Times*. (The Costume Research Centre, Bath)
207 below right Courtesy of Zapata Shoe Company, London.
208 Popperfoto, London.
210 David Wason Collection, London.
211 left Boldini: 'Lady Undressing Herself'. Lumley Cazalet Gallery, London. Copyright S.P.A.D.E.M., Paris. (Weidenfeld & Nicolson Archives, London)
211 right From *La Vie Parisienne*. (Mary Evans Picture Library, London)
212 left Courtesy of Edward Rayne, London.

212 right Photograph by Patrick Lichfield for *The Sunday Times*. (The Costume Research Centre, Bath)
214 left (Mary Evans Picture Library)
214 right (William Gordon Davis, London)
215 Photograph by Horst P. Horst for French *Vogue*. Courtesy of The Sonnabend Gallery, New York.
216 left Van Dongen: 'La Chemise Noire'. Marlborough Fine Art, London. Copyright S.P.A.D.E.M., Paris. (Weidenfeld & Nicolson Archives, London)
216 right Courtesy of Janet Reger, London.
217 Drawing by Philip Castle for *The Sunday Times*. (The Costume Research Centre, Bath)
218 The Mansell Collection, London.
220 Kodak Museum, Hemel Hempstead. (Weidenfeld & Nicolson Archives, London)
221 left (The Mansell Collection, London)
221 Photograph by Patrick Hunt for *The Sunday Times*. (The Costume Research Centre, Bath)
223 above From *The Throne and Country*. Courtesy of Mrs Doris Langley Moore, London.
223 below Photograph by Ronnie Hertz. (Camera Press, London)
224 above (Snark International, Paris)
224 below Keystone Press Agency, London.
225 left The Mander and Mitchenson Theatre Collection, London.
225 right Photograph by John Cowan for *The Sunday Times*. (The Costume Research Centre, Bath)
227 *Kent Messenger*, Maidstone (Weidenfeld & Nicolson Archives, London)
228 above Gibbs: 'Congleton War-Working Party'. Imperial War Museum, London.
228 below Still from *Millions Like Us*. (The National Film Archive, London)
231 left Imperial War Museum, London.
231 right Lords Gallery, London. (Weidenfeld & Nicolson Archives, London)
232 Cover of *La Femme Chic*. (Orbis Publishing, London)
233 Imperial War Museum, London.
236 left Photograph Hosefros. *The New York Times*.
236 right Photograph by Peter Phipp. Peter Phipp Studios, London.
237 Photograph by Ciancarlo Botti. (SYGMA/John Hillelson Agency, London)

The author and publisher have taken all possible care to trace the ownership of all illustrations in copyright reproduced in this book, and to make acknowledgment for their use. If any errors have accidentally occurred, they will be corrected in subsequent editions, provided notification is sent to the publisher.

Index

Page numbers in *italic* refer to the illustrations.